black feminism reimagined

NEXT WAVE New Directions in Women's Studies

A series edited by Inderpal Grewal, Caren Kaplan, and Robyn Wiegman

JENNIFER C. NASH

black feminism reimagined after intersectionality

Duke University Press   Durham and London   2019

Library of Congress Cataloging-in-Publication Data
Names: Nash, Jennifer C., [date] author.
Title: Black feminism reimagined : after intersectionality /
Jennifer C. Nash.
Description: Durham : Duke University Press, 2019. |
Series: Next wave | Includes bibliographical references and index.
Identifiers: LCCN 2018026166 (print)
LCCN 2018034093 (ebook)
ISBN 9781478002253 (ebook)
ISBN 9781478000433 (hardcover : alk. paper)
ISBN 9781478000594 (pbk. : alk. paper)
Subjects: LCSH: Womanism—United States. | Feminism—
United States. | Intersectionality (Sociology) | Feminist theory. |
Women's studies—United States. | Universities and colleges—
United States—Sociological aspects.
Classification: LCC HQ1197 (ebook) | LCC HQ1197 .N37 2019
(print) | DDC 305.420973—dc23
LC record available at https://lccn.loc.gov/2018026166

COVER ART: Toyin Ojih Odutola, *The Uncertainty Principle*, 2014. © Toyin Ojih Odutola.
Courtesy of the artist and Jack Shainman Gallery, New York.

CONTENTS

Acknowledgments vii

INTRODUCTION. feeling black feminism 1

1. a love letter from a critic, or notes
on the intersectionality wars 33

2. the politics of reading 59

3. surrender 81

4. love in the time of death 111

CODA. some of us are tired 133

Notes 139
Bibliography 157
Index 165

Over the course of writing this book, I moved to a new city, started a new job, and welcomed a new life into the world. It has been a long season of change—both delightful and disorienting—and in the midst of it, I have considered this project a reassuring constant. The poet Mary Oliver reminds us "Let me / keep my mind on what matters, / which is my work." Every day that I have met this work, I have been reminded that it matters because it has given me the freedom to ask questions, to explore, to dream, and to be in conversation with scholars whom I respect deeply.

I spent six years as an assistant professor in the American Studies Department and Women's Studies Program at George Washington University. I am deeply grateful for the friends I made there, particularly Dara Orenstein, Chad Heap, Calvin Warren, Naeemah Raqib (the patron saint of women's studies), Justin Mann, Kim Probolus, and the many fantastic cohorts of Varieties of Feminist Theory. I owe Emily Hirsch extra thanks for a friendship born from Varieties and sustained through two years of daily WhatsApps from Zambia. Tom Guglielmo is in a category of his own. He welcomed me to DC with tremendous warmth, and over the course of six years, our families became close friends. I am endlessly grateful for his big-heartedness and kindness and his sense of humor. Jim Miller created a departmental culture of generosity, a healthy irreverence for university bureaucracy, and a deep appreciation for March Madness. He is missed. Katie Rademacher Kein is one of my most cherished friends, and I owe her thanks for so much—a deep and always-growing friendship; Seinfeld references; daily e-mails and texts; cookies and waffles.

There isn't a day that has passed when we haven't talked about the smallest and biggest of things in our lives, and I am endlessly grateful for the ongoing conversation. Thanks to my new colleagues in the Department of African American Studies and the Gender and Sexuality Studies Program at Northwestern who have welcomed me into their community. And thanks, always and deeply, to my students who remind me why I do this work. Special thanks to Mishana Garschi for her careful reading of the final draft of this manuscript, for a friendship that I cherish, and for the shared love of cookies.

I have endless love and appreciation for my homegirls. Emily Owens has given me the joy of sisterhood. I am grateful for morning check-in e-mails and Skype sessions; for the intellectual pleasures of our many collaborations; for the celebrations we have shared and for the hard moments when we have been in each other's corner; and for all the ways that, for the last fifteen years, we have been witnesses to each other's lives. Samantha Pinto has read this horse more times than I can count, and always with encouragement, generosity, and her characteristic brilliance and insight. I thank her for the extraordinary pleasure of reading, writing, and thinking together; for texts and Skype sessions in the final months of this project that reminded me that there was something here worth saying; for her company, wisdom, and humor in the early years of parenting; and for all the moments she has helped me through existential dread by knowing just how to make me laugh. Amber Musser and I have been thinking together for over a decade—about big ideas and the stuff of everyday life—and this book simply wouldn't exist without her insightful and generous feedback, intellectual companionship, and treasured friendship.

Thank you to a remarkable group of dear friends: Amber Musser, Amy Hesse Siniscalchi, Attiya Ahmad, Emily Hirsch, Emily Owens, Jonathan Evans, Nikki Kadomiya, Katie Rademacher Kein, Peter Geller, Reshma Gardner, Samantha Pinto, Sarah Jane Cervenak, Sylvanna Falcón, and Tom Guglielmo. I appreciate all the lunches, dinners, cookies, teas, Scrabble games, supportive e-mails, and Skype dates.

Thanks to Sylvanna Falcón for long-distance feminist community, writing deadlines, the pleasures of collaborative writing, and many conversations on intersectionality and transnationalism. Thanks to Sarah Jane Cervenak for her deeply smart work, her generous spirit, and her generative feedback on this manuscript.

Thanks to the feminist writing circle for collegiality, smart feedback, and much-needed community: Attiya Ahmad, Libby Anker, Soyica Colbert, Ivy

Ken, Bibiana Obler, Samantha Pinto. Many thanks to Attiya for her generosity in every sense of the word, her pictures and texts from far-flung places, and for being a loving godmother to Naima. Many thanks to Ivy for her kindness and sense of humor, her important work on intersectionality, and for on-going conversations about mutual constitution (and for that unforgettable phrase: "death watch").

Thanks to Maria MacKnight, healer extraordinaire, for everything she did to keep my mind and body well. Thanks to Maricela Lloreda Manzano for lovingly caring for Naima from the very beginning, and for becoming part of our family. Thanks to the folks who have nourished Naima's mind, soul, and body—Kevin, Alma, Deonna, Taji, and especially Maria Pino Du-ran (my dear friend and *comadre*). This book simply wouldn't exist without the community they have made.

Thanks to mentors and teachers: Nicole Fleetwood served as my mentor during my fellowship year and gave tirelessly of her time, energy, and in-sightful feedback. In the many years since, she has consistently supported me and my work. She encouraged me to think about defensiveness in re-lationship to black feminism and thus set me on the path that birthed this book. She has also modeled for me a relationship to professional life that is rooted in generosity rather than competition, abundance rather than scar-city, joy instead of anxiety. Robyn Wiegman's work has challenged me in the most exciting ways, transforming the questions that I ask and demanding that I interrogate my attachments to those very questions. I am thankful for the tremendous intellectual generosity she has shown me, the critical questions she has posed at just the right time, and her deep support of my work. Sunday mornings with Ashutosh-*ji* Agrawal at Hindi University kept me grounded. I admire Ashu's genuine curiosity about people and ideas, his commitment to spreading his love of Hindi, and his passion for teaching. In the midst of my first Chicago winter, Lindsey Stranc helped me stretch my body and mind, challenging me to do things I didn't think possible while talking about MOOCs and the Middle East bakery. I am deeply grateful. Paulo Carvalho has introduced me to the joys of the piano and encouraged me to put a "little bit of Aretha" in everything I do.

The Woodrow Wilson Junior Faculty Career Enhancement Grant pro-vided a transformative year of research leave and supportive scholarly com-munity; Northwestern University's Faculty Research Grant, George Wash-ington University's Facilitating Fund, and George Washington University's Columbian College's Facilitating Fund provided research support; Elizabeth

Novara at the University of Maryland Library helped me access the National Women's Studies Association's archives. Thanks to editors and readers at *Social Text* and *Feminist Theory*; both journals published earlier versions of the work here, and anonymous readers helped me sharpen my arguments. Thanks to Duke University Press, especially Ken Wissoker and Elizabeth Ault, who shepherded this manuscript through the review process with profound care. Duke's review process models the best of academic life: a deep generosity with ideas. I owe endless thanks to the four reviewers whose rigorous, respectful, and thoughtful feedback pushed me forward in crucial directions.

Thanks to interlocutors who gave me space to try out ideas, and who posed exciting questions of this work: at the National Women's Studies Association's annual conference, the American Studies Association's annual conference, University of Massachusetts Amherst (especially Svati Shah), Rice University (especially Susan Lurie), Washington University (especially Amber Musser), Duke University's Feminist Theory Workshop (especially Robyn Wiegman), Ohio State University (especially Shannon Winnubst), the University of Michigan's Women's Studies Department (especially Joey Gamble) and American Culture Department (especially Stephen Molldrem), the University of California San Diego's Ethnic Studies Department, University of Pittsburgh, the University of Toronto's Critical Analysis of Law Workshop, UCLA's Critical Race Studies symposium, and Barnard College's Scholar and Feminist Conference (especially Attiya Ahmad).

Finally, I reserve these closing words for my family:

I stand on the shoulders of dear family members who labored so that I could have a life pursuing what I love. It is an honor to say their names here: Mae Thompson, Alfred Nash, Parthenia Nash, Christine Eastmond, Maurice Eastmond.

Amar Ahmad and I have had a very long journey to what has become a real and treasured friendship. Because our affection is hard-earned, it is all the more precious to me. I hope he knows that I consider it an immense gift to be his stepmother.

Naima Ahmad Nash has been a loving guide to this next chapter in my life. I owe her thanks for her patience with all I don't yet know, her sense of humor, and her deep curiosity and playfulness. She has taught me to enjoy birdies, bunnies, and doggies, to take time to stare with wonder at a plane or a shadow, and to appreciate the rumble of a trash truck. It has been an immense pleasure to see the world's ordinary magic through her eyes, and I am endlessly grateful for her beautiful presence in my life.

My parents, Carolyn and Douglas Nash, have made endless sacrifices so that I can thrive. My mother always makes time to say "I'm so proud of you," and my father has transformed the basement into the official Jennifer Nash archive (it is not surprising that this archive has yet to have any visitors except, of course, for my father). They find a way to communicate their love and affection, generosity and kindness, every single day. Thank you is far too small since they have given me the world, but it's what I can offer here. Thank you, Mom and Dad, for everything.

Amin Ahmad has done it all and then some. He supports me, cherishes my intellectual life, finds humor in my quirks, unleashes my silliness, and loves me fiercely. He inspires me every day with his commitment to making something beautiful with words, and with his pursuit of a creative life. He has traveled with me—often literally—to unfamiliar places to support my dreams, my work, and our visions of a different life, and he has done it with grace and generosity.

This project, like the one before, like the ones that will come after, is for Amin. It marks all that we have shared, and all that we share. It marks a love that grows with the years, the months, the days. It marks my unending gratitude for him, for the universe that allowed us to find each other, and for our love.

INTRODUCTION. feeling black feminism

In an article published in the *New Yorker* in 2016, Nathan Heller described intersectionality as the heart of contemporary student activism. He writes, "If the new campus activism has a central paradigm, it is intersectionality: a theory, originating in black feminism, that sees identity-based oppression operating in crosshatching ways."[1] A year later, journalist Andrew Sullivan's polemic against intersectionality was published in *New York Magazine*. He describes intersectionality as "the latest academic craze sweeping the American academy" and likened it to a "religion," one that produces a dangerous "orthodoxy through which all of human experience is explained— and through which all speech must be filtered."[2] If Heller envisioned intersectionality as the principle organizing campus activism, Sullivan treated it as a dangerous "academic craze" that "enforces manners" and "controls language and the very terms of discourse."[3] Both articles were largely— and correctly—condemned for representing students as hypersensitive and coddled, and for trafficking in deep misunderstandings of intersectionality's histories, critical and political aspirations, and roots in black feminist theory.[4] Yet what interests me about the articles—and the vociferous responses to them by scholars and activists on the US Left—is how "intersectionality," a term that "has migrated from women's studies journals and conference keynotes into everyday conversation, turning what was once highbrow discourse into hashtag chatter," acted as *the* window through which to view either the imagined problems (or, in the case of the articles' critics, the imagined progress) of the contemporary university.[5] In some ways, it is unsurprising that a term rooted in black women's intellectual production would be figured as a dangerous space of political excess, as an ideology that has colonized the hearts and minds of (vulnerable) college students, as this is precisely how black women's corporeal presences have been figured. Yet what is new, and even surprising, is the contention that intersectionality is at the center of the university's intellectual and political life, that an understanding of the contemporary university requires contending with intersectionality.

Black Feminism Reimagined is a project that carefully studies intersectionality's lives in the US university. The project was born from a deep curiosity about the variety of political and theoretical work that intersectionality is called upon to perform in the US academy, and in the peculiarly contentious battles that have been waged around intersectionality, battles which I argue implicate the body that haunts the analytic—black woman—even if she is not always explicitly named as such. If intersectionality functions as a barometer measuring—and calibrating—the political atmosphere of the US university, I argue that it has been most emphatically called upon to do corrective ecological work in the context of women's studies, and that it is in relationship to academic feminism that intersectionality's institutional life has taken shape. Indeed, in *Black Feminism Reimagined*, I treat intersectionality as women's studies' primary program-building initiative, as its institutional and ethical orientation, even as the field retains an ambivalent relationship with the analytic, always imagining it as simultaneously promising and dangerous, the field's utopic future and its past tense.[6] Thus, this book largely focuses on the complicated and contentious relationship between intersectionality and women's studies, arguing that studying the field's engagement with intersectionality allows a window into the discipline's longer and fraught relationship with black feminist studies, and with black feminists.[7] More than that, because women's studies has been a kind of laboratory for intersectionality's institutional life in the US academy, understanding feminist conversations about intersectionality as the remedy, the cure, the threat, or the peril enables an understanding of the debates that swirl around intersectionality in the university at large.

Black Feminism Reimagined explores what it has meant for black feminism —and black feminists—to have intersectionality come to occupy the center of women's studies and to migrate across disciplinary boundaries, to be both filled with promise and emptied of specific meaning. I ask how black feminists have made visible their collective feelings about intersectionality's "citational ubiquity" in and beyond women's studies, and about the black feminist affects that attend to the variety of hopes and perils that have been imaginatively tethered to the analytic.[8] Thus, I imagine black feminism as an affective project—a felt experience—as much as it is an intellectual, theoretical, creative, political, and spiritual tradition. *Black Feminism Reimagined* argues that there is a single affect that has come to mark contemporary academic black feminist practice: *defensiveness*. I treat black feminist defensiveness as manifested most explicitly through black feminism's proprietary attachments to intersectionality. These attachments conscript black feminism into a largely protective posture, leaving black feminists mired in policing intersectionality's usages, demanding that intersectionality remain located within black feminism, and reasserting intersectionality's "true" origins in black feminist texts. This book traces how defensiveness is largely articulated by rendering intersectionality black feminist property, as terrain that has been gentrified, colonized, and appropriated, and as territory that must be guarded and protected through the requisite black feminist vigilance, care, and "stewardship."[9] The project develops the term "holding on" to flag—and to unsettle—the set of practices that defensiveness unleashes, particularly the proprietary claim to intersectionality that continues to animate so much of black feminist engagement with intersectionality. In treating defensiveness as a defining black feminist affect, my intention is not to diagnose individual black feminists as defensive or to pathologize black feminist feelings. Nor is my impulse to ignore histories of antiblackness and misogyny—including the invisible labor of black women inside the academy that, quite literally, kills black female academics—that render black feminist defensiveness a political response to ongoing violence. I seek to ethically attend to that history even as I critique the proprietary impulses of black feminism in an effort to reveal how the defensive affect traps black feminism, hindering its visionary world-making capacities. If "holding on" describes the set of black feminist practices this project seeks to disrupt, "letting go" represents the political and theoretical worldview this project advances, a vision of black feminist theory that is not invested in making property of knowledge.

This book also argues that it is impossible to theorize black feminist defensiveness without a rigorous consideration of the place of black feminist theory generally, and intersectionality specifically, in women's studies. *Black Feminism Reimagined* situates black feminist defensiveness in the context of US women's studies, an interdiscipline that is organized around the symbol of black woman even as the field retains little interest in the materiality of black women's bodies, the complexity of black women's experiences, or the heterogeneity of black women's intellectual and creative production. Defensiveness emerges precisely because the symbol of black woman is incessantly called upon to perform intellectual, political, and affective service work for women's studies, much as black female faculty are called upon to perform diversity service work in women's studies and across the university.[10] This particular form of feminist service work is evident in the general sentiment that women's studies can be remedied—or already has been remedied—through the incorporation of black feminist theory into the field's canon, through the hailing of black feminist theory as the remedy to (white) feminism's ills, or through the ways that black female faculty are called upon to embody and perform the field's transformation. Rachel Lee captures how women of color are rhetorically summoned as proof of the field's evolution, noting "women of color remain eminently useful to the progress narrative Women's Studies wishes to create for itself, where the fullness of women of color's arrival within Women's Studies is always 'about to be.'"[11] Thus, black woman serves the discipline's "progress narrative," acting as a sign of how much the discipline has overcome its past exclusions and how deeply the discipline refuses so-called white feminism, and intersectionality's ubiquity in women's studies is often taken as evidence of how black feminism has transformed the discipline.[12] While this book remains deeply invested in a consideration of black feminism's relationship to the university generally, and to women's studies specifically, it is crucial to note that black feminism—and black feminists—have long been attached, optimistically or self-destructively (or maybe both)—to the university. Indeed, black feminist theory has a long history of *both* tracking the violence the university has inflicted on black female academics (often by demanding black women's labor—intellectual, political, and embodied labor) *and* advocating for institutional visibility and legibility. While black feminists have long traced the violence of the university, few have advocated for abandoning the institutional project of black feminism, despite long-standing and widely circulating texts theorizing how the academy quite literally cannibalizes black women, extracts their labor, and renders invisible the work they perform to establish fields. Thus, when I consider the violence the university has inflicted on black women's bodies, I want to underscore that black feminism has remained oriented toward the university *despite* this violence, and has largely retained a faith in the institution's capacity to be remade, reimagined, or reinvented in ways that will do less violence to black feminist theory and black feminists' bodies.

In naming defensiveness as a defining black feminist affect, *Black Feminism Reimagined* necessarily makes a claim about what constitutes black feminism. I treat black feminism as a varied project with theoretical, political, activist, intellectual, erotic, ethical, and creative dimensions; black feminism is multiple, myriad, shifting, and unfolding. To speak of it in the singular is always to reduce its complexity, to neglect its internal debates and its rich and varied approaches to questions of black women's personhood. I treat the word "black" in front of "feminism" not as a marker of identity but as a political category, and I understand a "black feminist" approach to be one that centers analyses of racialized sexisms and homophobia, and that foregrounds black women as intellectual producers, as creative agents, as political subjects, and as "freedom dreamers" even as the content and contours of those dreams vary.[13] I advance a conception of black feminism that is expansive, welcoming anyone with an investment in black women's humanity, intellectual labor, and political visionary work, anyone with an investment in theorizing black genders and sexualities in complex and nuanced ways. My archive of black feminist theorists includes black, white, and nonblack scholars of color who labor in and adjacent to black feminist theory. My contention is that these varied black feminist scholars can all speak on and for black feminist theory, and as black feminist theorists, even as they make their claims from different identity locations. To be clear, my capacious conception of black feminism is a political decision, one that is staged mindful of black feminists' long-standing critique of how the university "disappears" black women.[14] Shifting the content of black feminism from a description of bodies to modes of intellectual production might generate precisely the anxious defensiveness this book describes and aspires to unsettle. Nonetheless, I invest in a broad conception of black feminism—and black feminists—precisely because of my commitment to tracing black feminist theory's expansive intellectual, political, ethical, and creative reach, one that I see as always transcending attempts to limit the tradition by rooting it in embodied performances. Moreover, it is the ongoing conception that black feminism is the exclusive territory of black women that traps and limits black feminists and black women academics who continue to be conscripted into performing and embodying their intellectual investments.

The introduction unfolds in three parts. First, I offer an intellectual history of intersectionality. Then I turn to an institutional history of intersectionality with a focus on the term's relationship to women's studies. In this section, I make explicit the book's decision to root itself in US women's studies even as intersectionality specifically and black feminism more broadly have intimate connections to other interdisciplinary projects, particularly black studies. Finally, I turn to explicating black feminist defensiveness and to situating this crucial and relatively new affect in the context of what I term the "intersectionality wars."

Intersectionality: An Intellectual History

In 2007, Ange-Marie Hancock noted, "A comprehensive intellectual history of intersectionality has yet to be published, with . . . significant ramifications that affect scholars seeking to conduct intersectional research and those seeking to understand the intellectual contributions of intersectionality."[15] In the decade since Hancock's assertion, a number of scholars, including Brittney Cooper, Vivian May, Patricia Hill Collins, Sirma Bilge, and Anna Carastathis, have invested in historicizing intersectionality as a key strategy for understanding the term's varied disciplinary genealogies and interdisciplinary migrations. In my earlier work, I criticized the historical turn in intersectionality studies, suggesting that it is often undergirded by a search for a "true" intersectionality or by an attachment to a fictive past when intersectionality was practiced in ways that more "correctly" align with its foundational texts. As I argued, "The impulse toward historicization all too often becomes a battle over origin stories, a struggle to determine who 'made' intersectionality, and thus who deserves the 'credit' for coining the term, rather than a rich engagement with intersectionality's multiple genealogies in both black feminist and women of color feminist traditions."[16] Thus, I enter the terrain of historicizing intersectionality with a sense of caution and an awareness of the potential risks of fetishizing history as the preferable orientation toward understanding intersectionality's varied work. Here, I offer an intellectual history of intersectionality that emphasizes that intersectionality is part of a cohort of terms that black feminists created in order to analyze the interconnectedness of structures of domination. In other words, as Deborah King notes, "The necessity of addressing all oppressions is one of the hallmarks of black feminist thought," even as intersectional thinking has unfolded around different keywords, analytics, and theories.[17]

While intersectional histories have long included Combahee River Collective, Kimberlé Crenshaw, Patricia Hill Collins, Deborah King, and Frances

Beal, recent black feminist scholarship has centered Anna Julia Cooper's work as foundational to modern intersectionality theory. In many ways, Vivian May's scholarship ushered in a deep feminist investment in Cooper's work as a kind of intersectional praxis, one that has been taken up by other scholars like Brittney Cooper, who has advocated for Anna Julia Cooper's place in a genealogy of "race women," of black female intellectuals.[18] For May, centering Anna Julia Cooper is not only a crucial corrective to feminist historiographies that treat intersectionality as a "recent form" of feminist engagement but also a project of feminist education that makes visible the long intellectual and political labor of black women.[19] Indeed, May reads Cooper's *A Voice from the South* (1892) as "the first book-length example of black feminist theory in the US" that "tackles the racialized, gendered, and classed meanings of personhood and citizenship," and thus as an early articulation of intersectionality theory.[20] As May indicates, "Repeatedly, I have found that an inadequate understanding of intersectionality, even in its contemporary iterations, means that Cooper's innovative ideas and complex analyses are widely misunderstood. While Cooper articulates how race, gender, class, and region (and later, nation) interdepend and cannot be examined as isolated, many of her contemporaries and later scholars examining her work could not seem to fully grasp her arguments—in large part because Cooper's words and ideas were examined via single-axis frameworks, either/or models of thought, or measures of rationality that could not account for multiplicity."[21] May's work, then, is an important corrective that underscores the long roots of intersectional thinking in black feminist thought.

The Combahee River Collective's 1977 statement has also become a touchstone for black feminist engagement with intersectionality's histories. (Indeed, the celebrated fortieth anniversary of the collective brought a renewed scholarly and popular interest in centering Combahee as an—or perhaps *the*—inaugural intersectional text.) Combahee began its manifesto by noting, "The most general statement of our politics at the present time would be that we are actively committed to struggling against racial, sexual, heterosexual, and class oppression, and see as our particular task the development of integrated analysis and practice based upon the fact that the major systems of oppression are interlocking."[22] While Combahee practiced a black feminist politics rooted in a "healthy love" of black women, its manifesto offered a theory of power that was committed to understanding how sexism, homophobia, racism, and capitalism "are interlocking." As Combahee argued, eradicating sexism would require the deconstruction of other structures of domination. Writing a decade later, from a perspective rooted in critical historiography, Evelyn Brooks Higginbotham also underscored the "interlocking" nature of structures of domination. Higginbotham's work on the "metalanguage of race" sought to consider how gender, class, and sexuality are raced categories. She writes, "Race not only tends to subsume other sets of social relations, namely, gender and class, but it blurs and disguises, suppresses and negates its own complex interplay with the very social relations it envelops."[23] Thus, gender and class become racial categories that are given meaning through processes of racial domination. While Higginbotham's intervention is animated by a plea for historians to think differently about structures of domination and their constitution, it is also a call to fundamentally reimagine the very categories that form the basis of scholarly inquiry and political activism.

Other black feminist scholars of the same period were also developing theoretical frameworks that highlighted the mutually constitutive nature of gender, race, class, and sexuality. In 1969, Frances Beal developed the concept of "double jeopardy" to capture how race and gender collude to constrain the lives of black women. For Beal, double jeopardy describes how race and gender compound each other, making black women's particular experiences qualitatively different from those of both white women and black men, an experience marked by "double discrimination." Beal writes, "As blacks they suffer all the burdens of prejudice and mistreatment that fall on anyone with dark skin. As women they bear the additional burden of having to cope with white and black men."[24] Beal's crucial work produced the concept of "jeopardy" to treat gender and race as structures of domination that inflict violence on black women, and that collaborate to inflict that violence in particularly severe ways. In 1988, Deborah King built on Beal's work by developing the idea of multiple jeopardy to capture how "the dual and systematic discrimination of racism and sexism remain pervasive, and, for many, class inequality compounds these oppressions."[25] King sought to trouble the (potential) reading of "double jeopardy" as an additive model, one which suggested that race and gender simply compounded each other to produce a kind of double discrimination. For King, jeopardy is interactive and thus describes the dynamic interplay among structures of domination. King writes, "The modifier 'multiple' refers not only to several, simultaneous oppressions but to the multiplicative relationships among them as well. In other words, the equivalent formulation is racism multiplied by sexism multiplied by classism."[26] Beal's and King's respective engagements with "jeopardy" as a keyword in theorizing black women's subjectivities reveal a long-standing black feminist debate over how exactly race and gender interact, how to adequately capture the places where these structures of domination touch.

Though scholars debate intersectionality's origins, the term is often citationally and genealogically tethered to Kimberlé Crenshaw's two articles "Demarginalizing the Intersection of Race and Sex: A Black Feminist Critique of Antidiscrimination Doctrine, Feminist Theory and Antiracist Politics" (1989) and "Mapping the Margins: Intersectionality, Identity Politics, and Violence against Women of Color" (1991). As Brittney Cooper notes, "Taken together, Crenshaw's essays catalyzed a tectonic shift in the nature of feminist theorizing by suggesting that black women's experiences demanded new paradigms in feminist theorizing, creating an analytic framework that exposed through use of a powerful metaphor exactly what it meant for systems of power to be interactive, and explicitly typing the political aims of an inclusive democracy to a theory and account of power."[27] For Crenshaw, intersectionality is an analytic fundamentally rooted in black women's experiences, and it constitutes a theoretical, political, and doctrinal effort to do justice to the forms of violence that operate in raced and gendered ways in black women's lives. She writes, "I will center Black women in this analysis in order to contrast the multidimensionality of Black women's experience with the single-axis analysis that distorts these experiences. Not only will this juxtaposition reveal how Black women are theoretically erased, it will also illustrate how this framework imports its own theoretical limitations that undermine efforts to broaden feminist and antiracist analyses."[28] In "Demarginalizing," Crenshaw deployed the metaphor of intersectionality to describe the juridical invisibility of black women's experiences of discrimination, experiences that can be—though are not always—constituted by the interplay of race and gender.[29] In response to a set of legal decisions that obscured or wholly neglected black women's experiences of discrimination, Crenshaw offered the metaphor of the intersection: "Consider an analogy to traffic in an intersection, coming and going in all four directions. Discrimination, like traffic through an intersection, may flow in one direction, and it may flow in another. If an accident happens in an intersection, it can be caused by cars traveling from any number of directions and, sometimes, from all of them. Similarly, if a Black woman is harmed because she is in the intersection, her injury could result from sex discrimination or race discrimination."[30] Law's race-*or*-gender structure necessarily renders experiences "in the intersection" invisible, essentially telling those harmed by an accident—black women—either that no harm was done or that the harm that was inflicted cannot be remedied. In Crenshaw's hands, intersectionality is a way of responding to doctrinal invisibility with an insistence that law both recognize and redress black women's particular experiences.

While Crenshaw's intersection metaphor has circulated as a way of explicating the analytic's critical aspirations, Anna Carastathis's recent work calls attention to the second metaphor of "Demarginalizing," one where Crenshaw also elaborated intersectionality's theoretical and political urgency. Crenshaw writes:

> Imagine a basement which contains all people who are disadvantaged on the basis of race, sex, class, sexual preference, age and/or physical ability. These people are stacked—feet standing on shoulders—with those on the bottom being disadvantaged by the full array of factors, up to the very top, where the heads of all those disadvantaged by a singular factor brush up against the ceiling. Their ceiling is actually the floor above which only those who are not disadvantaged in any way reside. In efforts to correct some aspects of domination, those above the ceiling admit from the basement only those who can say that "but for" the ceiling, they too would be in the upper room. A hatch is developed through which those placed immediately below can crawl. Yet this hatch is generally available only to those who— due to the singularity of their burden and their otherwise privileged position relative to those below—are in the position to crawl through. Those who are multiply-burdened are generally left below unless they can somehow pull themselves into the groups that are permitted to squeeze through the hatch.[31]

This second spatial metaphor calls attention to the limits of the juridical. Here, Crenshaw reveals that conventional conceptions of discrimination that rely on a "but for" logic always leave black women in the proverbial basement, with their experiences of harm unaddressed. In this account, intersectionality shows that antidiscrimination law is itself a technology of discrimination, rather than an actual form of redress, a location that reproduces the violence it is supposed to upend.

While Crenshaw is citationally linked to intersectionality, Patricia Hill Collins is also tethered to the intellectual and political labor of intersectionality theory, especially in the social sciences, where her conception of the "matrix of domination" has become canonized.[32] Published at the same time as Crenshaw's twin articles, Collins's *Black Feminist Thought* introduced the concept of the matrix of domination, which attends to "how . . . intersecting oppressions are actually organized."[33] The "matrix" approach emphasizes how racism, sexism, capitalism, and heteronormativity are structurally organized and thus is allied with terms like "metalanguage of race" that sought to attend to structures of power rather than identity and subjectivity. While Collins roots the matrix of domination in a larger project of centering black women as knowledge producers, her conception underscores that there are "few pure victims or oppressors. Each individual derives varying amounts of penalty and privilege from the multiple systems of oppression which frame everyone's lives."[34] In this account, the labor of the matrix of domination is to describe the specificities of social location and the violence that structures of domination inflict, in various ways and in differing severity, on everyone.

My intellectual history of intersectionality foregrounds the variety of terms black feminists have deployed to capture the complexity of structures of domination. Given black feminists' long-standing investment in theorizing the "interlocking" nature of power, it is worth considering how and why intersectionality came to be *the* preeminent term for theorizing these structures. Perhaps it is the term's irresistible visuality, its ability to be represented—even if reductively—through the crossroads metaphor that has given it a life in and beyond women's studies, and well beyond its own investment in remedying forms of juridical violence and exclusion. Unlike Kathy Davis, who treats intersectionality's "success" as fundamentally rooted in its "vagueness," I speculate that it is the term's capacity to allow its reader to imagine its analytic import, to neatly and coherently represent a term that aspires to describe complexity, that has given intersectionality its ability to migrate across entrenched disciplinary divides and to become "the most important contribution women's studies . . . has made so far."[35]

Intersectionality's Institutional Histories

In this section, I engage in another kind of historicization of intersectionality, with a particular focus on what I term the "institutional life" of intersectionality. By institutional life, I am referring both to how intersectionality has become women's studies' primary program-building tool and institutional goal and to how intersectionality has been rhetorically and symbolically collapsed into diversity, and thus taken up as an inclusion project that resonates with the mission of the so-called corporate university.[36] To be clear, my investment in the term "institutional life" is not to suggest that intersectionality was once outsider knowledge wholly detached from institutions and now finds itself problematically located within the university. Instead, I ask how an analytic often tethered to black feminism and to black woman came to be a term that both universities and specific university departments embrace and extol. What do women's studies programs and departments mean when they articulate intersectionality as their core orientation, as animating their pedagogical approaches, their hiring strategies, and their curricula building practices? If intersectionality has myriad competing meanings, what do university administrators mean when they deploy the term? How have they effectively mobilized the term as something that moves alongside diversity and inclusion?

Women's Studies

These are introspective times in women's studies. Indeed, a number of now canonical anthologies, including *Women's Studies for the Future*, *Women's Studies on its Own*, and *Women's Studies on the Edge*, grapple with what Robyn Wiegman calls the "institutional project of academic feminism," posing questions like "Did we run the risk of affirming a system we sought radically to alter?," and examining whether institutionalized women's studies has ceded what Joan Wallach Scott calls "its critical edge," its "place of indeterminancy, at once exciting and precarious."[37] These queries have their own temporal logic, with many scholars treating the 1990s, the moment when women's studies programs labored for institutional recognition and status, as "amazingly productive and exciting years. . . . In that context, women's studies gained institutional footing and funding in the form of faculty lines and/or joint appointments, student majors, and even degree-generating graduate programs."[38] This "productive and exciting" time gave way to the emergence of what Scott terms feminist "orthodoxy" or what Wendy Brown theorizes as a "politically and theoretically incoherent, as well as tacitly conservative" disciplinary project.[39] This introspective narrative often organizes itself around loss—women's studies institutional gains are marked by a sadness at the imagined "incoherence" of the field, or a sense that the political energy of the field has been lost.

In recent years, the introspective turn has taken on another dimension, moving away from the ethics and politics of institutional life and instead probing the field's critical attachments, political desires, and prevailing narratives and engaging in corrective histories that resurrect terms like "lesbian," "woman," and "second wave feminism." Scholars like Wiegman, Hemmings, and Victoria Hesford have invited us to reconsider the "stories we tell" and to critically interrogate the affective pull of prevailing stories about our discipline(s), its histories and futures. I imagine my analysis of women's studies' long engagement with black feminism, and its specific engagements with intersectionality, as a contribution to the introspective turn that examines the discipline's *racialized* attachments and narratives. As part of my contribution to theorizing the field and its racialized "stories," I make two intimately related arguments about women's studies: First, women's studies has long constructed black feminism as a form of discipline inflicted on the field and has imagined black feminists as a set of disciplinarians who quite literally whip the field into shape with their demands for a feminism that accounts for race generally, and for black women specifically. Of course, in an account where black women's primary labor is to remedy—and perhaps even to save—the field from itself, the discipline treats black women, and black feminism, as a finite resource. Once the field has effectively reconfigured itself, black feminism is imagined as no longer necessary or vital. Nowhere has this simplistic construction unfolded more visibly than in the context of intersectionality, a term that is obsessively signaled by the field as precisely what is required to remedy feminism's histories of racism and exclusion. In other words, intersectionality is imagined as the flip side of "white feminism," the kind of ethical, inclusive, and complex feminism required for feminists to revive—and to complete—their political project. Second, intersectionality has become far more than a term with an intellectual history, a term that emerged out of a cohort of black feminist engagements with the "interlocking" nature of structures of domination. It has become women's studies' primary program-building goal. As I argue later in this introduction, black feminist defensiveness emerges from these institutional conditions, from a milieu where black women are imagined as both saviors and world-ending figures, and where intersectionality is both peril and promise.

Disciplining the Discipline

As I mentioned earlier, Hemmings's groundbreaking work invites feminists to consider and interrogate "the stories we tell." The dominant narratives that satisfy us politically and affectively become how feminists both narrate and understand our own history, how we introduce students to the histories of our field, and how we organize feminist knowledge production. For Hemmings, the primary accounts we offer are progress, loss, and return. Crucially, in at least two of these prevailing stories—progress and loss— black women and black feminism function as key figures either in making progress possible and visible or in foreclosing progress and engendering a feminist sense of loss. Hemmings writes, "The forward momentum from exclusion to inclusion is achieved by a variety of techniques of comparison and citation that situate black feminist critiques as essential to the transformation of Western feminist theory."[40] Here, the labor of black feminist theory is to serve women's studies, to ensure the discipline's "forward momentum" and "transformation." In the "progress" account, black feminism—and black women—are the literal and epistemological bodies that have made possible the transformation of the field from a focus on gender to an intersectional focus.

Nowhere is the "progress" that women of color generally, and black women specifically, are called upon to produce for the field more visible than in the women's studies classroom. Lee provides an explication of the place of "women of color" classes in the women's studies curriculum, arguing that they act as a "racial alibi" where "the bodies of knowledge produced by and about women of color are less important than the hailing of 'women of color' as a synecdoche for women's studies' own blindspots."[41] As Lee further contends, "Women's studies imagines itself as having, *in the past*, omitted a race-conscious perspective in its primary focus on gender and, *in the present*, as working toward a more inclusive analysis, considering the simultaneous subjectivizing discourses of race, gender, class, sexuality, nationality, and so forth. . . . [W]omen of color symbolize the potentiality of feminist studies' critical future."[42] For Lee, the "women of color" course performs crucial affective and political work in the women's studies curriculum, announcing the transformation of the discipline. That these courses often conflate bodies of knowledge and the racially marked bodies of the scholars regularly called upon to teach the courses suggests precisely the danger of the "racial alibi" that Lee maps. While making a very different argument, Wendy Brown also highlights the place of the "women of color" course in the women's studies curriculum, capturing how students often responded to it in "intensely emotional" ways. She notes, "Faculty, curriculum, and students in women's studies programs are in a relentless, compensatory cycle of guilt and blame about race, a cycle structured by women's studies' original, nominalist and conceptual subordination of race (and all other forms of social stratification) to gender."[43] Of course, this very "cycle" that Brown captures is the result not simply of the elevation of gender to the center of women's studies but also of the discipline's figuration of black woman as aggrieved subject demanding that she be accounted for, a demand that produces precisely the complex affects Brown traces, affects of "guilt and blame." Both Brown and Lee were writing before the "citational ubiquity" of intersectionality; now it has become abundantly clear that intersectionality stands as the paradigmatic example of feminism's progress. Indeed, if there is nothing more damning than the accusation of "white feminism," intersectionality stands as the field's primary corrective, its way of naming and labeling (even if not performing) a correct, ethical, and virtuous feminism.[44]

Of course, there is a flip side—or multiple flip sides—to the "progress" narrative. If black feminist theory enabled the field to "progress," and if black feminist theory's main contribution was a demand for inclusion, then the labor of the field is complete and black feminist theory is no longer relevant or required in the way it once was. As Hemmings suggests, the underside of progress is also loss, a melancholic sense that the imagined demands of black feminism, and of black women, have produced the loss of the simplistic and coherent category of gender as the centerpiece of our work. Black women's demands, then, have fractured feminism. This anxiety is particularly visible in debates about intersectionality's imagined goal of capturing an impossible "etc.," an account of the social universe that can attend to the unending complexity of both identity and the social world. Indeed, in her now famous diagnosis of the "impossibility of women's studies," Brown points to intersectional ethics as part of the incoherence of the field. She writes, "Subjects of gender, class, nationality, race, sexuality, and so forth, are created through different histories, different mechanisms and sites of power, different discursive formations, different regulatory schemes. On the other hand, we are not fabricated as subjects in discrete units by these various powers: they do not operate on and through us independently, or linearly, or cumulatively."[45] For Brown, complex theories of subject formation like intersectionality work through attempts at "greater levels of specificity," which she describes as "mapping the precise formation of the contemporary 'middle-class Tejana lesbian,'" but this strategy simply replaces simplistic shorthand with seemingly more precise shorthand. Here, intersectionality produces an account of power that fails to "historicize and theorize" and instead simply reproduces a thin conception of power invested in precisely the concepts it aspires to deconstruct.

In this account, the labor of black feminism is imagined primarily as a critique of women's studies. Brittney Cooper captures this characterization of black feminism, noting that "non-Black feminists reduce Black feminist knowledge production into the status of an intervention in the broader project of feminism. . . . Treating Black feminism as primarily an anti-racist intervention within feminism continues to render it as a disruptive and temporary event, to be addressed, responded to, and moved on from, back to the regularly scheduled course of things."[46] The continued blindness to black feminism *as an autonomous intellectual and political tradition* that has engaged in theorizing myriad questions, developed multiple analytics including intersectionality, and done far more than ask to be "accounted for" and included in feminist theory is what enables women's studies to continue representing black feminist theory as merely a critique.

Program Building

Intersectionality is now celebrated as "*the* primary figure of political completion in US identity knowledge domains," as "part of the gender studies canon," as "a new *raison d'être* for doing feminist theory and analysis," and as "the most cutting-edge approach to the politics of gender, race, sexual orientation, and class."[47] Indeed, nowhere has intersectionality's remedial promise been vocalized more forcefully than in feminism generally, and in women's studies specifically. As I consider the term's life in academic feminism's program-building initiatives, it is crucial to note that intersectionality has become absolutely central to US feminism's political life, something I discuss at greater length in the book's coda. The now familiar mandate that "if your feminism isn't intersectional, it's bullshit" suggests the ways that intersectionality has become a kind of article of faith, and here, my intention is not to resonate with Sullivan's contention that intersectionality is "religion" but rather to invite an interrogation of the notion of intersectionality as an unqualified ethical good and "more" intersectionality as an even better ethical good.[48] Even as intersectionality remains fluid—and perhaps even ambiguous—in its meaning, there seems to be consensus that it is women's studies' "big idea," its key intellectual and political contribution, and even proof of the importance of the discipline itself.[49]

When I describe intersectionality as women's studies' primary program-building goal, I refer to how departments and programs now regularly define their central mission as training students in intersectional theory, methods, and frameworks. Syracuse University, for example, describes the objectives of its Women's and Gender Studies Department as marked by a commitment to training students "to learn about gender with an intersectional and transnational approach. To study gender either in one's own society or in the world, one must come to understand how gender ideas and practices take shape in relationship with ideas and practices about race, class, cultural identity, sexuality, nationality, and religion. . . . The possibility of understanding and solidarity among women worldwide can only be achieved by an analysis of gender and gender oppression that places both within a global and intersectional framework."[50] Ohio State University's Women's, Gender, and Sexuality Studies Department describes its mission as "generat[ing] and transmit[ing] knowledge about the gendered nature of our lives and the ways gender, sexuality and other categories of identity shape and are shaped by culture and society."[51] Berkeley's Department of Gender and Women's Studies notes that it "offers interdisciplinary perspectives on the formation of gender and its intersections with other relations of power, such as sexuality, race, class, nationality, religion, and age."[52] Denison University's Women's and Gender Studies Program "fosters critical awareness and intellectual sensitivity to women's issues, the relationship between gender and other aspects of 'identity,' including race, class, age, religion and sexuality, methods inflected by the interdisciplinary of women's studies, and how the academic study of women's issues and gender has the power to transform lives."[53] What these varied descriptions reveal is an investment in intersectionality as inherent to the labor of women's studies in the university, or at least as inherent to the labor of women's studies programs and departments that have effectively come to terms with the challenges that black feminism poses. In other words, a training in intersectionality—however it is defined—becomes central to how the program or department produces feminist scholars, and to how a program or department defines its value and importance.

If intersectionality is central to how women's studies programs and departments narrate their distinctiveness, it has also become a strategy that programs and departments use to build their capacity through hiring. Recent years have been marked by a proliferation of women's studies tenure-track and tenured faculty job advertisements seeking "intersectional scholars." These advertisements range from encouraging applicants whose scholarship is rooted in intersectionality theory—"we welcome applications from those working in one of our three key areas of interest: . . . intersectionality/ critical race theory"—to "preference will be given to the candidate who demonstrates the ability to include intersectionality in all of their syllabi."[54] In this case, intersectionality as either an intellectual or a pedagogical commitment becomes a plus in the ruthlessly competitive and increasingly precarious academic job marketplace. In other cases, there are hires in the field of "intersectional feminism and critical praxis" where programs and departments seek scholars whose "research investigates the intersection of feminist politics, critical theories of difference, and questions of resistance." Intersectionality, then, becomes a legitimizing strategy that programs and departments can mobilize to secure resources and to make tenure-track and tenured hires.

I linger in the institutional work that intersectionality performs because it is here that its status as both overdetermined and emptied of any specific meaning becomes most lucid. Indeed, intersectionality can confer value on programs and departments, aligning them with institutional priorities around diversity and inclusion (something I discuss further later in the introduction) and can confer value on job seekers laboring to distinguish themselves in an intensely crowded and competitive job market. Here, intersectionality circulates far from its intellectual roots in black feminist investment in theorizing the complexity of structures of domination. Instead, it acts as something that confers value, that signals an alignment with intellectually and politically complex theories. It is this idea of intersectionality as a "value added," as a plus, as something that signals an ethical orientation that animates the analytic's institutional life.

Black Studies

While *Black Feminism Reimagined* focuses on the entanglements between intersectionality and women's studies, the analytic has also had a complex intellectual and institutional life in black studies, one that I take up briefly here because intersectionality's roots in black feminism place it at the tender (and sometimes contentious) places where women's studies and black studies touch. In other words, intersectionality is often imagined as something that emerges in the spaces where women's studies and black studies meet, as a critique of both the "race men" logic of black studies and the "white women" logic of women's studies. Ultimately, this project argues that intersectionality has animated a kind of anxiety in women's studies that it has not in black studies, and my endeavor here is to speculate about how and why that is. While it is beyond the scope of this project to engage in a history of black studies' treatment of black feminism, I do want to trace a few distinctions between women's studies' and black studies' respective relationships with both black feminism and the specific analytic of intersectionality.

As I have already argued, women's studies has long imagined intersectionality not only as field-defining but also as transformative, as precisely the kind of disciplining feminism requires to remake itself in ways that transcend the racist exclusions that have marked both academic and political feminism. Black studies has historically staked out a very different kind of relationship with intersectionality, one rooted in an investment in theorizing black women's intellectual and political labor, and interrogating the politics of citationality. This is unsurprising in a field that has labored to carve out an autonomous institutional space for black intellectual production. Indeed, unlike women's studies, which has largely figured black feminism's remedial work as a way of remaking feminism itself, and as a tool for creating more ethical (white) feminist political subjects, black studies has engaged more deeply with scholarship invested in theorizing the invisibility of black women's intellectual labor and describing the host of ways that the academy quite literally cannibalizes black women. As Grace Hong notes, black feminist theorists have captured a "bleak and ironic future, one in which the university's fetishization of black feminism as intellectual inquiry does not render impossible, and indeed in some ways facilitates, its systemic violence against black women."[55] For Hong, this "systemic violence" is deeply material as she ruminates on the black feminists who have worked in the academy and died—June Jordan, Audre Lorde, Barbara Christian, Claudia Tate, and I would add, Stephanie Camp. These deaths, Hong suggests, are part of the academy's systemic extraction of knowledge and service from black women, alongside the university's continued inattention to the structures of violence that mark black female faculty's day-to-day experiences. Arguably, women's studies' engagement with intersectionality is part of—rather than a departure from—the "fetishization" that Hong describes. This "fetishization" is one that Ann duCille diagnosed in her consideration of how black women are both desired and disavowed in the academy, and of how the field that black women produced—black feminist theory—has become imagined as a field without a history, without scholars, as an "anybody-can-play pick-up game performed on a wide-open, untrammeled field."[56] In other words, the labor—of love, of flesh, of spirit—engaged in by black female scholars has been replaced by the fetishization of the field of black feminist theory made visible in the one-off "women of color" courses that Lee describes, with no recognition of the work required to produce the field. In response to this simultaneous disavowal and fetishization, Barbara Christian called on black feminists to "be clear about the dire situation that African-American women academics face" and to "ask questions that at first glance may seem to have nothing to do with scholarship but are central to our survival."[57] It is not surprising that in an intellectual moment where black studies is preoccupied with death—social and material—and with the ways that the state functions on black disposability, that questions of survival are at the heart of how the field interacts with black feminist theory, imagining the university as a place that quite literally kills black female flesh. For black studies, then, an account of intersectionality's rootedness in black feminism, and its intimate connection to black women, is part of a long tradition of attempting to do justice to black women's intellectual and political labor.

Paradoxically, a field invested in black women's intellectual production has moved intersectionality to the discipline's past tense by insisting that only certain black feminist texts constitute the field's present moment. Indeed, the field's current orientation toward afropessimism engages black feminist theory largely through the work of Hortense Spillers, Saidiya Hartman, Christina Sharpe, and Sylvia Wynter, often at the expense of a robust engagement with other black feminist debates, dialogue, and disagreement. (The institutional projects of women's studies and black studies, then, share a practice of elevating certain black feminist theorists to canonical—and even sacred—status by insisting on the inclusion of only one iteration of the black feminist tradition in the canon in any given historical and political moment.) Drawing on this particular body of black feminist theory, afropessimist scholarship often unsettles the category of "black woman" entirely by foregrounding Spillers's concept of ungendering, a term that describes how the Middle Passage transformed gendered black bodies into ungendered black flesh. As Samantha Pinto notes, "The enthusiastic re-exercise of Spillers's vocabularies signals a critical desire to reanimate and realign Black feminist critical thought in a moment of political intensities that career across 'the living and the dying,' between suffering and the capacity for pleasure, sometimes pitching one against another."[58] This "enthusiastic" investment in ungendering unfolds in a moment when black feminism urgently theorizes the "dead and the dying," and when ungendering is mobilized to imagine how black life is lived alongside—or even within—spaces of death.[59]

Drawing on Spillers's conceptions of ungendering and flesh, Patrice D. Douglass deploys the term "black gender" to capture how gender itself is "a category for Humans. The violence of ungendering is a domain for the captive, those who died in the hold of the ship and continue dying by the wayside of gender."[60] Put differently, "black gender" reveals that gender—as a category of analysis—fails to describe both black bodies' location as outside of the Human, and the violent force of antiblackness. "Black gender," then, aspires to put analytic pressure on the utility of "gender" as a category for black subjects, and thus to problematize intersectionality's thought project of thinking race and gender (and other categories) simultaneously in an attempt to do justice to black women.

Calvin Warren's work furthers an afropessimist critique of intersectionality, arguing that an intersectional approach "seeks to understand blackness through forms of *equivalence* with human identity. In this instance, queerness and blackness are structurally aligned such that they become somewhat interchangeable forms of abstraction or are intelligible through each other. . . . We know queerness more accurately because we know blackness, and we know blackness more intimately because we know queerness, according to this approach. Put differently, the intersectional approach makes epistemological claims by presenting blackness and queerness (and other forms of difference) as ontologically equivalent."[61] For Warren, intersectionality operates through strategies of "equivalence," through presuming that blackness and "other forms of difference" are similarly constructed and produced. In a moment in which death has become a key term for black studies, intersectionality is often policed outside the parameters of black studies proper because of its imagined desire to treat identity categories and structures of domination as "ontologically equivalent," and because of its imagined refusal to recognize antiblackness as the "metalanguage." Moreover, for afropessimist scholars, intersectionality is imagined to presume that gender is a shared or collective category. Douglass asserts, "The archive of gender is structurally anti-black. Its assumptive logic, whether explicit in its presentation or not, maintains that all women have the same gender. This orientation of thought does more than render Black gender invisible or silent. It makes it conceptually impossible to think of gender violence as orienting more than the realm of gender."[62] Thus, Douglass advocates a divestment from "black woman" as a category and, implicitly, a divestment from intersectionality as a political and theoretical project.

Of course, inherent to intersectionality's analytic power has been a critique of the notion of gender as something that "all women" share in the same way. The very call to think intersectionally, to consider how gender is made through race (and vice versa), has always been a plea to imagine gender's racialized contours, and to theorize how gender is inhabited, lived, and negotiated in particular, distinctive, and varied ways. Thus, while this book's focus is on women's studies' engagement with intersectionality, I remain fascinated by an intellectual moment in which both women's studies and black studies, animated by distinct political desires and critical aspirations, have made intersectionality passé even as they deploy black feminist theory as a necessary investment.

It might seem that my account of black studies has painted the field in a favorable light that I deny women's studies. This is not at all my endeavor. Indeed, I find it curious and troubling that black feminism and black queer studies remain marginal in most black studies' programs and departments. Moreover, as black studies moves more squarely toward an investment in theorizing death as central to black subjectivity, and in considering perishment as constitutive of black experience, I remain concerned at the host of ways that the dead are always figured as black men, and black women are those who mourn, who grieve, and who make visible black male suffering.[63] There remains a gender problem in black studies, one related to the "sexual and epistemological conservatism" that continues to mark many black studies departments and programs, and that continues to relegate work on black erotics, black queers, black women, black trans folk, black "funky" desires, and black sexual freedoms to the intellectual periphery.[64] My impulse here, then, is merely to suggest that the way these "problems" manifest themselves in women's studies and black studies is distinct.

The Diversity and Inclusion Complex

Intersectionality often moves along a set of terms that are imagined to be allied: "diversity" and "inclusion." Here, I am referring to an array of phenomena, including the emergence of intersectionality centers at colleges and universities, the Association of American Colleges and Universities' advocacy of "intersectional frameworks" as part of larger strategies of diversity and inclusion, and the emergence of the language of intersectionality in university strategic plans.[65] As many scholars have noted, "The distinction between intersectionality and diversity remains blurry," and "the language of intersectionality is now associated with diversity," even as intersectionality scholars often critique the (il)logics of diversity.[66] In this project, I explore how intersectionality is thought to be a diversity project, and what that means for the analytic's institutional life.

Diversity has become the prevailing logic of the contemporary US university. As Roderick Ferguson has argued, the university has "cannibalize[d] difference and its potential for rupture," so that "differences that were often articulated as critiques of the presumed benevolence of political and economic institutions become absorbed within an administrative ethos that recast those differences as testaments to the progress of the university and the resuscitation of a common national culture."[67] For Ferguson, this "absorption" explains the institutionalization of black studies, women's studies, and other identity-knowledge projects and their incorporation into the university as signs of the institution's own commitment to inclusion. Alongside the incorporation of difference as evidence of an institution's transformation, diversity has become a key rhetoric animating an institution's self-presentation and organization.

Diversity has operated in an array of ways. In the wake of attempts to scale back affirmative action programs in higher education, "diversity" has emerged as a justifiable compelling state interest for maintaining affirmative action efforts, provided that racial and ethnic diversity is only one form of diversity that universities invest in. As the court explained in *Grutter v. Bollinger*, a US Supreme Court case assessing the constitutionality of the University of Michigan Law School's affirmative action program,

> The Law School's claim of a compelling interest is further bolstered by its *amici*, who point to the educational benefits that flow from student body diversity. . . . [N]umerous studies show that student body diversity promotes learning outcomes, and "better prepares students for an increasingly diverse workforce and society, and better prepares them as professionals." These benefits are not theoretical but real, as major American businesses have made clear that the skills needed in today's increasingly global marketplace can only be developed through exposure to widely diverse people, cultures, ideas, and viewpoints. What is more, high-ranking retired officers and civilian leaders of the United States military assert that, "[b]ased on [their] decades of experience," a

"highly qualified, racially diverse officer corps . . . is essential to the military's ability to fulfill its principal mission to provide national security."[68]

For the court, diversity's value lies not in its capacity to remedy past and ongoing racism and exclusion but in its ability to produce student-citizens prepared for an increasingly global workforce and for military global security service. The work of diversity, then, is not meant to transform social institutions but to insert bodies into existing structures and even to engage in "rebranding an organization."[69] Yet because diversity remains permissible ground for continuing the labor of affirmative action, it has become a kind of critical vocabulary for engaging in what some have positioned as radical work, and what others have imagined as "a way . . . of marketing the university" and "making the university into a marketplace."[70] The shifting logic of affirmative action from redress to diversity has led many scholars, including Sara Ahmed and Roderick Ferguson, to imagine diversity as a kind of "nonperformative." Feminists of color have been deeply critical of diversity logics, arguing that it is a practice of "benign variation" that "bypasses power as well as history to suggest a harmonious empty pluralism."[71] Banu Subramaniam describes the emergence of diversity as "an aesthetic of celebrating cultural variation and expressions of cultural difference within liberal discourse."[72] For Subramaniam, diversity—like cultural feminism—is a project of valuation that attempts to prioritize "cultural variation" and "cultural difference." Yet, Subramaniam argues, diversity has become corrupted in its "recent institutional incarnation," becoming "utterly domesticated and depoliticized and largely seen as 'good' because it has lost its political roots of structural issues of sexism and racism."[73] Like Subramaniam, Chandra Mohanty has underscored diversity's "benign variation" logic, and Ahmed recommends that we exercise "caution" around "the appealing nature of diversity" and interrogate "whether the ease of its incorporation by institutions is a sign of the loss of its critical edge."[74] Taken together, these scholars reveal the host of ways that diversity operates in apolitical and often antipolitical ways to selectively usher a few bodies into exclusive institutions.

Despite feminist of color efforts to problematize diversity, intersectionality remains a term that moves alongside diversity even as their respective projects are wholly distinctive and even opposed. Where diversity is a project of including bodies, intersectionality is an antisubordination project, one committed to foregrounding exclusion and its effects. Yet intersectionality's ascension within the university must be theorized alongside the ways it can take on the guise of diversity work, acting as a center-building initiative that can stand as evidence of an institution's commitment to difference and inclusion. May diagnoses our present moment as one where "intersectionality may be corporatized, used rhetorically to invoke 'good feeling' or manage institutional or national image, but not to address inequality. In the academy and beyond, it is being invoked as a means to allow 'business as usual' to go forward."[75] For May, intersectionality's easy conflation with diversity is an indication of how intersectionality "seem[s], for many, difficult to grasp or hold on to, easy to ignore or discount, or, perhaps viewed as ripe for extraction or expropriation."[76] Yet rather than treat intersectionality's conflation with diversity as evidence of practitioners' inability to comprehend intersectionality's complexity, I treat it as evidence of intersectionality's elasticity, which has made it relatively easy to institutionalize, to act as outsider knowledge, as institutional diversity project, and as evidence of the workings of the so-called corporate university that has incorporated a particular kind of investment in difference.

Ultimately, the university is deeply implicated in intersectionality's mobility, at least in part because of how intersectionality has been rhetorically mobilized as an ethic of diversity, and in part because naming intersectionality is often imagined to stand in for performing a kind of intellectual and political work. As Ahmed notes, "After all universities often describe their missions by drawing on the languages of diversity as well as equality. But using the language does not translate into creating diverse or equal environments. This 'not translation' is something we experience: it is a gap between a symbolic commitment and a lived reality. Commitments might even be made because they do not bring something about. I have used the term 'non-performativity' to describe this: how a commitment can be made to something as a way of not bringing something about."[77] Of course the "diversifying" mission—which is often articulated on the backs of black women—simply shores up the projects of elitism, exclusivity, and hierarchy that bolster the university. Yet speaking the language of diversity—which the university has again and again conflated with intersectionality—has become a primary strategy for garnering resources in the context of the corporate university, and so intersectionality has become a kind of lingua franca for university life. Finally, as the university is increasingly enlisted in pedagogies of citizenship—instructing students on how to desire, on how to be antiracist, on how to perform Left subjectivity—intersectionality has become, as the provocations that begin this introduction suggest, a keyword, transforming students into ethical political subjects.[78] It is, of course, crucial to note that the reproduction of intersectionality by the university was often made possible by women's studies programs and departments (alongside allied fields) that agitated for foregrounding intersectionality's demands for complexity and attention to difference, even as college campuses are now so saturated with the rhetoric of intersectionality *as* correct Left political subjectivity that the term's specific meanings and histories are lost.

Defensiveness and Intersectionality Wars

I am part of a panel at a small conference with a few other black feminist scholars, all of whom work on intersectionality. The mood is tense as we discuss the racial politics of intersectionality's circulation, its movement across the humanities and social sciences, and its status as women's studies' signature analytic. One scholar remarks that intersectionality's ubiquity reminds her of a passage from Ntozake Shange's choreopoem *For Colored Girls Who Have Considered Suicide / When the Rainbow Is Enuf* : "Somebody almost walked off wid alla my stuff."[79] The audience roars in delight, and I find myself fascinated both by the deployment of Shange's provocative image of theft and by the audience's enthusiasm. This book was born of questions that emerged that day: Why had the idea of intersectionality as something stolen resonated so deeply? How might we understand the racial politics of this scene, one where a canonical black feminist work is used to theorize the violent theft of another canonical black feminist work? Who owns intersectionality, and who steals it? What might this encounter—the use of Shange, and the audience's reaction to it—reveal about the affects of contemporary academic US black feminisms? What does it mean when an anticaptivity project like black feminist theory claims ownership as a primary model for conducting black feminist inquiry?

I treat this scene as a point of departure to capture what I argue is a distinctively contemporary academic black feminist affect: defensiveness. I read defensiveness as a practice of a certain kind of agency—indeed, I argue that it is the primary form of agency that black feminists exert in the US academy. It is a form of agency that is seemingly exercised on behalf of black women's intellectual production, and on behalf of black women as subjects worthy of study, and one that does its work through an exertion of ownership. It is, though, ultimately a dangerous form of agency, one that traps black feminism, and black feminists, rather than liberating us, by locking black feminists into the intersectionality wars rather than liberating us from those battles, and enabling us to reveal how deeply problematic these battles are. The defensive posture produces a kind of impasse for black feminist theory, one that keeps us fundamentally stalled, and that frustrates black feminism's political projects. Indeed, the defensive position is constitutive of the impasse, the "holding pattern," that marks black feminist theory.[80] Despite evidence that the attachment to the defensive position is toxic, the attachment persists because it offers the sense of collective world-making, and because it is the exertion of a certain form of agency.

The defensive posture unfolds not only through a territorial hold on intersectionality but also in and through black feminism's ongoing attachment to the university, *even as* black feminist theorists have long captured the violence of the university. In other words, black feminist theorists retain both a deep critique of the university and its violence—including the imagined violence of intersectionality's circulation apart from black women and black feminism—and a continued faith in the university as a space that can be reformed and reimagined to do justice to black women's intellectual labor. Indeed, very few black feminist theorists have called for a wholesale rejection of the university, or a profound investment in doing black feminist theoretical and practical work outside of the killing engine of the university, even as black feminist theorists including Ann duCille, Barbara Christian, and Grace Hong have posed crucial questions of the university, like the provocation "Can black feminism survive the academy?"[81] Thus, black feminist defensive tactics around intersectionality take hold in the context of a larger theoretical tradition attached—optimistically, self-destructively, or both—to the university.

My understanding of defensiveness is also indebted to Sianne Ngai's work on "ugly feelings." For Ngai, ugly feelings are "petty, amoral, and noncathartic feelings" that "offer no satisfactions of virtue, however oblique, nor any therapeutic or purifying release. In fact, most of these feelings tend to interfere with the outpouring of other emotions." The "ugliness" of the "ugly feelings" indexes social conditions of marginality and "state[s] of obstructed agency."[82] What appeals to me about Ngai's formulation is not simply the idea of "ugliness," the sense of a negative affect that is nonproductive (though, unlike Ngai, I view black feminist defensiveness as *deeply* cathartic, and as deeply appealing in the sense that it is an ethical and virtuous practice staged on behalf of black women's intellectual production). I am also drawn to the idea of defensiveness as indexing an "obstructed agency," which for Ngai is not a personal (or psychic) condition but a social one. In other words, ugly feelings are a sign of the social conditions that allow for obstructed agency to be the only form of agency imaginable. Here, I argue, is the richness of Ngai's work for my purposes—it helps us understand black feminist defensiveness as an attempt to exercise agency, as a willful form of territorial exertion in the service of autonomy, but one that is frustrating and frustrated.

Ultimately, this book treats black feminism not simply as an intellectual, political, creative, and erotic tradition but also as a way of feeling. The felt life of black feminism is varied and complex, but what I hope to underscore here is that the felt life of black feminism is shaped by black feminism's institutional location in women's studies. In making this claim, it is not my contention that black feminism is a subsidiary of women's studies. Indeed, black feminism has its own lives outside of women's studies—in allied disciplines, including black studies, that have embraced black feminist theories, methods, and analytics—and outside of the academy. But it is precisely because women's studies has imagined black feminism as central to its institutional project, because the field is marked by a preoccupation with black woman, that I imagine black feminism and women's studies as bound up, and that, I argue, means that the felt experiences of academic black feminism are necessarily rooted in women's studies. When I describe the felt experience of black feminism, my investment is in considering how the tradition is felt by those attached to it, by black feminists themselves. It is clear that nonblack feminists also *feel* black feminism in certain ways, viewing it as a place of hope, retreat, anxiety, disgust, imagining it as both world-making and world-ending simultaneously. These are feelings projected onto black feminism and black feminists, often in ways that are supported by the field of women's studies. My own investment in tracing the felt life of black feminism, though, is in considering the structures of feeling that attend to and underpin the practice of black feminism in the academy by black feminists themselves.

In treating black feminism as a felt experience, I am attempting to honor the panoply of scholarship rooted in the intellectual tradition that has voiced the ecstasies, frustrations, longings, and fatigue of scholars who organize themselves around the sign black feminism, including Patricia J. Williams, Rachel Lee, Tiffany Lethabo King, Brittney Cooper, and Amber Jamilla Musser. These scholars have, in varied ways, named the complex experiences of performing black feminism in the academy. For example,

Cooper captures the experience of describing herself as a "black feminist theorist" and notes that she often receives "looks of confusion, eyebrows crinkling into question marks, and long awkward pauses, as colleagues wait for me to clarify. . . . This kind of ambivalence does not usually attend to my white feminist colleagues' declarations that they are 'feminist theorists,' or that they 'do feminist theory.' Even if they have to give specifics, feminist theory names a universe of possibility that Black feminist theory apparently does not."[83] If Cooper's description of the "ambivalence" (or, I would argue, disbelief) that attends to reactions of her investment in black feminism, it also describes the experience of being a black feminist in the academy. To be invested in black feminist theory in the academy, Cooper reveals, is to inhabit a position that is subject to scrutiny; it is to require an additional explanation, or to be prepared to be challenged. In other words, the experience of being a black feminist engenders certain kinds of feelings in its practitioner, feelings of fatigue, of sadness, of anger. What Cooper's account underscores is that to claim black feminism as one's academic home is an experience that has an affective charge.

Ann duCille's work also emphasizes the felt life of black feminism:

Today there is so much interest in black women that I have begun to think of myself as a kind of sacred text. . . . Within the modern academy, racial and gender alterity has become a hot commodity that has claimed black women as its principal signifier. . . . This attention is not altogether unpleasant, especially after generations of neglect, but I am hardly alone in suspecting that interest in black women may have as much to do with the pluralism and even the primitivism of this particular postmodern moment as with the genuine quality of black women's accomplishments and the breadth of their contribution to American civilization.[84]

DuCille's analysis of black women's curious place in academic life focuses on the felt life of black feminism and the paradox of being both "a sacred text" and "neglect[ed]." That is, race and gender are "hot commodities" while the fleshy materiality of black women's bodies continues to be theoretically neglected. DuCille's insight reveals that the place of black feminists in the academy is marked by an experience of what Lee terms "fetishized marginality," being both desired and disavowed simultaneously.

In flagging black feminism as having a felt experience, I am also situating it within the broad tradition of affect studies. Affect studies, as a field, has been notoriously inattentive to questions of race, and to the specific contributions of black feminist scholars in theorizing death, loss, grief, and ambivalence, to name just a few. My own desire here, then, is to craft alternative genealogies of affect theory that recognize and center the long attachment of black feminist theory to the felt life. Though a history of the affective turn falls outside of the scope of the project, I will flag that the recent investment in affect is often intellectually tethered to queer theory. Ann Cvetkovich, for example, argues that scholarship on affect is marked by an "interest in everyday life, in how global politics and history manifest themselves at the level of lived affective experience, [and this] is bolstered by the role that queer theory has played in calling attention to the integral role of sexuality within public life. Moreover, our interest in negative affects draws inspiration from the depathologizing work of queer studies, which has made it possible to document and revalue non-normative ways of living."[85] I aspire to complicate genealogies of affect studies that downplay or entirely neglect the affective work of black feminism, and its centrality to making visible the importance of affect to creative and political lives, by emphasizing both how black feminism has treated racism and sexism as felt experiences and how black feminists have theorized what it feels like to do labor that is both desired and devalued inside an academy that was not designed to celebrate or even support black women's intellectual work. Instead, I ask what it might mean to tell the story of affect theory centering, for example, Patricia J. Williams's *Alchemy of Race and Rights*, Audre Lorde's *Cancer Journals*, and Ntozake Shange's *For Colored Girls*. How might terms like "survival," "loss," "pain," "spirit," "grief," and "desire" look (and feel) different when black feminist texts are centered at the heart of the tradition?

Moreover, one of the tremendous insights of affect theory has been its invitation to consider how structures of domination feel, and to suggest that simply naming structures fails to do justice to how they move against (and inside of) our bodies. Following Kathleen Stewart's call to take notice, to inhabit, and to observe the workings of "ordinariness," recent scholarly work has turned its attention to capturing what academic life feels like. Cvetkovich, for example, characterizes academia as a location "where the pressure to succeed and the desire to find space for creative thinking bump against the harsh conditions of a ruthlessly competitive job market, the shrinking power of the humanities, and the corporatization of the university."[86] Cvetkovich reads (white academic) depression—the affect at the center of her theory-memoir—as indexing a set of social conditions that mark academic life for both graduate students and faculty on the seemingly endless grind of the tenure track. This depression is steeped in ordinariness, marked by the seemingly banal texture of an everyday life spent researching, writing (or, not writing), responding to student e-mails, performing "service" labor, and teaching. Black feminists alongside women of color feminists have offered rich ethnographies of the felt experiences of academic life, a project that continues with celebrated volumes like *Presumed Incompetent* and *Telling Histories: Black Women Historians in the Ivory Tower*.[87] This work has foregrounded practices of racialized and gendered pedagogies, theorizing how questions of authority, hierarchy, and power shape the experiences of women of color in the classroom. For example, Paulette Caldwell's work on the felt experience of black female law school faculty asks how it feels to be "the subject of a law school hypothetical," a way of reframing W. E. B. Du Bois's question "What does it feel like to be a problem?"[88] As Caldwell begins to teach *Rogers v. American Airlines*, a case centered on American Airlines' purportedly neutral ban on employees' braided hairstyles at work, she theorizes her own discomfort. She writes, "I had carefully evaded the subject of a black woman's hair because I appeared at each class meeting wearing a neatly-braided pageboy, and I resented being the unwitting object of one in thousands of law school hypotheticals."[89] Caldwell introduces the "problem" of the body for female faculty of color, the ways in which our bodies must be mitigated, performed, inhabited, toned down, and played up in a variety of ways depending on institutional and student demands. Williams describes these competing demands: "I am expected to woo students even as I try to fend them off; I am supposed to control them even as I am supposed to manipulate them into loving me. Still I am aware of the paradox of my power over these students. I am aware of my role, my place in an institution that is larger than myself, whose power I wield even as I am powerless, whose shield of respectability shelters me even as I am disrespected."[90] Williams's description of the central paradox of pedagogical life for faculty of color—how to "woo students" while "fend[ing] them off," how to claim power in an institution that systematically "disrespects" bodies of color—beautifully captures the conditions of the present. Indeed, this body of scholarship has usefully posed questions like: What are the felt experiences of teaching when one is "presumed incompetent"?

Yet what interests me about this black feminist work on the felt life of academia is its tendency to efface the affective labors of intellectual production, research, and writing. Teaching, it seems, is the space where racialized and gendered labors are most visibly performed. Research and writing are imagined as a kind of solitary refuge, or at least as spaces that are less fraught than the performative and affective task of pedagogy. This book asks: What does it feel like when analytics that one imagines as one's own—such as intersectionality—become popularized, institutionalized, ossified? How does one come to imagine an analytic, method, or tool as one's own? What does it feel like when one's scholarly work becomes termed a "buzzword" or is mobilized by universities in ways that feel at odds with one's own work? And what does it mean to feel that the symbols of one's body and intellectual production have become the cornerstone of women's studies programmatic ambitions and wills to institutionalism? My work intervenes in this conversation by treating defensiveness as the black feminist affect that attaches to the popularization and circulation of intersectionality. I understand defensiveness to be a space marked by feelings of ownership and territoriality, and by loss and grief. The book, then, theorizes defensiveness as the feeling that emerges when intersectionality is thought to be a lost object or, worse, a stolen object. It is also a book that seeks to encourage and imagine other ways of feeling black feminist, other ways of being black feminist and doing black feminist labor in the academy that eschew defensiveness and its toxicity.

ONE. a love letter from a critic,
or notes on the intersectionality wars

I discovered something about myself when reading a recently published edited volume: I am a "vocal critic of intersectionality."[1] To be hailed as one of intersectionality's critics is to inhabit deeply uncomfortable terrain. Jasbir Puar notes that the "claim to intersectionality as the dominant feminist method can be produced with such insistence that an interest in exploring other frames . . . gets rendered as problematic and even produces WOC [women of color] feminists invested in other genealogies as 'race-traitors.'"[2] Puar reveals that scholars who pose questions about intersectionality's critical limits, or who "explore" other analytics, are often marked as traitorous. To have one's work deemed criticism is to feel as though one has been removed—excommunicated, even—from the boundaries of black feminism precisely because one is imagined as inflicting harm on the very intellectual, political, ethical, and creative terrain that black women have labored to carve out. My impulse, then, was to understand "vocal critic" as much more than an intellectual critique: this was an allegation challenging my political commitments to the project of black feminism. My desire was to seek to defend myself from these charges, to insist that I admire intersectionality, that my work endeavors to be generative, not destructive.

This chapter aspires to suspend that critical desire, even as I am deeply intrigued by it. What are the intellectual and political conditions that permitted me to understand the word "critic" as an allegation? Why has the term "critic," in the context of robust scholarly debate about intersectionality, taken on such a powerful charge? Rather than resist the term or refuse its interpellation, this chapter follows the word "critic" around the black feminist theoretical archive, endeavoring to carefully trace to whom it attaches, and what makes that attachment possible. My investment in tracking the meanings embedded in the term "critic" follows Claire Hemmings's call to trace the "stories we tell." In so doing, this chapter asserts that black feminist theorists emphatically retell a singular story about intersectionality: the analytic is the subject of vicious and inaccurate attacks, the victim of an intense "backlash" marked by "a remarkable degree of epistemic intolerance."[3] In this account, one group of scholars supports intersectionality—black feminists—and another powerful chorus of scholars is opposed to the analytic: the critics. This is a deeply compelling narrative: it has a victim (intersectionality; or, perhaps more broadly, black feminism) and a villain (the ubiquitous critic). The story also has a moral imperative: intersectionality must be saved, and black feminists must defend intersectionality from these unwarranted and misguided attacks. This affectively saturated narrative has come to animate the intersectionality wars, the contentious battles that swirl around intersectionality and that garner their urgency and ethical legitimacy from attempts to protect intersectionality from the "loveless and world-ending" figure of the critic.[4]

Yet, as I argue in this chapter, this compelling narrative is the site of various projections and fantasies. A close engagement with black feminist citational practices reveals that intersectionality's critic, always constructed by black feminism as outside black feminism's critical and ethical reach, is actually imaginatively produced *by* black feminists as they are locked into practices of holding on. In treating the critic as an imaginative projection, I am careful not to argue that black feminists are engaged in dreaming up something that is not there; instead, I consider how women's studies' positioning of black feminists as disciplinarians who demand that the field offer an account of black women actually gets performed by black feminists as they contend with intersectionality's movement to the field's center by guarding intersectionality from the phantasm of the critic. In other words, black feminists are enlisted in becoming precisely what the field imagines them to be—relentless, demanding, policing disciplinarians—as they expose and condemn the critics who are imagined to fail to adequately and fairly account for intersectionality, for black feminist theory, for black women's intellectual production. The constant invocation of the malicious critic as a pernicious outsider becomes a crucial rhetorical, theoretical, and ethical strategy through which black feminists reassert their territorial claim to intersectionality and perform their collective desire to shield intersectionality from violent criticism. Ultimately, this chapter shows what happens when black feminists—who have long been part of a movement against captivity in its myriad forms—hold captive intersectionality in the face of an imagined dangerous critic.

In the first section of the chapter, I engage the intersectionality wars, arguing that the prevailing story I have traced here is the centerpiece of those wars. In the second section, I aspire to determine how black feminists decide who—or what—constitutes traitorous critical labor. In so doing, I argue that the critic's production supports black feminism's defensive posture and suggest that the psychic life of black feminism is, once again, worthy of sustained attention. In place of entrenching black feminism's territorial relationship with intersectionality, one that responds to the analytic's centrality to women's studies through asserting a proprietary claim to the analytic and guarding it from imagined outsiders, this chapter asks what would happen if we—black feminists—considered intersectionality's critics as figures who lovingly address us, who generatively bring (rather than destructively take), and who offer their participation in black feminism's long-standing world-making project. This chapter, then, is an attempt to interrupt the black feminist disavowal of intersectionality's critics, figures who are the absent-presences that haunt black feminist engagement with intersectionality, and to instead argue that the spectral figure of the critic might provide an opportunity to embrace precisely the letting go the book celebrates.

The Intersectionality Wars

At the 2014 American Studies Association (ASA) conference, a panel entitled "Kill This Keyword" asked: "What kind of work do the commonplace keywords of current American studies endeavors do? (How) Can critical leverage, incisive edge, be returned to commonplace terms, or to the ideas to which they refer? What terms have fallen out of favor that might be reanimated in the face of the demise of another?"[5] Panel members were invited to reflect on widely circulating scholarly terms like "precarity," "neoliberalism," and "affect," and to determine if these terms should be "killed"—banished from our scholarly lexicon—or "saved." Nothing generated more anxiety than intersectionality, which was immediately declared dead. Moments after a collective performance of intersectional fatigue, a scholar voiced discomfort with "killing" intersectionality because to do that would be to "kill" black feminism, or perhaps even to "kill" black woman as object of study. The room grew quiet at the prospect of symbolically killed black women. As intersectionality slipped into black feminism slipped into black woman, the analytic moved from dangerous to desirable, from peril to promise, and the audience that had been quick to kill had been convinced to rescue.

The term "intersectionality wars" describes the discursive, political, and theoretical battles staged in this scene. Indeed, as this ASA encounter makes visible, debates about intersectionality all too quickly become referendums on whether scholars are "for" or "against" intersectionality (rather than attempts to refine, nuance, complicate, or even think through intersectionality's contours and migrations). And debates about whether one is "for" or "against" intersectionality almost always seem to become referendums on whether one is "for" or "against" black feminism, and perhaps "for" or "against" black woman herself.[6] These slippages—between black woman and black feminism, between intersectionality and black woman, between intersectionality and black feminism—animate the intersectionality wars because they ensure that discussing intersectionality's critical limits is always already to debate racial politics and allegiances. Undergirding the ASA scene, and the intersectionality wars more broadly, are the affective dimensions of the prevailing narrative I described earlier, one where intersectionality is under siege and must be saved, one where a group of critics who are characterized in various ways—ranging from misguided careerists to antiblack or anti–black feminist—have made it a mission to undermine black feminists' intellectual contributions.

I am drawn to the term "intersectionality wars" because of its echo with feminism's other wars, most particularly the sex wars. Waged in the 1980s, and reaching a feverish pitch around the time Barnard's 1982 Scholar and Feminist Conference focused on "pleasure and danger," the so-called sex wars *seemed* to be battles over pornography.[7] These "wars," though, were about much more than pornography; the "sex wars" were bound up with accusations of policing sexual minorities and attempts at censorship, especially in light of Catharine MacKinnon and Andrea Dworkin's attempt to pass antipornography legislation and the Feminist Anti-Censorship Taskforce's decision to file an amicus brief in *American Booksellers v. Hudnut.* Even the casting of widely circulating and complex debates about pornography as a "war" suggests that feminists defined themselves exclusively as "for" or "against" pornography, eliding myriad feminist work that sought to stake out a complex analysis of pornography's meanings, pleasures, and cultural significance. Similarly, the intersectionality wars *seem* to be fights over intersectionality's meanings, circulations, origins, "appropriation," and "colonization," but these fights are *actually* battles over the place of the discipline's key sign—black woman—in the field imaginary. These wars are fights over questions like: Will black women "save" so-called white feminism with an insistence on intersectionality as the analytic that will free feminism from its exclusionary past and present? Will black women undo feminism with a demand for a complex account for difference? Will black women's efforts to discipline the field finally—and even redemptively—exculpate the field from its racist past? What is intersectionality's ultimate theoretical and political goal?

If the "sex wars" were rooted in the sexual culture—and sexual panics— of the late 1970s and early 1980s, the intersectionality wars that I trace in this book are relatively recent battles, rooted in intersectionality's "citational ubiquity," its movement across disciplinary borders, across administrative/intellectual boundaries, and across academic/popular boundaries.[8] I date the intersectionality wars to intersectionality's institutionalization, to the rise of Kimberlé Crenshaw's articles "Mapping the Margins" and "Demarginalizing the Intersection of Race and Sex" to near-canonical status, and the movement of intersectionality to the center of women's studies. I also date it to intersectionality's circulation in popular feminist conversations as a way of signaling a critical practice attentive to (certain forms of) difference, as a way of disciplining so-called white feminism and white feminists, and as a strategy for naming ethical practices of feminism. As more scholars have laid claim to intersectionality, as more disciplines have come to value—at least rhetorically—intersectionality, the intersectionality wars have escalated, with black feminists increasingly stepping into the fray to defend the analytic from imagined misuse and abuse, from improper circulations and devaluations.

Like the sex wars, the intersectionality wars have been waged in contentious ways. The sex wars were played out through public confrontations— debates over Barnard's "Pleasure and Danger" Diary, battles over the proposed antipornography legislation, civil rights hearings led by MacKinnon and Dworkin, and protests against antipornography legislation; the intersectionality wars have been played out in increasingly contentious scholarly battles waged at conferences, in journal articles, and at myriad symposiums celebrating intersectionality and its interdisciplinary cache. In describing these battles as contentious, I am particularly drawn to considering the tone of these scholarly debates as the location where the deep antagonisms of these battles are most visible. My turn to form—and to tone—is indebted to the work of Janet Halley, who argues that "political ideas have prose styles" and that "you can find out something about your political libido by feeling for whether you are turned on or off by a political idea's way of addressing itself to you."[9] The intersectionality wars are produced through particular kinds of appeals that work on the reader's "political libido" through language that underscores the violence inflicted on intersectionality by "critics." In other words, these "wars" are waged through exposure: black feminists reveal the violence of critics' work through language that is itself forceful. For example, Brittney Cooper describes Jasbir Puar's work as an "*indictment* of intersectionality."[10] Nikol Alexander-Floyd argues that Leslie McCall's widely cited article "The Complexity of Intersectionality" "*disappears* black women and their scholarly contributions; more pointedly, her analysis *does violence* to the progenitors of intersectionality by subverting their aims and objectives."[11] She also warns, "Barely a decade into the new millennium, a new wave of raced-gendered *occultic commodification* is afoot, one focusing not on black female subjectivity per se, but on the concept of intersectionality."[12] Sirma Bilge writes, "Intersectionality, originally focused on transformative and counter-hegemonic knowledge production and radical politics of social justice, has been *commodified and colonized* for neoliberal regimes."[13] The Crunk Feminist Collective notes, "Intersectionality without women of color is a *train wreck*. Call us parochial if you want to, but we should remember that in the case of both these theories, they grew out of the lived political realities of marginalized people."[14]

I put these distinct quotes next to each other to call attention to something that permeates black feminist entanglement in the intersectionality wars: the language used to describe and capture the violence performed by intersectionality's critics—disappearing, commodification, colonization, and "train wrecks"—suggests that criticism is a violent practice. The impulse undergirding these readings of intersectionality's critics is prosecutorial: it exposes, indicts, and condemns. This reading practice works on readers' "political libido" by representing an intersectionality under siege, rendered vulnerable by the labor of critics, and ultimately salvaged by the labor of black feminists themselves. The labor of black feminist scholarship, then, is to incite the reader to protect intersectionality from a set of forces— colonization, appropriation, gentrification—that are undeniably violent. It is intersectionality's vulnerability that demands a protective response. In noting that this language works on the "libido," my intention is not to suggest that it produces only political arousal—it might just as easily produce disgust, boredom, or unhappiness. Rather, my interest is in how these battles are waged in a language that reproduces intersectionality's vulnerability in the service of enlisting readers in the battle to preserve and protect the analytic.

If the intersectionality wars are contentious, what precisely is being fought over? What are the battles that are unfolding under the sign of intersectionality?

Origin Stories

The intersectionality wars are often waged over competing origin stories that narrate the genesis of intersectionality. When I describe origin stories, I capture how black feminism often tethers intersectionality to a coherent, legible origin, describing a particular moment of intersectionality's creation. Origin stories work by presuming that intersectionality emerged not through debate or collaboration but through a *singular* voice, historical moment, or foundational text. In this way, origin stories are distinct from intellectual genealogies that trace how concepts emerge from multiple traditions or that analyze how different theoretical traditions treat the same concept differently. Intersectionality's origin stories circulate in (at least) two ways. First, they respond to women's studies' "whitening" of intersectionality by centering the analytic's origin in black feminist studies.[15] They often insist on intersectionality's presence in black feminist theory well before the term was coined or emphasize intersectionality's long roots in black feminist scholarship and activism. In so doing, they underscore both the term's historical underpinnings and its fundamental connection to black feminist scholarship. Second, origin stories function as debates internal to black feminism about who coined the term, who its inaugural scholar is, and whose terrain intersectionality "originally" was.

What origin stories share, despite their varied investments in intersectionality's "original" location, is an insistence on intersectionality's place *in* black feminist thought, thus correcting the widely circulating notion that intersectionality is the "product" or intellectual contribution of women's studies. They directly counter the "whitening of intersectionality," which, as Sirma Bilge notes, refers not "to the race of intersectionality practitioners, but to the ways of doing intersectionality that rearticulate it around Eurocentric epistemologies."[16] One of the central ways this "whitening" unfolds, according to Bilge, is through the now commonplace claim that intersectionality was "in the air," that it was nascent in women's studies long before it was named.[17] This proprietary feminist claim to the analytic ignores "the historical fact that intersectionality was developed by black women activists and intellectuals *against* white-dominated feminism, as much as against the male-dominated black liberation movement, against capitalism and heterosexism."[18] Anna Carastathis offers a similar critique of women's studies' historically inaccurate claims about intersectionality, noting that "the appropriation of intersectionality by 'women's studies' and 'feminist theory' (which remain white-dominated discourses) can serve to obscure its origins in Black feminist thought."[19] The black feminist response to this "whitening" is to assert, as Jean Ait Belkhir does, that intersectionality is "one of the greatest gifts of *black women's studies* to social theory as a whole."[20] In Belkhir's account, intersectionality is not only a product of black feminist theory but also an indication of black feminist generosity, since intersectionality is a crucially important "gift" bestowed upon women's studies by black feminists. For my purposes, what is fascinating about the response to women's studies' proprietary claims to intersectionality is black feminist theory's own proprietary claims to the analytic. The subject of debate, then, becomes who truly owns intersectionality, who gets to claim the term as their property.

The labor of reiterating and emphasizing intersectionality's rootedness in black feminist thought is a critical response to women's studies and its imagined "appropriation" (a term I will discuss later in this chapter) of black feminist scholarship. It is also a practice of black feminist holding on, a corrective claim that retells intersectionality's history in an ostensibly accurate way, one that honors the analytic's location in black feminism and its intimate connection to black women's intellectual labor. It is through corrective labor that defensiveness garners its affective and political charge; it offers the promise of speaking on behalf of black women, black women's intellectual production, and black feminism in the face of critical practice that is imagined to efface black women. Thus, black feminist origin stories counter a circulating (institutionalized) feminist origin story with a counter–origin story, one that emphasizes the analytic's "subaltern and liminal origins."[21]

While origin stories are a strategy for countering women's studies' narratives about the analytic, they often produce their own sets of debates and contests. Indeed, black feminists also consider intersectionality's history among themselves, often posing the question: Who invented the term "intersectionality"? As I mentioned in the introduction, within black feminism, origin stories are often amplified in disciplinary-specific ways. Black feminist social scientists, for example, regularly perform intersectional origin stories through Patricia Hill Collins's work on the "matrix of domination," while black feminist humanists often perform these origin stories through Crenshaw's work on intersectionality.[22] Still others perform their origin stories through engagement with the historical underpinnings of intersectionality, emphasizing earlier intersectional innovators like the Combahee River Collective, Deborah King, Frances Beal, and/or Anna Julia Cooper. Oftentimes these appeals to earlier black feminist scholarship seek to locate intersectionality's arrival in a moment that long predated the arrival of anti-essentialist feminism *or* to complicate the narrative that anti-essentialist feminism only arrived in the 1970s. Importantly, all these origin stories perform political work—they take complicated intellectual genealogies and reduce them to a single story, engaging in corrective labor that rewrites circulating narratives about intersectionality. They emphasize that "intersectional ideas have repeatedly been misconstrued or treated reductively" and thus historicize the analytic while asking why "intersectionality concepts have had to be reiterated for well over a century."[23]

Even as these debates unfold in disciplinarily specific ways, it is crucial to note that Crenshaw's work has remained a touchstone. Some black feminist scholarly work describes her two articles as the site where intersectionality "was introduced and later elaborated."[24] For example, Devon Carbado notes that Crenshaw's "Demarginalizing" article "introduced what would become an enormously influential theory—intersectionality," Vrushali Patil describes intersectionality as "delineated by Kimberlé Crenshaw and elaborated by subsequent authors," and Barbara Tomlinson notes that the analytic was "emanating" from Crenshaw's work.[25] In other words, a substantial part of the labor of black feminist origin stories is to center Crenshaw, to insist on her fundamental centrality to intersectionality's intellectual genealogy, and to emphasize her role as *creator* of the analytic. According to this rich body of scholarship, Crenshaw's articles are intersectionality's urtexts, and Crenshaw is intersectionality's creator.

Yet other black feminist work seeks to challenge and to correct the centrality of Crenshaw to intersectional histories. Collins, for example, upends the "stock" intersectional origin stories that emphasize Crenshaw because, in those accounts, "Crenshaw was Columbus. . . . She came back from the native lands from far, far away with the gift of intersectionality. Wow, she brought us a present!"[26] For Collins, prevailing narratives of intersectionality's origins obscure the analytic's true birthplace: social movements and activism. In their collaborative work on intersectionality, Collins and Bilge emphasize that intersectionality has undergirded black feminist practice for generations, including the work of Frances Beal, Sojourner Truth, Anna Julia Cooper, Toni Cade Bambara, and the Combahee River Collective. According to this counter–origin story, one attentive to intersectionality's long historical roots, intersectionality was always present in black feminist work, particularly black feminist activist work, even if was not named as such. This impulse toward historicizing intersectionality is not to capture the variety of kinds of intellectual and political labor black feminists have engaged in but instead to emphasize that black feminists have *done* intersectionality for decades. Yet this historical narrative—one that emphasizes intersectionality's long presence—has another effect, which is to suggest that all black feminist intellectual and political work has always been intersectional.

My reading of these widely circulating, albeit disciplinary-specific, competing black feminist origin stories presents a different account of debates over intersectionality's histories than Robyn Wiegman's work, which argues that black feminist engagements with intersectionality's genealogies break "with the general habits of feminist critical practice, which routinely confer on *the namer* much more than citational status and rarely posit a scholar's articulation of a term in the lower register that 'coinage' infers."[27] Wiegman suggests that black feminist work on intersectionality "refuses the lure of the signature in favor of a history of collective critical and political endeavor."[28] The insistence on citing scholars *before* Crenshaw is treated as indicative of a (radical?) refusal of the singular, a critical practice that relishes the collective and disrupts the logic of "coinage." Yet, I argue that black feminist defensive work too rarely "refuses the lure of the signature," even as black feminist scholarship is divided over whether the analytic originated with Crenshaw, Collins, Higginbotham, Combahee, or Cooper, and too often is seduced by the narrative of singularity. While some black feminist scholars locate intersectionality *before* Crenshaw, the preoccupation with locating intersectionality in a singular moment, and the ongoing battles over who coined it, reflect the profound "lure" of the origin narrative, particularly in the context of the intersectionality wars. Insisting on intersectionality's "correct" origins and its long-standing practice is an effort to carefully guard the analytic from abuse.

Ultimately, if origin stories offer a single narrative that performs its own elisions, they also participate in—rather than critically disrupt—the intersectionality wars. In their insistence on correcting feminist narratives by insisting on intersectionality's roots in the bodies of black women, they continue the battle over ownership and territoriality that plagues these wars, rather than critically interrogating how and why women's studies has "laid claim" to intersectionality, and examining when, how, and why intersectionality has come to have value for women's studies. These questions engender a critical shift within black feminist debates; rather than insisting on correct citational practices and "accurate" genealogies, they ask us to consider how and why citing intersectionality became the gold standard of feminist work, and even to consider what it is we mean when we talk about intersectionality and its value.

Appropriation

Undergirding the debate about the "whitening" of intersectionality is a broader claim: that intersectionality is terrain that has been taken over—colonized—by (white) women's studies. Black feminist scholars regularly mobilize language like "gentrification," "appropriation," "commodificiation," and "colonization" to describe how intersectionality "travels" in troubling ways. The intersectionality wars are often waged through attempts to highlight—and police—intersectionality's "appropriations." These scholars insist on reading the analytic's movements across disciplinary borders, and its movement to the center of women's studies, as evidence of misuse, wrongful circulation, and theft. If intersectionality has been taken—or, perhaps in the language of these scholars, *stolen*—then the task of black feminism is to expose the theft and to reclaim proper ownership of the analytic. The language of "appropriation" and "commodification" performs this exposure and reveals the necessity of a black feminist reclamation of the analytic. For example, Alexander-Floyd warns, "Barely a decade into the new millennium, a new wave of raced-gendered occultic commodification is afoot, one focusing not on black female subjectivity per se, but on the concept of intersectionality."[29] Alexander-Floyd's insights—linking intersectionality's circulation to a form of "occultic commodification"—are a point of departure not simply for considering intersectionality's current iterations in women's studies but also for uncovering the *feelings* that intersectionality's institutionalization engenders in black feminist theory and in black feminists. If intersectionality has been *commodified*, it is to suggest that the analytic, the result of intellectual labor, has been imbued with value, and that it has been rendered a product for sale (or for theft) in the marketplace of ideas. Here, intersectionality comes to stand in for black women—both of which are sites of magical value and incessantly devalued. It is this paradox, what Rachel Lee terms the space of "fetishized marginality," that the language of appropriation underscores.[30]

Feminist scholarship pointing to problems of commodification often highlights how intersectionality's circulation allows scholars to *pretend* to engage in intersectional labor. Rachel E. Luft and Jane Ward, for example, write: "When not joined to intersectional practice, intersectional intonations function as a kind of credentialing, an appropriation used to mask an anti-intersectional orientation. . . . [T]he language of intersectionality can serve to inoculate against charges of racism. It distracts from the speaker's resistance to the struggle for racial justice, like other liberal and/or color-blind disclaimers. A generation and more ago, the primary intersectional error was omission. Today it is joined by appropriation, and the failure is one of justice, of commitment to feminist, racial, economic, and sexual social transformation."[31] Like Bilge, Luft and Ward advance a historical argument: if, in feminism's past, intersectionality emerged to remedy "omission," an inattention to women of color, in feminism's present, intersectionality has been "appropriated," stripped of radical meaning and instead used to "credential" and to "mask an anti-intersectional orientation." Similarly, Carastathis bemoans "the *appropriation* of intersectionality by 'women's studies' and 'feminist theory' (which remain white-dominated discourses)," arguing that the mobilization of the term "can serve to obscure its origins in Black feminist thought."[32] In other words, intersectionality is used to disguise, to cover, and to "mask" "white-dominated discourses." Intersectionality not only is severed from its "true" origins but also is used to undermine its very project.

While commodification is one rhetorical device through which defensiveness is ethically mobilized, colonization is another. The language of colonization, often paired with commodification, positions intersectionality as a territory that has been wrongfully, problematically, and even violently taken by outsiders. Bilge writes, "Intersectionality, originally focused on transformative and counter-hegemonic knowledge production and radical politics of social justice, has been *commodified and colonized* for neoliberal regimes."[33] Here, Bilge is engaged in an origin story (intersectionality *once* was radical and "transformative" and has been stripped of its political edge) and a story about wrongful possession, but she is also engaged in a story about theft, about the reclamation of the analytic by outsiders. In this act of colonization, intersectionality paradoxically works to enable scholars who are not "actually" performing intersectional work to make intersectional claims, or to disguise their work in the guise of intersectionality, all the while maintaining the status quo. Colonization allows scholars to lay claim to intersectionality, and the idea of virtuous feminist labor that attaches to intersectionality, without *actually* performing the demanding work of intersectional work. The language of colonization also points to the necessary decolonial labor of black feminist theory. To return intersectionality to black feminists, and to black women, is to effectively undo long-standing practices of feminist colonialism. It is, then, a practice of justice.

Yet the language of appropriation leaves two central questions unanswered. First, it is unclear how "appropriation" is different than the "travel" or migration of theories. Intellectual ideas circulate; of course, their circulation is made possible by structures that confer value on certain concepts and devalue others, by the institutional and geographic contexts in which ideas emerge. But this work has yet to distinguish appropriation from the variety of uses to which any theory will be put by scholars of differing theoretical and political traditions. Second, where this scholarship succeeds is in its rigorous display that the capacity to call one's work intersectional is a claim to value, hence the ways that scholars who perform a variety of forms of theorizing have attempted to make use of the term "intersectional" to describe their work. However, this body of scholarship has yet to clearly reveal—and then dismantle—the system of value that aligns "intersectional" with "good feminist work," that presumes that intersectional scholarship is politically virtuous. Instead, it reinvests in intersectionality's value by attempting to limit who can rightfully access the analytic.

I have carefully mapped the terrain of the intersectionality wars, revealing that while they seem to be waged over origin stories and accounts of appropriation, they are undergirded by a common and compelling narrative. This is a story of villains (critics) and saviors (black feminists). The intensity of the intersectionality wars is made possible because of the affective pitch of this story, and at stake in the intersectionality wars is black feminist labor to speak for black feminist theory, to speak for black women's intellectual labor, to speak for black women. This "speaking for" takes the form of advocating for intersectionality in the face of myriad challenges levied at the analytic.

Intersectionality's Critics

The remainder of this chapter turns to the figure of the critic, who is represented as both ubiquitous and destructive, relentlessly attacking intersectionality in precisely the moment that the analytic has achieved "success" and interdisciplinary cache.[34] To be clear, my interest in carefully tracing how the term "critic" circulates in black feminist scholarship is not to imply that there are *no* criticisms of intersectionality. Indeed, there are a number of "critiques" of the analytic that have circulated in scholarly literature across the humanities and social sciences, ranging from a sense that the analytic is too focused on the race/gender intersection, to the notion that the analytic is tethered to fixity rather than motion, to the idea that it relies on precisely the categories it could—and should—disrupt.[35] The emergence of so-called post-intersectionality, especially in the context of the legal academy, suggests that a number of scholars have raised important questions about intersectionality and its applicability and have imagined refashioning intersectionality to unleash its utility and analytic power.[36]

I also read the black feminist preoccupation with the critic as apart from scholarly engagement with intersectionality's institutionalization. For example, Maria Carbin and Sara Edenheim note that intersectionality "has moved from being a sign of threat and conflict to (white) feminism to a consensus-creating signifier that not only made the concept successful but also enabled an institutionalization of a liberal, 'all-inclusive' feminism based on a denial of power as constitutive for all subjects."[37] Their insight centered on intersectionality's "consensus-creating" status invites rigorous feminist engagement with how and why intersectionality has come to occupy the center of US women's studies (and, according to them, European women's studies as well). My interest is in something different: not in a set of critical queries posed about intersectionality and its "successes" but in how the critic has emerged as a singular figure who is imagined to be both *outside* of intersectionality and *destructive* to the analytic.

What marks the critic? What are her critical practices? The critic, according to black feminist scholarship, is marked by her "cavalier treatment" of intersectionality and by the production of work that is "damaging to feminist antisubordination scholarship and activism."[38] The critic's work is destructive precisely because it is "insipid, apolitical, one dimensional, anodyne."[39] If the critic is engaged in a violent act, she is also involved in a trendy practice, since critique has become "all the rage."[40] As May argues,

"Intersectionality critiques have become something of their own genre—a form so flourishing, at times it seems critique has become a primary means of taking up the concept and its literatures."[41] Critique thrives, then, because of institutional politics that value dissent more than generative critical practice; intersectionality's critics, then, are careerist. As Tomlinson notes, "Rhetorical misrepresentations of intersectionality emerge in part from professional pressures, reward structures, and credentialing mechanisms. Scholars are eager to publish. Displacing and supplanting previous knowledge conforms to the structures of professional reward. Scholars may exaggerate criticisms to draw on the prestige of the appearance of novelty and innovation in ways that are destructive rather than constructive and competitive rather than contributive."[42] Rather than posing important questions about intersectionality and its limits, the critic's queries about intersectionality are motivated by an unrelenting willingness to yield to the demands of the corporate university. While the critic's work is "produced under the dispassionate guise of theoretical disagreement," it actually "broadsides against black feminist theorizing."[43] Critique is not only oppositional to intersectionality but oppositional to the project of black feminism more broadly.

While black feminists have carefully pointed out the ubiquity of critiques, there has been considerably less care in naming the critics who supposedly proffer and circulate these critiques. For example, Tomlinson regularly names "the critic," describing the myriad forms of violent work this subject performs:

> Critics may argue, for example, that intersectionality should be set free from the identities of the marginalized women of color who originated it. Critics may claim that intersectionality has not yet revealed as much as it ought to about identities or has not examined the most important identities, one's own identity, enough identities, too many identities, or identities in a complex enough way (Staunæs 2003; Prins 2006; Taylor, Hines, and Casey 2011). They may assume that intersectionality is legitimated by an individual's conscious awareness and balancing of individual aspects of identity rather than revealing structures of power (Carastathis 2008; Weston 2011). In consequence, critics may assume, rather than argue, that eliminating subordination is no longer necessary or no longer a feminist goal (Hancock 2007a; Nash 2008), treating intersectionality's originating interest in structural power as

readily disposable and self-evidently no longer of concern. Critics may even argue as if intersectionality's critique of structural power interferes with its more important use for developing general theories of identity (Prins 2006; Nash 2008).[44]

I linger in two moments in Tomlinson's description of the critic's varied and dangerous labor—first, the ubiquity of the term "critics." Critics are presumed to be monolithic in their labor; all critics (who are named in clustered parenthetical citation to collapse any distinction or variation in their work and to shore up a vision of the monolithic and dangerous critic) perform the same intellectual and political work. Indeed, *all* critics seem to perform *all* of the labor that Tomlinson references: effectively undermining intersectionality's antisubordination efforts and ensuring intersectionality's vulnerability.

Second, though "critics" are mentioned in parenthetical citations, it is often unclear *how* they perform the labor they are alleged to engage in, and which critics engage in which problematic practices. Instead, the reader encounters a list of critics' names that conjures the ubiquity of all of the problematic work critics perform. Take, for example, the contention that "critics may assume, rather than argue, that eliminating subordination is no longer necessary or no longer a feminist goal." How do the critics parenthetically cited perform that work? Do we do it in the same way? Through what kind of work have we ventured that the task of antisubordination is over? How do critics "assume" rather than "argue" this claim? The practice of parenthetical citations, which clusters scholars whose work on intersectionality is actually quite complex and varied, secures the notion of an intersectionality under siege, vulnerable to the all-encompassing labor of critics.

While Tomlinson's analysis produces the critic as ubiquitous through a citational practice that collapses differences among scholarly projects, May's work presents the critic's labor as so odious that any feminist scholar or activist would have to reject it. She notes that critique can "feel remedial in nature, even quasi-Eugenic."[45] Indeed, she argues that many of the ways that intersectionality has been critiqued "evoke the hyper-surveillance and micro-aggressions faced by women of color in the culture at large but also in the academy."[46] As is the case with Tomlinson's account, absent from this analysis is precisely *what* these critiques are and *who* is proffering them. Yet the notion of critique as a practice that bolsters and enforces "hyper-surveillance" and racist "micro-aggressions" necessarily requires the reader to reject critique and to align herself with black feminist attempts to safe-guard the analytic. Similarly, May notes, "Intersectionality turns up reg-ularly in the critical literatures as akin to a destructive, unruly Sapphire figure (who needs to be tamed/taken down); a theoretically unsophisticated concept (while, at the same time, often lauded as experience's poster child); a dated idea in need of a makeover; or a deficient body of thought in need of a remedial/eugenic cure."[47] In May's account, critiques of intersectionality are deeply racist, transforming the analytic into an "unruly Sapphire fig-ure" in need of disciplining. This account operates on the reader's "political libido" by enlisting the reader to recognize the deeply racialized work of critiquing intersectionality.

Finally, some "pro-intersectionality" scholars insist that critiques of in-tersectionality are so commonplace, so "standard," that they need not be cited at all. Devon Carbado, for example, examines "standard criticisms" of intersectionality that permeate feminist conversations about intersection-ality. This list includes the following:

1 Intersectionality is only or largely about Black women, or only about race and gender.
2 Intersectionality is an identitarian framework.
3 Intersectionality is a static theory that does not capture the dy-namic and contingent processes of identity formation.
4 Intersectionality is overly invested in subjects.
5 Intersectionality has traveled as far as it can go, or there is noth-ing more the theory can teach us.
6 Intersectionality should be replaced by or at least applied in con-junction with [fill in the blank].[48]

The only "critique" that warrants engagement with the work of a specific scholar is the sixth, about which Carbado notes:

This brings me to the final criticism, which is not a criticism at all but rather a suggestion (against the backdrop of the preceding criti-cisms) that scholars should replace intersectionality with, or at least apply the theory alongside, some alternative framework. Among the candidates that advocates of this view have marshaled to perform this work are "cosynthesis" (Kwan 1997); "inter-connectivity" (Valdes 1995, 26); "multidimensionality" (Valdes 1998; Hutchinson 1999, 9; Mutua 2006b, 370); and, most recently, "assemblages" (Puar 2007).

Proponents of these theories implicitly and sometimes explicitly suggest that each has the inherent ability to do something—discursively and substantively—that intersectionality inherently cannot do or does considerably less well.[49]

Carbado's approach to describing intersectionality's critique—simply listing a set of widely circulating criticisms without reference to specific scholars—suggests that these criticisms are so familiar that they are simply truisms. If each "criticism" references a rich body of debate within the field of intersectionality studies, Carbado elides those debates, instead presenting each as a way in which intersectionality is undone by critics.

Though these scholars offer varied descriptions of critique, all have positioned their scholarship as a way of protecting intersectionality from the dangerous and destructive task of the critic, as a project of speaking on behalf of intersectionality. In other words, these texts perform the prevailing narrative that marks black feminist theoretical engagement, one marked by a problematic villain who systematically undoes intersectionality, often with questionable intellectual motives. In this account, the critic is ubiquitous, omnipresent, powerful, and dangerous, and the task of black feminist theory is to rescue (something I take up more in the next chapter).

Yet, despite the contention that the critic is ubiquitous, that intersectionality is quite literally under siege, the texts share a lack of specificity about the figure of the critic as each presumes the critics' omnipresence yet refuses to name specific critics, or to attach particular critical labor to particular scholars. There is, though, one critic who is named repeatedly in black feminist scholarship that guards intersectionality: Jasbir Puar. Puar is often figured in *both* scholarly and popular work as the paradigmatic critic of intersectionality.[50] Carastathis, for example, treats Puar's work as "the most influential critique of intersectionality," and Patrick Grzanka calls Puar one of "intersectionality's most committed critics."[51] In his cogent analysis of intersectionality and black feminism, James Bliss describes Puar's scholarly contributions as critiques:

> Over the past decade, Jasbir Puar has offered a field-defining series of critiques of intersectionality through her explication of assemblage theory. . . . Puar critiques intersectionality as, first, anachronistically located in and of regimes of discipline; second, collusive with the post-9/11 national security state; and, finally, regressively attached to identity. . . . [M]y interest lies in what falls outside of Puar's

description of her critique of intersectionality: namely, an anxiety that manifests as hostility toward the project of a radical Black feminism. What critical readers of Puar have caught in her several interventions on intersectionality is a tendency to align Black feminism with state violence generally, and the post-9/11 US imperial project specifically, something far different from an anxiety about the political stakes of leaving intersectionality behind. . . . While not at all limited to Puar, it is this animating desire to displace Black women and Black feminist theorizing that troubles the turn to assemblage theory.[52]

Here, Puar's engagement with assemblage as an alternative conception of theorizing relationality, subjectivity, and sensation is imagined less as a generative intervention and more as a practice of unsettling intersectionality. Indeed, in Bliss's retelling of Puar's contributions, Puar is figured as largely invested in dismantling intersectionality, a project that "manifests as hostility toward the project of a radical Black feminism." Similarly, Tiffany Lethabo King reveals that Puar's work is "one of the most well-circulated critiques in the humanities" and notes that "without trying to, Puar's non-post-intersectional critique is immensely effective at encouraging people to consider transcending and moving past intersectionality."[53] Puar is not only the analytic's key critic but also foundational to a larger devaluation of intersectionality.

I attend to scholars' preoccupation with Puar as critic not as part of a project of rescuing Puar from the title of "critic" but to interrogate *both* what it means that her work has come to stand for a set of practices that undermine intersectionality, that her name has come to signal myriad scholarly attempts to unsettle intersectionality, *and* what it means that the critic is imagined to be a ubiquitous figure, and yet the only critic regularly cited is Puar. While some insist that attention is given to Puar because she has offered, in Amy L. Brandzel's words, "one of the most thorough critiques of intersectionality," my provocations here are designed to ask about the institutional politics that have made it such that Puar's work *stands for* a critique of intersectionality.[54] What is it about both Puar and black feminist theory that has enabled the notion of Puar as *the* critic to circulate and to flourish? What role does Puar—as paradigmatic critic—play in enabling the intersectionality wars to flourish?

Puar's status in the literature on intersectionality as *the* critic is particularly surprising because of her own uneasiness surrounding intersectionality, and her desire to think anew about relationality in ways that intersectionality may not (or may!) be able to accommodate. Indeed, it is crucial to read Puar's engagement with intersectionality twice—first in *Terrorist Assemblages* and then, later, in "'I Would Rather Be a Cyborg Than a Goddess.'" *Terrorist Assemblages* ends by setting assemblage, the analytic Puar champions, against intersectionality. Puar writes:

> As opposed to an intersectional model of identity, which presumes that components—race, class, gender, sexuality, nation, age, religion—are separable analytics and can thus be disassembled, an assemblage is more attuned to interwoven forces that merge and dissipate time, space, and body against linearity, coherency, and permanency. . . . We can think of intersectionality as a hermeneutic of *positionality* that seeks to account for locality, specificity, placement, junctions. As a tool of diversity management and a mantra of liberal multiculturalism, intersectionality colludes with the disciplinary apparatus of the state—census, demography, racial profiling, surveillance—in that "difference" is encased within a structural container that simply wishes the messiness of identity into a formulaic grid.[55]

Here, Puar offers an account of intersectionality that underscores its collusion—or potential collusion—with the state, the fact that it is (or can be) enmeshed with logics of counting, numeracy, measurement, and fixity.

In "'I Would Rather Be a Cyborg Than a Goddess,'" though, Puar carefully traces her ambivalence about how intersectionality has come to be deployed in the space of institutionalized women's studies. She writes, "But what the method of intersectionality is most predominantly used to qualify is the specific 'difference' of 'women of color,' a category that has now become, I would argue, simultaneously emptied of specific meaning on the one hand and overdetermined in its deployment on the other. In this usage, intersectionality always produces an Other, and that Other is always a Woman Of Color (woc), who must invariably be shown to be resistant, subversive, or articulating a grievance."[56] The critical questions she poses about intersectionality and its usages center on its dominance in women's studies, its place as the field's prevailing method, and the fact that questioning intersectionality results in precisely what has happened to Puar, the placement of the theorist (and her frameworks) as "traitorous." Here, what Puar performs is less critique than a critical inquiry surrounding intersectionality's circulation and institutionalization.

Why, then, are Puar's ambivalent engagements with intersectionality's racial and institutional politics forgotten in the service of representing her work exclusively as damning critique? How can we make sense of how a scholar's ideas change, shift, transform, and are presented differently? In other words, how can we track the evolution or shift of Puar's work on intersectionality from *Terrorist Assemblages* to "Cyborg" with a deep recognition of the fact that our collective scholarly endeavors are rooted in larger disciplinary conversations that might result in different presentations in our ideas *or* shifts in our thinking? While my endeavor here can only be speculative, it is worth noting that one of intersectionality's only named critics—and the analytic's imagined preeminent critic—is not black and is often positioned as either a nonblack feminist, an antiblack feminist, or a queer theorist (rather than a feminist). The practice of reinscribing Puar as intersectionality's quintessential critic, then, has the potential effect of shoring up the notion that intersectionality and "black woman" are synonymous, and that intersectionality's critics are outsiders *both* to the analytic and to black feminism. Here, I want to linger in a consideration of the fact that Puar's status as critic—as *the* critic—is secured and sutured through both her body and her imagined identity. In so doing, I trace how a potent "critique" of intersectionality might be argued to flourish precisely because it was articulated by a nonblack woman of color feminist, and I ask how black feminists have constructed Puar as the paradigmatic critic because of her imagined status as an outsider to black feminism (a status that is conferred not simply because of her scholarship but because of certain readings of her imagined identity).

My consideration of Puar's status as an outsider to black feminism unfolds alongside how my own work gets described as "critique." Our respective "critical" projects are differently described, circulated, and received in the field. While some of my earlier work, particularly my article "Rethinking Intersectionality," is described as a "critique" of intersectionality, it is largely understood as emerging in and through an affection for black feminism (and for black women's intellectual production), a fact that might be tethered to my own scholarly work but also to the ongoing collapses between racially marked subjects' bodies and their objects of study. When, for example, Brittney Cooper describes my work, she situates it as a *black feminist* critique of intersectionality, one that, then, emerges from "inside" the imagined location where intersectionality was born.[57] My location as a black feminist, and as a black woman (and, of course, these two identities are often collapsed), means that my critiques of intersectionality are imagined as practices of love and affection rather than hostility, and are thus treated with a kind of generosity.

I understand my own treatment—one marked by a sense that the work I do is animated by an investment in black feminism—as markedly different than how Puar's ambivalent engagement with intersectionality is received. Indeed, the notion of Puar as an outsider to black feminism has been echoed by larger critiques of her work as antiblack; one critique of *Terrorist Assemblages* noted that the book has an "anxious intent to sidestep blackness," positioning Puar as a stranger to the intellectual and political projects of black studies. Egbert Alejandro Martina notes, "For Puar, intersectionality is a stand-in for an unacceptable radical Black feminist politics. Beneath the terrorist is the queer, and beneath the queer is the Black, a mode of being too monstrous even for Puar to *pretend* to encounter in good faith," and suggests that underpinning Puar's questions about intersectionality is a larger "hostility" toward black feminism.[58] Puar's status as nonblack feminist, as someone outside of the tradition from which intersectionality emerged, can deepen the conception of intersectionality's critiques as particularly problematic because they are born beyond the critical practice of black feminism and are motivated by hostility and animus.

If Puar's critiques are imagined to emerge from a nonlocation in black feminism, she is also often positioned as an outsider to the feminist project itself, with her roots in queer theory underscored. Lynne Huffer, for example, notes that Puar "shifts her focus away from intersectionality to queer assemblage. . . . In doing so, she directly challenges the unquestioned stability of the subject implicit in feminist intersectionality theory."[59] Rather than reify an imagined distinction between feminist theory and queer theory, I ask how Puar's imagined location *within* queer theory, a tradition that is still often described as *outside of* feminist theory, amplifies the conception of her "critique" as formed by an outsider, and thus makes intersectionality particularly and problematically vulnerable. Puar is treated as not just a queer theorist but also a queer of color theorist, part of a vibrant cohort of interdisciplinary scholars who have considered "social formations as the intersections of race, gender, sexuality and class, with particular interest in how those formations correspond with and diverge from nationalist ideals and practices."[60] If black queer studies "throws shade on the meanings of queer," queer of color studies, in Jafari Allen's words, "takes seriously Third World or women of color feminist politics of, for example, Chandra

Talpade Mohanty, Chrystos, Gloria Anzaldúa, Cherríe Moraga, Norma Alarcon, Chela Sandoval, and others who consistently made connections in their local scholarship, artistry, and activism, with state practices and sites within and beyond their own ethnic or racial borders."[61] Indeed, queer of color critique has insisted on the centrality of woman of color feminisms—particularly black feminism—to queer theory, and thus emphatically placed scholars like Lorde, Anzaldúa, and Moraga in the queer canon. Roderick Ferguson and Grace Hong write: "Much of what we now call 'women of color feminism' can be seen as queer of color critique, insofar as these texts consistently situate sexuality as constitutive of race and gender. . . . Women of color feminism and queer of color critique reveal the ways in which racialized communities are not homogeneous but instead have always policed and preserved the difference between those who are able to conform to categories of normativity, respectability, and value, and those who are forcibly excluded from such categories."[62] For Ferguson and Hong, women of color feminists—including Lorde—*are* queer theorists whose work indexes a commitment to "set about creating something else to be," and whose theoretical contributions examine the intimate relationship among race, gender, and sexuality.[63] Yet it is crucial to underscore that queer of color theory often claims its intimacy with black feminist theory through a retrospective gaze rather than through engagement with contemporary black feminist scholarship. Queer of color theory's citational trajectory is primarily tethered to black feminist work from the 1970s and early 1980s, and it sutures the (queer of color) present to an earlier moment in black feminism's past, not to black feminism's unfolding present. Indeed, queer of color critique often moves sideways to intersectionality, insistently *not* engaging it and embracing seemingly anti-identitarian analytics generated by black feminists "earlier" than Crenshaw and intersectionality. By sideways, I refer to a citational practice that does not reject intersectionality or its "inaugural" scholar, Kimberlé Crenshaw, but instead adopts some of intersectionality's core investments while disidentifying with intersectionality itself, and while situating other scholars—particularly Lorde—as intersectionality's early (or perhaps earliest) practitioners. I term this "reading sideways" because I argue that this strategy produces a new genealogy that neither rejects nor accepts intersectionality but instead sidesteps it entirely. Reading sideways, then, is a performance of ambivalence made manifest through silence. Puar is located in a queer of color tradition that embraces black feminism, but only black feminist work from an earlier historical era than intersectionality. It is this location as a queer of color scholar, as part of a tradition that has sidestepped intersectionality, that also allows black feminists to position Puar as an outsider to intersectionality, a critic who might be easily represented as having an investment in rendering intersectionality vulnerable.

In revealing that the critic is rarely named—and, when she is, is so often Puar—I seek to suggest that black feminists *produce* the critic rather than *expose* the critic. Indeed, while the critic is regularly described by black feminists as an omnipresent threat, she is actually *one scholar* who is relentlessly cast as an outsider to intersectionality and to black feminist theory, a framing of her work that requires a refusal to engage her scholarship on intersectionality's complex institutional locations and racial politics. The figure of the critic is, then, an imaginative projection of black feminist defensiveness, a figure that animates and justifies the defensive affect *even as* that figure is a fantasy, rather than an actual threat. The constant production of the threatening critic makes the labor—the moral thrust—of black feminism abundantly clear: to rescue black feminist territory, to protect it from these outsiders who neither understand nor value the intellectual and political labor of black feminism.

Love Letter from a Critic

This chapter began with my anxieties about being hailed as a critic. It has unfolded as a rumination on the figure of the critic, an imaginative villainous projection who I argue is central to the intersectionality wars, and thus animates the defensive territoriality that I term "holding on," the structure of feeling that undergirds contemporary US black feminism. The critic is the outsider, the hostile stranger, who seeks to encroach on territory, on property, on hard-earned intellectual turf that is not hers. But why would the practice of constructing the critic be appealing to black feminists? Why repeatedly produce the figure of the critic, and why participate in the intersectionality wars?

Part of my contention is that the figure of critic locks black feminism into the logic of what Alison Peipmeier terms "besiegement." She writes, "As WGS practitioners debate the focus of the field, recount its history, or plan for its future, they present themselves as fighters and the discipline of WGS as under fire—besieged."[64] For Peipmeier, besiegement affects how women's studies narrates itself, producing a story in which feminist scholars located in women's studies are "academic outlaws, or at least outsiders." Yet as Peipmeier begins to probe this narrative, she asks how much of an outsider women's studies can be when its classes regularly fill, when it often has core and affiliated faculty, and when it hosts myriad events on campus. How can an institutionalized field retain its claim to outsiderness when it is so deeply embedded in the university? And why do scholars laboring in women's studies retain a deep commitment to naming their marginalization when they have often secured institutional recognition, visibility, and resources? Indeed, Peipmeier reveals that the narrative of besiegement is necessary to women's studies' conception of itself even as that account no longer always captures women's studies' institutional situatedness. Following Peipmeier's work, I ask how the figure of the critic, and the narratives of "besiegement" it can produce, is an alluring one for black feminism, particularly when the critic is imagined primarily as Puar, a figure represented as outside of the boundaries of black feminism and perhaps outside of the boundaries of feminism more broadly. The image of a vulnerable intersectionality, a literal space that needs to be protected from colonizers and gentrifiers, positions black feminism as not only an intellectual and political tradition but also an ethical intervention that speaks on behalf of black women, in the service of protecting their intellectual labor. There is nothing more virtuous, then, than protecting intersectionality from the critic. Yet this same alluring narrative locks black feminism into a problematic location in women's studies, one that makes the theoretical tradition primarily oriented toward protecting its turf. Indeed, the kind of paranoid readings advanced by black feminist practitioners invested in exposing the critic play out in the context of a field that continues to offer black feminist theory an incredibly limited role in the intellectual and political project of the field—a corrective. If the tradition is designed merely to correct, rather than to exist as its own vibrant field of debate, then it is logical that black feminists find themselves mired in the impasse of the present, one marked by the intersectionality wars that again attempt to tether black feminism to one intellectual product—intersectionality—and to reduce and collapse "black woman," "black feminism," and "intersectionality."

As I indicated in the opening paragraphs of this chapter, I enter this debate not merely as a scholar invested in a robust black feminist theory but also as a scholar whose name is often included in the list of "critics." This chapter, then, has for me prompted a desire not to upend the category of the critic, but to spend time with the villain in black feminism's prevailing narrative, to sit with the imagined colonizer, appropriator, gentrifier, and critic. Indeed, this chapter is a rumination on what black feminists can garner from sitting with, sitting *beside*, this disavowed figure. My investigation has prompted in me a desire to envision a black feminism that can love the critic and can interpret the critic as engaged in a loving practice rather than a malicious one, a generative act rather than a destructive one. Rather than attempting to rescue intersectionality from imagined outsiders who purport to damage and defang the analytic, I invite us to treat the critic as giving us an offering, a way of picturing black feminism's relationship with intersectionality and with the field of women's studies otherwise. The critic's offering might even include compelling black feminist theory to come to terms with its own narrative about a dangerous outsider determined to undermine our theoretical innovations.

What is it that the critic might offer? And how might black feminists cultivate the critic, effectively seeing what she offers not as a threatening gesture, but as a kind of love letter, one that, in Lauren Berlant's words, offers us a chance to imagine "becoming different"?[65] Part of the critic's offering is a rigorous engagement with the psychic structure of our tradition, a structure that has empowered us to locate danger everywhere. The critic's offering also includes compelling black feminist theory to come to terms with our prevailing story about a dangerous outsider determined to undermine our theoretical innovations, and our current preoccupation with narrativizing our field around a sense of our besiegement. The critic also offers us a chance to refuse the lure of territoriality, a form of imagined agency that always brings us to an impasse rather than liberating us from the destructive intersectionality wars. Instead, what might be possible if we began to imagine new forms of agency, and perhaps even embraced—rather than relentlessly rejecting—the vulnerability that intersectionality's movements can make some of us feel. Part of this offering is also compelling a critical attention to how we, black feminists, construct who is "inside" and "outside" the boundaries of our own creative, political, and intellectual tradition, pushing us to interrogate how our anticaptivity project has become its own boundary-policing exercise. Ultimately, what the critic sends us is not a threatening world-ending message, but an invitation to embrace the possibility of other ways to *be* and *feel* black feminist.

TWO. **the politics of reading**

At the end of her intellectual history of intersectionality, Ange-Marie Hancock urges scholars to "read, read, read across disciplines, across continents, and across communities of engagement so that we might engage in careful and responsible management of a burgeoning field of study that has been entrusted to our care for future generations."[1] I want to linger on two portions of Hancock's plea: the call for more reading, and the idea of care. This chapter is an exploration of how black feminists have imagined "good" reading practices as strategies of guarding intersectionality from misuse and as tactics of care. In other words, the chapter explores how "care" has two meanings for black feminists mired in the intersectionality wars. First, it means to read faithfully, to exercise a deep fidelity to the analytic's foundational texts. In this sense, care is a method for reading and a commitment to an intimate relationship between the reader and the analytic's key texts. Second, it means to manifest a certain kind of regard for intersectionality. To read carefully is to practice care for intersectionality, to nurture it, to cultivate it, to treat it with respect and affection.

Rather than assume that careful reading has an inherent meaning, this chapter seeks to interrogate *both* the claim that careful reading and textual fidelity are synonymous and the notion that certain kinds of reading practices manifest an affection for intersectionality. In this chapter, I develop the term the "politics of reading" to explore how and why certain kinds of reading practices have become imagined as a display of respect for intersectionality, and how and why intersectionality has come to be figured as a vulnerable object in need of loyalty and care. To make a claim to care in this historical moment—one marked by newly emphatic rhetorics of self-care as strategies of black survival, and new scholarly and political attention to caring for the black dead—is to make a powerful political plea. Indeed, I finish writing this chapter in a moment when Representative Maxine Waters's phrase "I am reclaiming my time" has become a kind of black feminist and black queer slogan that epitomizes self-care, self-love, and self-regard as strategies of resistance and radical refusal. Acts of "reclaiming time" are increasingly hailed as practices of self-maintenance and survival, particularly in the midst of the Trump era and its emphatic antiblack, misogynist, and homophobic violence. Thus, the black feminist assertion that careful reading manifests a deep care for intersectionality is an affectively saturated rhetorical strategy, one that conflates the survival (or even thriving) of black women's bodies with intersectionality as an object of study and a method of analysis.

The battles over how to read intersectionality's foundational texts have become only more politicized in the last few years. In the wake of the twentieth anniversary of Kimberlé Crenshaw's articles, an array of special issues, edited volumes, and conferences have celebrated the term's history. In my earlier work, I referred to the proliferation of texts honoring intersectionality's anniversary as the "commemorative genre" and argued that this new form seeks not only to celebrate intersectionality but also to reiterate the importance of correct usage of the term.[2] This body of scholarship is often marked by what I called the "corrective gesture," an investment in correcting misuses of intersectionality and in policing how the term circulates.[3] Commemorative work declares the importance of careful reading, which is an assertion of respect for the analytic, a respect that is all the more valued in a genre celebrating intersectionality's interdisciplinary importance.

This chapter explores the contentious politics of reading by taking as a point of departure interventions like Anna Carastathis's, which asks, "Is 'intersectionality' . . . appropriated without deep engagement with Crenshaw's work, and used in ways that distort and even invert the meaning of the concept?"[4] The first section of this chapter develops the concept of "intersectional originalism" to make sense of what constitutes "deep engagement" and to interrogate the value that is conferred upon this "deep" engagement. I ask: How do scholars argue for deep engagement as a practice of care that treats intersectionality as a vulnerable object? How do we discern the presence (or absence) of the requisite care? This portion of the chapter roots its analysis in two entries in the vast archive of commemorative work on intersectionality: special issues of *Signs* and the *Du Bois Review* devoted to intersectionality. The special issue of *Signs*, from 2013, positions itself as producing a new synthesis of intersectional work and as rejuvenating the use of intersectionality in "furthering our understanding of some of the most important issues facing contemporary society."[5] The *Du Bois Review*'s special issue on intersectionality, also from 2013 and guest-edited by one of the *Signs* editors and two of the *Signs* contributors, takes up many of the questions raised in the *Signs* articles but engages with them through the lens of social science methodology and theoretical frameworks. The second section of the chapter unfolds as a rumination on the notion of textual fidelity as care. I investigate what intellectual care looks like and ask how attempts to practice a deep form of care are often imagined as radical but actually reinscribe the logics of property and the attendant affects of defensive holding on they attempt to sidestep. In making this claim, I am not suggesting that care is always a proprietary act. Indeed, a host of scholars, including Christina Sharpe, have persuasively argued for the importance of care as an ethic animating black feminist practice, including scholarly production. Instead, I want to investigate how care often masks its territorial labor, and consider how this masking unfolds in the moment when care and love (I take up love more in the book's last chapter) have become the prevailing aesthetics and rhetorical devices of black feminist theory, thus obscuring the problematic labor they can, at times, perform.

On Carefulness: Performing Intersectional Originalism

Intersectional originalism describes an interpretative framework that confers value on "deep engagement" with Crenshaw's articles, invests in the notion that these articles have a singular meaning that can be ascertained through sustained practices of close reading, and contends that later work "distorts" that true meaning through careless readings. Originalism, then, operates as a methodological tool *and* as a political strategy. As a method, it insists on close reading as a practice and as *the* primary way of accessing and unleashing intersectionality's "true" meanings. It suggests that intersectionality's critics are plagued by misreadings of the analytic and argues that close(r) reading is required to bring us nearer to intersectionality's truths.

As a political strategy, originalism operates to "un-gentrify" intersectionality and to perform that deeply politicized labor through the seemingly neutral and apolitical guise of close reading. Though I trace intersectional originalism as a singular interpretative practice, the texts I discuss here emerge from differing disciplinary traditions, deploy distinctive methods, and maintain particular theoretical and methodological relationships to intersectionality. What these texts share, though, is a purported investment in textual fidelity as a response to intersectionality's "critics," and careful reading as a practice of treating a vulnerable intersectionality with loyalty. They collectively invest in the notion that returning to intersectionality's origins will unleash the analytic's true power and effectively save it from current perceived misuse. Close reading is hailed as a practice that will get us out of the impasse of the present *even as* the close-reading practices that are championed are their own rereadings of intersectionality's foundational texts.

I use the term "intersectional originalism" in hopes of drawing out resonances between the battles unfolding around intersectionality and those staged in the legal context where originalism is often pitted against something termed "judicial activism." In the juridical context, originalism is regularly described by its practitioners as *merely* a practice of close reading that champions doctrinal faithfulness, as opposed to "judicial activism," which is often conceptualized as a politicized practice of reinterpretation that attempts to make doctrine resonate with the politics of any period. Yet originalism is its own interpretative strategy, one that hides its interpretative work. Much like the judicial context, intersectional originalist strategies make claims to power through assertions of close reading, and reading becomes the terrain where contests over politics and power are played out. As in the judicial context, though, originalism is its own interpretative practice, one that reads intersectionality's foundational texts in particular ways, with particular investments, even as it insists that good reading is neutral, apolitical, simply an act of staying close to the text, displaying care for it. In this section, I trace three facets of intersectional originalism's interpretative framework: evaluation, rescue, and forgetting. Following the aims of the previous chapter, my impulse here is not to condemn the workings of intersectional originalism; instead, I am invested in how its relationship to ideas of care makes it a compelling interpretative practice and a powerful strategy for black feminists to assert a kind of agency, even as I treat that form of agency as obstructive.

Intersectional originalism is a diagnostic reading practice; it evaluates feminist work to determine which articulations and practices of intersectionality most closely align with intersectionality as articulated by Crenshaw's two canonical articles. In other words, the excellence of contemporary scholarship is measured by its faithfulness to intersectionality's original texts, and faithfulness is manifested through a politics of citationality that explicitly references Crenshaw, and through a steadfast refusal of contemporary "critiques" of intersectionality. Barbara Tomlinson, for example, describes the desired proximity between contemporary work and Crenshaw's articles "telling the truth."[6] A work's closeness to the truth, its fidelity to Crenshaw's articles, becomes the measure of the quality of the work and a litmus test distinguishing good and less good feminist scholarship. Of course, the fact that determining the meaning of a text is an interpretative exercise, and the fact that Crenshaw's articles, like any scholarly piece, do not contain a singular essence or truth that can simply be deduced through careful reading remain neglected by this position.

"Truth-telling" is often secured through correct citationality, through a rigorous commitment to citing the analytic's foundational texts. As Vivian May notes, "Even if cited, earlier intersectionality texts may not be given nuanced readings but treated casually or deemed theoretically underwhelming. This dynamic can also be relatively subtle: today, for instance, the secondary intersectionality literatures often are more widely referenced and taught than are many foundational writings and practices."[7] For May, contemporary work on intersectionality neglects "nuanced readings" of the analytic's key texts or engages earlier work in an "underwhelming" way. Far worse, contemporary work often wholly neglects intersectionality's founding articles, instead relying exclusively on secondary literature. Similarly, Cho, Crenshaw, and McCall simply state, "Our sense is that some of what circulates as critical debate about what intersectionality is or does reflects a lack of engagement with both originating and contemporary literature on intersectionality."[8] The notion that contemporary scholarship and "critical debate" are somehow unfaithful to "originating . . . literature" becomes a way that originalist readings evaluate existing feminist scholarship on intersectionality, distance themselves from certain feminist scholarship, and embrace other seemingly more faithful scholarship. Of course, as I argued in the introduction, this emphasis on "correct" citationality comes from the long-standing devaluation of black women's scholarship and the continued practice of extracting intellectual labor from black women while disavowing that labor. Thus, the retreat into assertions of "correct" citationality is deeply understandable; it is a response to ongoing institutional violence. Yet I aspire to reveal how this evaluative work also performs territoriality and an ultimately problematic defensiveness, by insisting that there is a singular correct and "true" way to narrate the story of intersectionality, and by arguing that citation *is* care.

Evaluative work is often practiced through exposure; it locates and reveals commonly circulating critiques of intersectionality and diagnoses them as *mis*readings, as dangerous deviations from the original texts. Tomlinson, for example, argues that "many critics approach intersectionality . . . through meta-commentary and complaint and through recommendations to bring its radical critique under control by advocating recourse to specific disciplinary methods. . . . Critics assume that their task is to *critique intersectionality*, not to *foster intersectionality's ability to critique* subordination."[9] Tomlinson aligns "careless," "complaint," and "metacommentary," positioning critique as oppositional to "fostering intersectionality's ability to critique subordination." As I argued in the previous chapter, critique is not imagined as a generative labor, as a significant component of feminist scholarly conversation; instead, to the extent that it moves away from intersectionality's inaugural texts, critique hinders intersectionality's analytical capacities. Sirma Bilge offers a similar diagnosis of the current state of intersectionality research. Like Tomlinson, Bilge contends that the *doing* of intersectionality has become corrupted, though she locates these problems in the corporate university and in what she terms "disciplinary feminism." She writes: "I contend that what may at first appear to be an enthusiastic reception of intersectionality is a significant reflection of the need by disciplinary feminism to contain it, to neutralize its politics. For disciplinary feminism to 'take on' or 'take over' intersectionality serves to marginalize those trying to reconnect intersectionality with its initial vision which was grounded in the political subjectivities and struggles of less powerful social actors facing multiple intertwined oppressions."[10] Indeed, Bilge warns against an "ornamental intersectionality" that is far from "benign" and instead acts as a "disarticulation of radical politics of social justice."[11] Bilge, like Tomlinson, argues that contemporary practices of intersectionality that "take over" the analytic are a troubling departure from its "initial vision" and a problematic remaking of the analytic.

Ultimately, evaluation is a practice of measuring feminist scholarship by its fidelity to—or distance from—intersectionality's original texts. It is a reading practice that insists on careful engagement with intersectionality's key writings and that performs its care for intersectionality through its loyalty to the analytic's founding scholars. In so doing, evaluative approaches presume that intersectionality is currently vulnerable, and thus in need of the requisite amount of both loyalty and veneration to ensure its continued vitality.

Rescue

If intersectional originalism assesses contemporary intersectional scholarship based on its imagined fidelity to (or infidelity to) earlier writing, it also aspires to rescue intersectionality from feminist work that is deemed "damaging to feminist anti-subordination scholarship and activism."[12] Intersectional originalism endeavors not simply to value its inaugural texts but also to imagine intersectionality as a body in need of saving. It is, in Bilge's words, a call to "stop doing intersectionality in ways that *undo* it."[13] Evaluation and rescue are the flip side of the same coin; evaluative work identifies problematic deviations from intersectionality's founding texts, and rescue work saves intersectionality from misuse, either by revealing the problematic work of critics or through insisting that intersectionality's true analytic potency has not yet been unleashed.

Rescue work often begins with proving that critiques are misreadings, and then with revealing intersectionality's original vibrancy. In other words, rescuing intersectionality from critique is a process of reanimating and revitalizing the analytic. For example, Devon Carbado lists six widely circulating critiques of intersectionality, including that "intersectionality is only or largely about Black women" and that "intersectionality is an identitarian framework."[14] He then begins to "clear the ground," effectively refuting these critiques so that he can "radicalize and reinvigorate intersectionality by first moving the theory back to its initial articulation and then moving it forward to new sites and concerns."[15] Carbado's insistence on "clear[ing] the ground" reveals that it is necessary to "challenge the . . . narrow readings of intersectionality" before advancing new articulations of intersectionality or extending the theory into new sites.[16] In short, he quite literally pulls intersectionality theory away from circulating critiques, saving it by showing that those critiques are false and then projecting intersectionality safely into feminism's future.

Rescue work also endeavors to save intersectionality from problematic academic politics. Sumi Cho attempts to liberate intersectionality from "post-intersectional" critiques, a set of questions about intersectionality that have emerged in the legal academy. Post-intersectionality theory has generated new analytics—including multidimensionality and symbiosis—as a way of honoring the political investments of intersectionality while attending to intersections "beyond" race/gender. Cho reveals that post-intersectional legal scholars turned away from intersectionality because of a perception that intersectionality was "not theoretically suited to engage issues of sexuality," and because intersectionality was part of an institutionalized critical race tradition that was imagined to be largely uninterested in questions of sexuality.[17] Cho's emphasis on perception suggests that post-intersectionality theory is rooted in an imagined shortcoming in intersectionality theory. Cho moves from the diagnostic labor of evaluation to full-fledged rescue, exposing the fact that the post-intersectional turn is *actually* animated by pernicious politics, by what she terms "extratextual factors."[18] Indeed, she argues that intersectionality is an object of condemnation because "it has become a 'pink ghetto,' overly populated by feminists (mostly of color)."[19] Thus, the challenges levied against intersectionality in the legal academy are actually undergirded by academic racism and sexism, by a scholarly desire to distance oneself from work that is devalued because it is produced by, or associated with, women of color.

Rescue, then, operates alongside evaluation to identify problematic readings and to ensure intersectionality's continued vitality. It attempts to care for intersectionality by saving the analytic from misuses, criticisms, bad readings, and appropriations, and critically interrogates the politics undergirding critiques of intersectionality. Ultimately, rescue becomes a critical strategy for moving intersectionality into feminism's future, even though it does this through casting a retrospective gaze, looking back to intersectionality's foundational texts.

Forgetting

Intersectional originalism is an exercise in forgetting. I use the term "forgetting" to describe intersectional originalism's simultaneous *investment* in questions of how power shapes academic life and its *disinvestment* in how the context of the "corporate university" has shaped intersectionality's relatively easy institutionalization within the American university. While scholars including Kathy Davis, Robyn Wiegman, Sara Ahmed, and Nick

Mitchell have, in different ways, attended to intersectionality's ubiquity and institutionalization, there remains too little engagement with how intersectionality's status as "buzzword" is enabled by the analytic's resonance with universities' rhetorical investment in diversity, difference, and inclusion, or with how its ascension has been made possible, as I traced in the book's introduction.[20] In other words, intersectionality's appeal, spread, and interdisciplinary movement are often treated as *intrinsic* to the analytic—as is the case in Davis's widely cited work on intersectionality's "vagueness"—rather than as reflective of a set of structural changes in the US academy or in women's studies programs and departments.

This practice of forgetting is most evident in what is perhaps the most commonly used word in the originalist lexicon: "travel." Intersectionality is often described as an analytic that has simply, benignly, and perhaps even by chance, moved across disciplinary borders—"traveled." Cho, Crenshaw, and McCall note, "As intersectionality has emerged in a number of discursive spaces, the projects and debates that have accompanied its *travel* have converged into a burgeoning field of intersectional studies" and "as intersectionality has *traveled* questions have been raised regarding a number of issues."[21] Tomlinson writes, "It [intersectionality] has served as a frame, heuristic, and tool for a variety of analyses and arguments, *traveling* across discourses and disciplines, countries and contexts, and taking on many different meanings in diverse situations."[22] Similarly, Carbado asserts, "Crenshaw's articulation of these dynamics should not lead one to conclude that there is an already-mapped terrain over which intersectionality must and only can *travel*."[23] Despite the growing body of literature attending to what I view as the institutional life of intersectionality, the term "travel" still permeates the field of intersectional originalist frameworks, making intersectionality's movements seem accidental.

What is the appeal of this term, and what does it obscure? The notion of travel, in addition to making intersectionality's movements seem either accidental or intrinsic to the term itself rather than the result of structural forces that have elevated intersectionality to an article of faith, obscures the varieties of kinds of movements intersectionality enjoys. At times, travel seems to refer to intersectionality's disciplinary movements, its unusual capacity to have value in the humanities and social sciences. This kind of travel is, in fact, increasingly valued as universities extol interdisciplinarity as an intellectual virtue, and often as an intellectual virtue that can garner funding and resources. Yet intersectionality's other travels are often less analyzed and, at times, neglected in feminist conversations. Intersectionality has enjoyed the unusual capacity to move across academic/administrative boundaries within the university, enabling the term to act both as theoretical framework and as diversity mandate. This form of travel has often happened on the backs of black women who themselves traverse the academic/administrative boundary as they are conscripted into (or hailed by) the task of diversity work. While intersectionality is imbued with value because of its imagined interdisciplinarity, its administrative travels, and its complex relationship with institutionalized diversity discourses, these forms of migration which produce substantial feminist anxiety are far less theorized, analyzed, and discussed.

Moreover, the language of travel ignores the fact that intersectionality's institutionalization has been facilitated from its emergence from a US context, and that its travels have been enabled by US universities' hegemonic location in women's studies, and in academia more generally. Nivedita Menon argues for the importance of a critical feminist interrogation of how "concepts developed in the global North are assumed to have universal validity."[24] In the context of intersectionality, Menon notes that "the 'single axis framework' was never pre-dominant or unchallenged in our parts of the world. New identities continually arose then, and do now, from different contexts, forcing recognition on our part that all political solidarities are conjunctural and historically contingent."[25] In other words, her analysis emphasizes that intersectionality's now "citational ubiquity" and easy travels cannot—and should not—be imagined apart from the geopolitical and academic politics that make certain concepts seem universally applicable and that hide the intellectual and creative labor emerging from locations in the global South. Vrushali Patil's notion of "domestic intersectionality" underscores this point, noting that "while the concept of intersectionality has indeed been feminism's 'success story,' much like the concept of patriarchy, applications of intersectionality also continue to be shaped by the geographies of colonial modernity."[26] Taken together, these claims argue for the importance of considering intersectionality's "travels" as intimately related to its institutional and geopolitical origins.

In underscoring evaluation, rescue, and forgetting as hallmarks of intersectional originalism, I show that originalism is not simply an insistence on close reading and a celebration of textual fidelity. It is an *interpretative strategy* that operates to secure the boundaries of the analytic, to rescue intersectionality from critique, to expose misreadings of intersectionality, and to systematically ignore the conditions that have permitted intersectionality to move across entrenched and policed boundaries. It is also its own reading practice embedded in a particular historical and institutional moment, one that endeavors to project intersectionality's disciplinary significance into women's studies' unfolding future, even as it masks this labor and insists that it is *merely* adhering to Crenshaw's seminal articles. To be clear, intersectional originalist strategies, like all readying practices, are interpretative, even if they mask their interpretative work in the name of textual fidelity. Yet these strategies have a particular appeal because they seem to operate on behalf of black women's intellectual production through insisting on a sustained engagement with Crenshaw's work, through arguing for citational practices that take seriously black women's labor. In naming and describing intersectional originalism's affective lure—namely, the appeal of reading correctly, properly, faithfully—I aspire to unsettle it. My claim is *not* that there are no good—or better—readings. Clearly, texts can be misread and misinterpreted. Instead, I am interested in the collective amplification of good reading as the practice that can get black feminism out of the predicament it finds itself in, and invested in tracing how this notion of reading *right* necessarily produces a black feminist impulse toward policing and surveilling scholars' work.

Intersectional Originalism as Rereading

If intersectional originalism constitutes a reading practice that masks its labor of rereading, it also constitutes an explicit reworking of the analytic. My emphasis in thinking through how intersectional originalist strategies reread intersectionality's foundational texts is *not* to argue that intersectionality itself has a set of predetermined meanings that originalist reading practices ignore or neglect. Instead, I underscore that *all* readings are interpretations, whether they imagine themselves as such or not. In this section, I show that the very practices that champion textual fidelity actually emphasize certain aspects of intersectionality and downplay others, often to make the analytic resilient in the face of new "critiques" and new trends in the humanities and social sciences. They perform this interpretative work in and through a language and ethic of care, as a loving practice defending a vulnerable intersectionality.

The Ethic of Inclusivity

Intersectional originalism has reimagined intersectionality, transforming it from an analytic particularly invested in subjects who are multiply marginalized into a broad and expansive framework that describes *all* subjects' social location. If black women were "imagined to prove a theoretical value-added . . . to expose the specters of racism and sexism which leave their traces even in progressive analyses," intersectionality has been reimagined as an analytic whose value comes through its ability to capture and describe all subjects' experiences, locations, and identities.[27] Through a purported performance of textual fidelity, intersectionality gets shifted away from an *ethic of redress*, a specific intervention invested in validating the distinctive epistemological and the juridical standpoint of black women, and toward an *ethic of inclusivity* that both dramatically expands intersectionality's explanatory reach and ushers intersectionality into feminism's future by producing a tool through which all subjects can locate themselves. Curiously, though many black feminist scholars have, as I have shown in the previous chapter, critiqued the "whitening" of intersectionality, the ethic of inclusivity dramatically broadens the conception of the intersectional subject *from* black women to *all* subjects. In noting the valuing of inclusivity, I situate my work differently than scholars like Alexander-Floyd, who notes that "people refer to her [Crenshaw's] famous analogy between an automobile crash at an intersection and the interplay of racism and sexism, for instance, but ignore her call to center on women of color's experience."[28] My contention is *not* a critique of the ethic of inclusivity that argues that black women *should* have a privileged relationship to intersectionality; instead, I am invested in revealing that, though originalism names its fidelity to Crenshaw's inaugural texts and those texts' investments in black women, the analytic is increasingly moving away from the subjects who formed the core of Crenshaw's analysis, *even as this unfolds* through the language of care for intersectionality and careful protection of Crenshaw's work.

The advent of an expansive intersectionality is not something practiced exclusively by those invested in originalist reading strategies. Nancy Ehrenreich, for example, advocates a "hybrid intersectionality," one attentive to the intersectional experiences of subjects who are *not* multiply marginalized, particularly white women. Ehrenreich imagines that an intersectionality attentive to these "hybrid" subjects offers an important window into how power works and reveals that "while singly burdened individuals are clearly benefited by their privilege, that privilege also (paradoxically) makes them vulnerable. In that sense, the system that *subordinates them is supposed by the system that* privileges them."[29] Indeed, Ehrenreich emphasizes that an intersectionality-like theory constructed around white women's particular experiences would yield an analytically rich account of how privilege and oppression work together. Similarly, Ange-Marie Hancock advocates an intersectionality that is wholly detached from the specificities of black women. She asks, "What if, as noble a pursuit as it is, I do not wish to study women of color? What can I gain from intersectionality? I think intersectionality can help us better conceive research designs and data collection through its attentiveness to causal complexity."[30] While it is worth interrogating why studying women of color is constructed as "noble," it is also important that, for Hancock, intersectionality can—and should—move apart from the specific experiences of women of color. I read both Ehrenreich's and Hancock's respective commitments to an expansive intersectionality as something that circulates apart from originalism (indeed, I would argue that both are explicit about their interest in remaking intersectionality).

Intersectional originalism produces genealogies of intersectional thought that shift black women from the center of the analytic to its periphery, even as black women's particular experiences at the metaphorical intersection of race and gender yielded the productive metaphor that has become the centerpiece of intersectionality theory. For example, Carbado argues that though black women were "the particular juridical and political sites in which Crenshaw sought to intervene," he refutes the argument that "intersectionality is only or largely about Black women, or only about race and gender."[31] In other words, though black women were foundational to intersectionality's formation, the analytic is no longer "only" or even "largely" about the materiality of black female flesh, or black women's experiences of discrimination and harm. This argumentative move allows him to position intersectionality as an analytic that refuses to "privilege any social category," as a framework that can—and does—speak about all subjects' social locations.[32] Here, rather than interrogating an epistemological universe that refuses to allow black women to speak from or for the universal subject position, Carbado emphasizes that intersectionality's analytic power is not tied to black women's imagined particularity.

The refusal of black women's centrality to intersectionality theory requires Carbado to craft an alternative genealogy of intersectional thought.

As I have argued earlier in this book, genealogical work is at the heart of black feminist defensiveness strategies. Black feminist defensive genealogies attempt to exert territorial claims to the analytic and its movement by constructing singular, narrow origin stories that necessarily tether intersectionality to black feminist thought; thus, it is my contention that it is crucial to attend to the political and racial work of intersectional genealogies, particularly those that purport to, in Tomlinson's words, engage in "truth-telling." Though many scholars have treated Crenshaw's work as an extension of earlier black feminist work on "jeopardy"—particularly Frances Beal's "Double Jeopardy" and Deborah King's "Multiple Jeopardy"—Carbado treats intersectionality as a rupture with rather than a continuation of earlier black feminist work on the intersections of race and gender. He writes:

> While I do not presume to know precisely why some scholars view intersectionality as a theory concerned only with Black women or race and gender, one plausible explanation is that these scholars conflate intersectionality with a particular line of argument in the "double jeopardy" theory. Roughly, this argument forwards the idea that the greater the number of marginal categories to which one belongs, the greater the number of disadvantages one will experience. Women of color and Black women in particular figure prominently in this scholarly domain based on the view that, at the very least, they experience the double jeopardy of racism and sexism.[33]

Carbado constructs an alternative genealogy that positions Crenshaw's work as a significant break from earlier black feminist work. In Carbado's hands, intersectionality is not a theory of multiple marginalization, like jeopardy; instead, it is a theory of how privilege and oppression coincide to make the lives of all subjects.

If Carbado creates a genealogy that treats intersectionality as a break from earlier black feminist work on the intimate connections between race and gender, other scholars offer genealogies that also seek to disrupt the centrality of black women to intersectionality theory, particularly dispersal narratives. These accounts suggest that intersectionality *began* with black women and moved *beyond* black women, a testament to its explanatory power. In this account, intersectionality's power emerges from its capacity to capture multiple subject positions. Tomlinson, for example, notes that intersectionality emerged from "a specific problem facing Black women plaintiffs in employment discrimination cases" and "has served as a frame, heuristic, and tool for a variety of analyses and arguments, traveling across discourses and disciplines, countries and contexts, and taking on many different meanings in diverse situations."[34] In this account, black women's particular experiences of discrimination were a point of origin for a theory that now broadly describes structure and power, not identity. Carbado et al. offer a similar story, locating intersectionality's origins in Crenshaw's two seminal articles and noting that since the publication of those articles, "scholars and activists have broadened intersectionality to engage a range of issues, social identities, power dynamics, legal and political systems, and discursive strategies in the United States and beyond."[35] Black women's experiences, then, provided a kind of analytical and political basis for intersectionality theory, but the analytic has moved well beyond the particularity of black women.

Nowhere is this push toward inclusivity more visible than in the invocation of the mythical "white heterosexual man" who, some scholars invested in intersectional originalism reveal, can also be the subject of intersectionality. Devon Carbado and Mitu Gulati, for example, argue that "all of us have intersectional identities, including White, heterosexual men. This is why Carbado has argued that we should differentiate between 'intersectionally marginalized groups' (or IMGs) and 'intersectionally privileged groups' (or IPGs). Doing so would help us to disrupt the extent to which some scholars perceive intersectionality as only about marginalized social categories."[36] Here, intersectionality's explanatory power comes from the fact that it describes "all of us," including "White, heterosexual men." Intersectionality is imagined not as a theory of multiple marginalization (or "multiple jeopardy") but as a theory of the interplay of privilege and oppression.

My claim in tracing the presence of these alternative intersectional genealogies is not to argue that intersectional originalism *should* fashion a vision of intersectionality committed exclusively to black women, or to assert that intersectionality should remain specifically tethered to black women's bodies. Indeed, the larger project of this book is to practice an ethic of letting go and to disrupt the claims of territoriality and defensiveness that I argue have come to animate black feminist academic practice. Instead, I show how laying a claim to textual fidelity masks certain kinds of interpretative work performed by intersectional originalism, particularly a commitment to crafting a broad and expansive intersectionality, despite a long-standing black feminist commitment to locating intersectionality theory in black women's specific experiences of violence, discrimination, and harm.

Subjectivity and Structure

Intersectionality theory has enjoyed a long-standing debate as to "whether intersectionality should be limited to understanding individual experiences, to theorizing identity, or whether it should be taken as the property of social structures and cultural discourses."[37] Intersectional originalist reading practices come down squarely on the side of structure and make this appeal through claims to textual fidelity. Cho, Crenshaw, and McCall begin the special issue of *Signs* by underscoring the structural dimensions of intersectionality. They note: "We emphasize an understanding of intersectionality that is not exclusively or even primarily preoccupied with categories, identities, and subjectivities. Rather, the intersectional analysis foregrounded here emphasizes political and structural inequalities. The recasting of intersectionality as a theory primarily fascinated with the infinite combinations and implications of overlapping identities from an analytic initially concerned with structures of power and exclusion is curious given the explicit references to structures that appear in much of the early work."[38] Cho, Crenshaw, and McCall are engaged in two related argumentative moves. First, they argue that intersectionality is an analytic that has long been invested *not* in identities or subjectivities but in structure. In other words, they make a historical argument about intersectionality's intellectual and political labor. Second, they locate their claim—that intersectionality is preoccupied with the structural rather than the identitarian—in the "early work." In so doing, they make an originalist assertion that returns to "much of the early work" as an articulation of intersectionality's true meaning and suggest that readings of intersectionality as an identity-based framework are *mis*readings that fail to adequately engage the analytic's foundational texts.

Other times, originalist practitioners offer a very clear distinction between identitarian work and structural work as a way of securing intersectionality's claims to the structural. Tomlinson, for example, notes, "If critics think intersectionality is a matter of identity rather than power, they cannot see which differences make a difference."[39] Similarly, Jennifer Jihye Chun, George Lipsitz, and Young Shin pithily observe, "[Intersectionality] primarily concerns the way things work rather than who people are."[40] Yet the distinction between "the way things work" and "who people are" or between "identity" and "power" is not as clear as intersectional originalist reading practices often suggest. What sparks my interest about this pair of quotes are the stark distinctions drawn between identity and structure, distinctions that neglect how experiences of embodiment; projects of self-making and self-performing; sensations of pleasure, pain, injury, desire, and so on are always fundamentally altered, shaped, and constituted by social location, experiences of power and disempowerment. To put it simply, "who people are" can never be understood apart from "the way things work," despite the insistence of this scholarship that these two categories are distinct.

Importantly, the move toward a structural intersectionality is often advanced alongside the plea for an inclusive intersectionality. Carbado, like Ehrenreich, advocates a vision of intersectionality that embodies expansiveness and focuses entirely on structure: "colorblind intersectionality." This form of intersectionality "refers to instances in which whiteness helps to produce and is part of a cognizable social category but is invisible or unarticulated as an intersectional subject position. For example, white heterosexual men constitute a cognizable social category whose whiteness is rarely seen or expressed in intersectional terms."[41] Carbado uses the expression "high-status intersectionality" to refer to "white male heterosexuality," and uses intersectionality to refer *not* to disadvantage or marginalization but to the ways that structures coincide to produce privilege or disadvantage. In short, "Intersectionality applies even where there is no double jeopardy. Indeed, the theory applies where there is no jeopardy at all. Thus, it is a mistake to conceptualize intersectionality as a 'race to the bottom.'"[42] Intersectionality, then, is a map of social structure that accounts for both "the bottom" and "the top," the privileged and the oppressed, the margins and the center. Instead of describing multiple marginalizations, centering the experiences of the multiply marginalized, or foregrounding the embodied knowledges of the multiply marginalized, intersectionality is instead posited as an analytic that describes the systems of domination that ensnare us all, even as we are ensnared in different and socially contingent ways. While the investment in intersectionality's structural dimensions is treated as something intrinsic to intersectionality and its foundational texts, it is clear that sidestepping the identitarian and the subjective has taken on a particular charge in light of sharply voiced critiques of so-called identity politics. Indeed, if "identity politics" has become the kind of dirty term of the Left (and of the humanities), an emphasis on intersectionality as a theory of social structures rather than identities effectively rescues the term from a political affiliation that is seen, at best, as passé and, at worst, as dangerous. Yet the political context in which the disavowal of intersectionality's identity work unfolds is obscured when intersectional originalist reading practices insist that they are merely reading intersectionality's foundational texts *as they were meant to be read.*

In this section, I have argued that in safeguarding intersectionality from critique through a purported textual fidelity, intersectional originalism contains a set of racial politics. Intersectional originalism has fashioned intersectionality as a broad, inclusive, and expansive analytic that has no particular analytical or political investment in the "margins," that describes the variety of ways that social structures work on bodies to produce privilege and oppression. Indeed, the specter of the "white heterosexual man" *as intersectional subject* haunting intersectional originalism interpretative practices reveals an investment in untethering intersectionality from black female bodies *even as* it purports to take care of black women's intellectual production as it cites black feminist scholars as intersectionality's "original" authors, and from an interest in redressing specific racial and gendered injuries, toward crafting a broad descriptive analytic. Of course, this impulse toward crafting a broad and inclusive intersectionality in response to critiques of intersectionality's identitarianism necessarily poses important questions: Why is it that intersectionality's status as "field defining" emerges in a moment when the analytic is remade to include everyone? Why is intersectionality's hold on feminism's future dependent on its ability to offer theoretical and political space for all subjects? Why are black female bodies imagined as the quintessential identitarian subjects? Or, to ask it another way, why would an analytic centered on black women not be palatable or desirable as a field-defining analytic? In posing these questions, I endeavor to center the importance of understanding the institutional rationales for this remaking of intersectionality, one that argues for the analytic's importance by producing the analytic apart from black women's bodies. Ultimately, intersectional originalism is marked by an intense proliferation of calls for careful citations and "right" readings of Crenshaw's work as a way to take care of intersectionality, *yet* this same reading practice suggests that the analytic's "travel"—a sign of its political power—hinges on its ability to be untethered from black women's bodies.

The Politics of Care

The intersectional originalist reading practices that I have described here are underpinned by a black feminist ethic of care, a deep sense of responsibility and loyalty to intersectionality, and to black women's intellectual production more broadly. This section more deeply interrogates the notion of close reading *as* care, examining the political and affective lure of the imagined care work of careful reading. Hancock's discussion of intersectional "stewardship" epitomizes the kinds of calls for care I am invested in exploring. Hancock develops stewardship as a way of advancing care, rather than ownership, as the defining relationship between black feminist scholars and intersectionality. She writes, "If we think of a steward as someone entrusted with caring for valuables that she does not herself own then my role is to not only disavow ownership of intersectionality, but to remember that while I am permitted to use it, I must do so ethically, which entails producing projects that hopefully leave intersectionality scholars better equipped to engage in knowledge production projects in intersectionality studies."[43] Stewardship, then, means "being entrusted with the care of such a precious and complicated phenomenon like intersectionality."[44] To be a "steward" of intersectionality is to recognize one's place in a long lineage of scholars and activists who carefully and lovingly preserve the term for future generations. Hancock urges intersectional stewards to develop an attention to intersectionality's "global reach" and distinctive local practices, to recognize the panoply of forms that intersectional theory and practice can take, and the variations in these forms according to place, space, and historical moment.[45] In other words, stewards need deep knowledge of the analytic's interdisciplinary reach and myriad meanings. Similarly, stewards should understand intersectionality's long "historical arc," one that includes Crenshaw and Collins, and other women of color feminists including Maria Stewart, Sojourner Truth, Gloria Anzaldúa, and the Combahee River Collective.[46] This enables stewards to attend to "intersectionality-like thought," to a long tradition of intellectual and activist work grappling with the interconnectedness, complexity, and contingency of difference. Ultimately, Hancock suggests that a deep and broad understanding of intersectionality *facilitates* the preservationist attitude toward intersectionality she advocates, a caring and loving stance.

For Hancock, stewardship's ethic of care is imagined as an interruption to potentially alluring logics of ownership. As a steward, one never possesses intersectionality, one simply cares for the precious intellectual tradition to enable its ongoing vitality. This act of care enables scholars to lovingly pass intersectionality from black feminist generation to generation, ensuring the continuity of the term's life. Yet I want to interrogate how this form of care—one that includes careful reading and careful engagement with intersectionality's histories—can actually produce and reinscribe logics of ownership, property, and territoriality. What marks Hancock's caring conception of stewardship is a sense that there is an "ethical" way to do intersectional work, yet it is left unclear how we determine what constitutes a correct (or "ethical") way to do intersectionality. How do we discern ethical usage of an analytic? And what are the exertions of territoriality and defensiveness that even the idea of "ethical usage" can produce? If, following Hancock's logic, intersectionality constitutes a kind of "precious" valuable passed carefully from generation to generation, how do we decide which uses of intersectionality might damage it, diminish its value, or wholly destroy it? The notion of ethical intersectional practice, of lovingly caring for and cultivating the analytic, might not effectively disrupt the notion that there is a correct (or even better) way to do intersectional work. It is precisely this investment in correct—and less correct—intersectional practices that entrenches the conception of the analytic as vulnerable territory in need of black feminist protection.

Despite the fact that stewardship refuses to interrupt ownership and property in the ways that it aspires to, it mobilizes a deeply powerful rhetoric on behalf of intersectionality: care. Black feminist theory has become newly and emphatically preoccupied with care. It is crucial to think of this new preoccupation as swirling around at least two phenomena—one is the proliferation of scholarly and popular writing on black feminist practices of self-care *as* black feminism's primary agenda for survival; the second is the context of the Black Lives Matter movement, a renewed interest in black social death as the condition marking the present, and a renewed investment in care in the face of death (and care as a practice of black life in the face of black death). In making a claim that there is a new interest in care, I do not seek to efface black feminists' longer investment in care—including scholarship on the racial, gendered, and sexual politics of care work, on the care performed by fictive kin and other-mothers, on homegirls and the political importance of black female friendships. Instead, I hone in on a particular proliferation of work on self-care as political practice, as revolutionary act, a body of scholarship (and activist work) that has circulated with greater speed in recent years and that has often circulated alongside Audre Lorde's statement "Caring for myself is not self-indulgence, it is self-preservation, and that is an act of political warfare."[47] As Kai Green and Marquis Bey note, "Black feminist scholarship rescues self-love from pathology and instead imagines it as politically, erotically, and creatively generative."[48] Green and Bey underscore that self-love is particularly transgressive for black women because of "cultural prohibitions" on black love, and they urge black women to "create new systems of value that attempt to rescue the self from internalizing a capitalist logic that allows one to only see oneself in terms of wealth, use value, or object."[49] The investment in black women's self-love as a radical act of self-valuation is echoed in popular venues, where commentators advocate self-care as a "radical feminist act" for black women because "we've spent generations in servitude to others. In fact, Black women have often been considered properties of our communities."[50] Taken together, these texts collectively underscore the importance of rhetorics of self-love, self-care, and self-preservation to contemporary black feminist theory and politics.

In our current moment, care and death are entangled in the black feminist theoretical imagination. Christina Sharpe, for example, treats care as fundamental to the concept of "wake work" that she develops. For Sharpe, wake work is an analytic about survival and death, and their inextricable link. It captures a mode of cultural production, creative praxis, and daily practice that attends to how "we are Black peoples in the wake with no state or nation to protect us, with no citizenship bound to be respected," and to how we live, survive, imagine, dream, and do in the midst of the afterlives of slavery and the persistence of racial violence.[51] She writes, "I want to think 'care' as a problem for thought. I want to think care in the wake as a problem for thinking and of and for Black non/being in the world. Put another way, . . . [this] is a work that insists and performs that thinking needs care ('all thought is Black thought') and that thinking and care need to stay in the wake."[52] For Sharpe, care performs myriad forms of work: it is a way of "defending the dead," a strategy of thinking through black death and our endless proximity to it (or perhaps the fact that we reside in it), and a tool for theorizing "Black non/being in the world."[53] Care is a practice for tending to what has already been lost and what might be lost, a political tool for the maintenance of self and collective, that is always oppositional to the logic of the state (something I will return to in the book's fourth chapter). It is thus a practice of being deeply attuned to historical and ongoing violence, and to living in the midst of it, a strategy of examining black life and the structures that seek to constrain that life. Sharpe's work reveals not only that an ethic of care has particular appeal to black feminists in "the wake of" Black Lives Matter, but that part of its appeal is the long shadow of death, a new and deepened investment in tracing emphatically the "afterlives of slavery" that are evident in spectacular national events, including white supremacist violence in Charlottesville, the acquittal of George Zimmerman for the murder of Trayvon Martin, the election of Donald Trump, the racial violence thrust at Barack and Michelle Obama, *and* in quotidian acts of what Patricia J. Williams terms "spirit murder."[54]

It is crucial to link Hancock's conception of careful stewardship to newly proliferating calls for black care—self-care, collective care—as strategies for living "in the wake." Thus, to argue for careful reading, for care for intersectionality, is to make a deeply political claim. Under this logic, reading is not merely reading; it is an articulation of a commitment on behalf of intersectionality and on behalf of black women. Like Hancock, Vivian May mobilizes the language of care to advocate for black women, noting, "In the end, my goal is to underscore the degree to which intersectionality's historical and intellectual origins, diverse philosophical premises, and range of political nuances need to be attended to . . . with far more care."[55] This call for "care," for acting in care, with care, in the context of a moment where care signals a strategy of resisting antiblack sexist violence, makes a powerful claim on behalf of intersectionality. To care for intersectionality, then, is to care for black women's intellectual production and to care for black women as knowledge producers, as subjects. Despite the allure of care, and the importance of black feminist work theorizing black thriving "in the wake," this book again and again emphatically interrogates moments where care, love, and affection mask a pernicious possessiveness, a refusal to let intersectionality move and transform in unexpected and perhaps challenging ways. The remainder of this book takes up the political pull of care and tries to reanimate it, asking how we might display our care—our affection, our regard, our love, even—for intersectionality differently, in ways that exceed the deep pull of the proprietary.

The organizers of the 1994 National Women's Studies Association (NWSA) conference, "Women Working in a Global Context," described the urgency of "global" feminist engagement:

> The situation of women around the globe — in the former Yugoslavia, South Africa, Southeast Asia, in U.S. inner cities — compels us to reconceive our work in a global context. Therefore, NWSA invites feminist scholars and activists to examine gender, race, ethnicity, class, religion, sexuality and nationality in a global context. We encourage presenters to examine the experiences, lives and work of women in all cultures and countries and to reconsider their own work, their disciplines, their areas of interest and fields of action in this expanded context. We want this conference to challenge our understanding of "global" and to shatter our narrow conception of it as exclusively "international" or "third world." We hope that the conference will bring together diverse women from as many countries as possible.[1]

That year's conference was celebrated for its inclusion of plenary speakers from Bulgaria, Canada, Egypt, India, and Nigeria and for its demand that feminists reckon with the "global context" in which US feminist intellectual and political work is staged. Bethania Maria, a representative of the NWSA's Women of Color Caucus, urged conference participants to imagine a feminism that would "find a common ground . . . and a common language."[2] This "common language," to borrow Adrienne Rich's oft-cited phrase, had a grammar that centered the "global" and imagined the transnational as a remedy for the racial exclusivity that had long plagued both the organization and the discipline.

The centrality of the "global" to a complex, robust, and inclusive feminism was echoed at subsequent NWSA conferences in 1996 ("Borders, Crossings, Passages: Women Reinterpreting Development"); 1997 ("Currents and Crosscurrents"); 1998 ("Foundations for the Twenty-First Century"); 2004 ("Women in the Middle: Borders, Barriers, Intersections"); and 2008 ("Resisting Hegemonies: Race and Sexual Politics in Nation, Region, and Empire").[3] In her 2003 presidential address, NWSA's president Magdalena Garcia-Pinto noted that it was "important for the future of Women's Studies" to engage "theoretical contributions of feminist theorists that emerge from geographical locations beyond US borders. United States feminism, so instrumental in inspiring feminist movements in many regions of the world, will find new challenges by establishing more active contact with international feminisms, with third-world feminisms."[4] Garcia-Pinto's plea for an engagement with "international feminisms" was echoed by Colette Morrow's presidential address the following year, which called for "accelera[ting] the globalization of women's studies."[5] These appeals emphasized that the theoretical and political project of women's studies should be oriented toward an "international" feminism that would connect US feminisms with the "many regions of the world," that would analyze the global context in which feminist work unfolds, and that would undo the violent traces of racism and colonialism from feminist practice.

Though the language of the global came to animate the discipline's annual conferences in the mid-1990s, another narrative has emerged about the discipline's preoccupations during this period: the 1990s were marked by the salvific arrival of intersectionality. This history is rehearsed by a number of scholars with varied investments in intersectionality: Nikol Alexander-Floyd notes, "The 1980s and 1990s brought with it an explosion of interest in black women's studies, particularly by white feminists, black men, and others who were not black feminists"; Carolyn Pedwell argues, "Intersectionality was initiated through Black feminists' potent critiques of white middle-class bias within mainstream feminist theory and practice . . . in the 1970s and 1980s"; Jasbir Puar asserts, "Intersectionality emerged from the struggles of second wave feminism as a crucial black feminist intervention challenging the hegemonic rubrics of race, class, and gender within predominantly white feminist frames"; Roderick Ferguson argues, "Whether located within the late seventies or the late eighties, the term has become a signature feature of the critical vocabularies of queer studies and academic feminism"; and Leslie McCall asserts, "The methodology of anticategorical complexity was born in this moment of critique, in which hegemonic feminist theorists, poststructuralists, and antiracist theorists almost simultaneously launched assaults on the validity of modern analytical categories in the 1980s."[6] The recent scholarly interest in historicizing intersectionality has also led to the repetition of this oft-cited truth, even as historically oriented projects are increasingly invested in theorizing intersectionality's long theoretical and political roots in earlier black feminist work. Wholly absent from these disciplinary stories is an engagement with the field's investment in transnationalism and the "global" during the 1990s.

If the NWSA was deeply invested in transnationalism in the 1990s, why is intersectionality tethered to this period in women's studies' stories about itself? Why has telling intersectionality's history seemed to require forgetting transnationalism? This chapter asks what it might mean to tell a different story about women's studies' histories and its key analytics, and for black feminism to be at the vanguard of this different kind of telling. Indeed, as I argue in this chapter, women's studies has long rehearsed a story about itself that presumes that intersectionality and transnationalism are wholly separate analytics, each embodied by a particular racially marked subject. This story is particularly surprising as both analytics are similarly deployed by the field to make certain racialized bodies into signs of the promise of feminist inclusivity, complexity, and "political completion"—and into signs of fatigue, frustration, and even political depression.[7] In other words, I trace a paradox where, on the one hand, intersectionality and transnationalism have been imagined to perform similar remedial work for the field, and on the other hand, they have been represented in women's studies as discrete theoretical and political projects competing for the meager intellectual and material resources allotted to women of color.

In this chapter, I imagine a black feminist theoretical and political project that could surrender its territorial hold to intersectionality and permit the analytic to move untethered from the imagined specificity of black woman. My understanding of surrender is indebted to Kevin Quashie's work on black interiority, which complicates the prevailing notion that surrender is "a passive term, the counterpart to being conquered, dominated, or defeated."[8] Instead, Quashie argues that surrender can be "expressive and active," "a deliberate giving up to another, the simultaneous practice of yielding and falling toward what is deeply and largely unknowable."[9] Drawing on Quashie, I treat a black feminist surrender of intersectionality *not* as a form of "defeat" but as the beginning of reimagining black feminist theoretical and political life, as a deep act of generosity that unleashes connections between black feminism and women of color feminism, enabling black feminism to imagine itself otherwise. Indeed, this chapter endeavors to energize a black feminist politics of surrender by asking what if we surrendered the notion that black woman is intersectionality's key sign? What if we insistently despecified intersectionality? What if we embraced a vision of intersectionality that was capacious enough to center women of color generally and that insisted on the intimacies between transnationalism and intersectionality in terms of both their construction and use by women's studies and their creative world-making possibilities? What if intersectionality could be mobilized to theorize arrangements of power beyond US black woman, and thus as a generative space of intimacy among women of color? In other words, I treat a despecified intersectionality, one that does not necessarily reference black woman, as a critical response to how women's studies has imagined *both* intersectionality and transnationalism, and as an opportunity for black feminists to imagine a kind of intimacy with both transnationalism and the broader category "women of color." This form of letting go, effectively ceding a proprietary relationship with intersectionality, allows for new forms of intimacy, allegiance, and alliance and promotes a form of black feminist agency that is far from the defensive posture I trace in the first half of the book.

My method for thinking through the discipline's construction of intersectionality and transnationalism is historical. Unlike other chapters in this book, my engagement is closely centered around a particular organization—the National Women's Studies Association—and its archive. My investment is not in treating the NWSA as representative of women's studies' formations at all programs and departments at US colleges and universities; instead, I am interested in the NWSA as the discipline's institutional home, its organizing force, and as a critical actor in feminism's institutional histories. I examine the agendas that were charted for the field in and through the organization's annual conferences, spaces that have consistently brought together feminist scholars and activists to discuss the field as it is and to chart future visions for the discipline. It is also a space where the tensions in the discipline—the activist/theory binary, the queer theory/feminist theory debate, and the politics of racial difference—have been played out in both quotidian and spectacular ways, and so it provides a rich window onto the racial politics of US academic feminism.

Archiving the NWSA

In its early years, the NWSA imagined its primary labor to be cultivating an antiracist feminism, a project that required feminists to undertake a rigorous form of self-labor; feminists *should* work on themselves to fight racism, the NWSA's annual conferences advocated. And a feminist *should* endeavor to, in Audre Lorde's words, "reach down into that deep place of knowledge inside herself and touch that terror and loathing of any difference that lives there."[10] Over the course of the organization's history, the NWSA's investments shifted from the notion of antiracist work as a labor of self toward a conception of antiracist work as an institutional task that required thinking through systems and structures of white dominance. In this section, I trace how the NWSA imagined this institutional labor, arguing that it was first staged through the "transnational" and "global" and only later through intersectionality, even as the discipline offers a historical account that foregrounds intersectionality at the expense of transnationalism. My aim in this section, then, is to trace two shifts: first, a shift toward a conception of racism as structural, not individual, and second, a shift from antiracist confrontations to transnationalism, and then to intersectionality, as a "cure" for feminist racism.

The NWSA was founded in 1977, and its early years were marked by organizational precarity; its annual conferences, which were held during the summer months, marking it as untethered to the academic calendar, were labors of love staffed by volunteers and "troubleshooters" who were learning how to run a conference as they went. In one letter to future volunteers, the organization's marketing manager described "NWSA" as an acronym for "Not What She Anticipated," a description that captured the on-the-ground troubleshooting that was an integral part of volunteering for the conference. During this era, the association's annual conferences were preoccupied with cultivating a feminist antiracism in deeply particular ways.[11] For example, annual meetings often featured prominent black feminist scholar-activists exposing the prevalence of racism in women's studies and challenging so-called white feminists to engage in the labor of reforming their selves. Under this logic, white feminists were imagined to *need* the remediation the conference provided as a way of perfecting the practice of their feminism, and black female attendees were imagined to be agents of remediation, instructing white women on the development of an anti-racist self. For example, in 1979, the same year that the NWSA's Women of Color Caucus was formed, Barbara Smith delivered her now-canonical "Racism and Women's Studies" speech at the closing session of the conference. She said:

> For those of you who are tired of hearing about racism, imagine how much more tired *we* are of constantly experiencing it, second by literal second, how much more exhausted we are to see it constantly in your eyes. The degree to which it is hard or uncomfortable for you to have the issue raised is the degree to which you know inside of yourself that you aren't dealing with the issue, the degree to which you are hiding from the oppression that undermines Third World women's lives. I want to say right here that this is not a "guilt trip." It's a fact trip.[12]

Smith's widely cited speech marks the NWSA's early approach to the question of racism. First, it positions racism as located in the hearts and minds of white women. Racism, in Smith's hands, is individual, not institutional; it is "in your eyes," not in the very structure of the discipline, the academy, or the organization. Second, it envisions racism as something that can be dismantled through its recognition. A "fact trip," or a recognition of black women's lived, embodied, and quotidian experiences of racism, can undo racism itself. The labor of the conference, then, is to allow white women to recognize their own racism and to provide them with tools to undo that racism. Finally, Smith's speech situates black women—the "we" who speak (back) to the "you" in the audience—as truth-tellers whose experiences can lead to a vision of feminism that "lift[s] oppression off of not only women, but all oppressed people: poor and working-class people, people of color in this country and in the colonized Third World. If lifting this oppression is not a priority to you, then it's problematic whether you are a part of the actual feminist movement."[13] While Smith's speech was a plea for feminist practitioners to recognize how women's studies itself was steeped in racism, it was also a call for *white feminists* to engage in "changing their behavior." This scene—one where black women were called upon to mark racism and to demand redress—would be replayed at the NWSA for many years and formed the basis of the organization's prevailing approach to the politics of difference during the 1980s.

The association's 1981 conference, held at the University of Connecticut, was organized around the theme "Women Respond to Racism," and, as Becky Thompson notes, "All conference members were expected to attend daily two-hour consciousness-raising groups that lumped all women of color into one group but allowed white women to choose from a differentiated list of groups: working-class women, Jewish women, immigrant women, educated women, and so on."[14] Though the consciousness-raising groups were clumsily constructed, they established antiracism as a critical and time-consuming labor of self, and as a project particularly geared toward white women.[15] That same year, one that the NWSA later described as "ground-breaking," Adrienne Rich delivered her widely anthologized speech "Disobedience and Women's Studies."[16] Like Smith's "Racism and Women's Studies" speech, Rich's talk was delivered as an exposé, one that revealed white women's problematic investment in racism. She noted:

> So long as we identify only with white women, we are still connected to that system of objectification and cruelty called racism. And that system is not simply a "patriarchal mindfuck," an idea, which the feminist can assume she has tossed out along with "mankind" and "God the Father." It is a material reality of the flesh and nerves, and our relation to it as white feminists is a complex function. . . . Only as white women begin to understand both our obedience and complicity, and our rebellions, do we begin to have the tools for an ongoing response to racism which is neither circular, rhetorical, or resentful.[17]

In encouraging "disobedience," Rich, much as Smith did the year before, cast the labor of challenging white racism as a labor of self, a recognition and dismantling of white female "complicity."[18] For Rich, the labor of the NWSA was to confront and dismantle the "obedience" that "white feminist[s]" had developed, and to cultivate an ethic of radical disobedience that would begin with a liberation of self.

The NWSA's conception of racism as a problem of self that could be overcome through rigorous and demanding labor was fundamental to how organizers *imagined* the meetings. In 1985, Ann Russo's letter to the NWSA Planning Committee detailed an attempt to commence a "White Women Confronting Racism" workshop at the next conference—a workshop that would be "exclusive to white women" and that would "facilitate discussion of racism both from intellectual and personal perspectives."[19] This vision of a workshop *exclusive* to white women is, in many ways, resonant with

Smith's call to "take some frightening risks" and with her plea that "you [white women] have got to comprehend how racism distorts and lessens your own lives as white women, that racism affects your chances for survival too and that it is very definitely your issue. Until you understand this no fundamental change will come about." The potential "White Women Confronting Racism" workshop again painted "confrontation" as the key to remedying racism, consciousness-raising and workshops as critical methods for countering racism, and self-work as essential to feminist practice. It also imagined the space of the NWSA conference as one where white women worked on their selves to actively combat racism and to produce a newly antiracist, and thus appropriately feminist, self. It is, then, clear that the 1980s were an era in which the NWSA institutionalized "connecting women," confronting racism, and challenging white privilege as essential to the mission of the organization, to the practice of women's studies, and to both academic and political feminisms. In this moment of the NWSA's history, black women were the organization's primary symbol; their inclusion signified progress, they emblemized the challenges facing feminism and the possibilities of a multiracial, egalitarian feminist future, and their bodies made possible the kinds of confrontations the organization felt necessary in the construction of a new antiracist discipline.

If the NWSA long sought to remedy racism through intensive self-labor and consciousness-raising, and through black women exposing white women's "complicity" and "obedience," its infamous "Feminist Education: Calling the Question" conference at the University of Akron in 1990 revealed the profound shortcomings of this individualized approach to eradicating racism. Caryn McTighe Musil, NWSA's then executive director, described the Akron conference as follows: "After nearly a quarter of a century of the second wave of the women's movement, more than two decades of formal Women's Studies Programs, and five years since the end of the UN Decade of Women, it is time to call the question. The need for feminist education is no longer subject to debate. What is under discussion are the strategies, theories, and structures of feminist education and how to use its potential to alter inequitable arrangements of power."[20] Yet "inequitable arrangements of power," particularly within the NWSA's ranks, would come to define the Akron conference.

When conference attendees arrived in Akron, they were greeted by scholars and activists wearing buttons that posed the question "Where is Ruby Sales?" For those who had not heard of Sales, the question was a provocation, and by the end of the few days in Akron, everyone knew who she was. Sales was the NWSA's first full-time black employee, and she had been terminated before the Akron conference. Sales alleged that her termination was racially motivated, and she filed a complaint with the county's Human Relations Commission. Musil insisted that Sales was terminated for personnel reasons; in an interview, she noted, "It's easy to make that charge (of racism) of almost every organization in the country."[21] Conference participants, though, were not satisfied by Musil's response, and some suggested that Sales's termination was indicative of larger racial problems within both the organization and the discipline. In an "Open Letter to the Lesbian Caucus," Rosemary Curb and Bette S. Tallen—two self-identified "white lesbians"— write, "[Sales] challenged the implicit racism of white women's ways of getting on with things everywhere it appeared. . . . With Ruby in NWSA there was no way it wouldn't change. . . . Can we call ourselves an organization for all women if only white women work in the national office? How far have white feminists really come in confronting our racism?"[22] For Curb and Tallen, Sales's termination was evidence that the kinds of labor NWSA participants were supposed to be constantly involved in—consciously confronting white supremacy—had failed.

In response to growing concern about Sales's termination, the NWSA Steering Committee circulated papers that offered the association's "active record on affirming racial difference and opposing racism."[23] The NWSA's Women of Color Caucus quickly responded with its own statements, including one which charged that "NWSA, like the society in which it is embedded, is a system of institutionalized oppression. While the oppressions manifested within NWSA are several, race oppression is its archetype."[24] The Women of Color Caucus urged NWSA to "clean its own house" and warned that, "in the meantime, 'we are outta here.'"[25] Sales also drafted an open letter to the NWSA published in *off our backs* in which she urged the organization to "reconsider its history and its future" and to "reckon with the reality that there is no monolithic woman, that women's lives differ according to race, class, and skin color. NWSA must explore the paradoxes of what it means as white females to be both inside and outside the circle of power."[26]

Much like the Barnard "Women and Sexuality" conference in 1982, Akron quickly became a divisive flash point in larger feminist debates, with Sales's departure acting as a way of considering the organization's—and the discipline's—relationship to so-called difference. Indeed, looking back on Akron, a number of its participants describe the conference as a turning point for the organization: Sara Evans calls it the year when the NWSA experienced its "self-destruction."[27] Maria C. Gonzalez writes, "What erupted in Akron is always hard for me to describe."[28] And Barbara Scott writes, "Now when I think of NWSA and Akron in 1990, I think not so much about white women and racism but of home. With women of color I feel something very familiar, very nostalgic, very spiritual, and something very protective and safe that reminds me of home."[29] After Akron, the NWSA's "Feminist Horizons: Crossing Borders" conference, scheduled for 1991, was canceled, Musil resigned, and, as Robin Leidner notes, "NWSA lost a substantial number of members, the entire national staff resigned, a governance-reorganization committee struggled to redefine the political structure of the association, and a search committee hired an interim national coordinator . . . to pursue community linkages and to make NWSA more inclusive."[30] Before her departure, Musil polled women's studies' program chairs and directors about what they wanted to see at future NWSA conferences; many indexed an investment in developing strategies that would help the NWSA "survive." In that fractious moment, the continuity of the organization was on the line, and the meaning of antiracist feminist politics was newly subjected to debate.[31]

In the years after Akron, a new feminist strategy was born. In calling it a strategy, I do not mean to imply that NWSA officials gathered to select a singular approach to recovering from Akron. Instead, the organization's conferences, mission statements, presidential addresses, and reconceptualization of its structure in the wake of the Akron meeting collectively reveal a profound shift in how the organization responded to questions of racism and the politics of difference. By 1994, the third post-Akron conference, the question of the "global context" was placed squarely on the NWSA's agenda, and for the next decade, the global played an important *remedial* role at NWSA conferences. The global was not simply a new location for staging feminist inquiry but a terrain on which inequality could be both mapped and remedied, a space in and through which US women's studies could effectively be transformed into an anticolonial and antiracist project. The "global" not only promised the NWSA a way to talk about feminism expansively and to dream about feminism's "common language" (while critiquing ideas of "global sisterhood") but also was imagined to remedy the problems of essentialism and exclusivity that had marked earlier feminist projects, including the NWSA's conference at Akron. The "global" effectively replaced the association's earlier investment in antiracist labors of self, and transformative confrontations that jarred white women into embracing an antiracist consciousness.

The NWSA's embrace of global analytics was part of an era in which transnational feminism "emerged"—a term I use in quotation marks to highlight how the "stories we tell" seem to hinge on emergence and disappearance rather than on institutional and geopolitical contexts that make particular concepts desirable in certain moments—when the academic and political practices of feminism were fundamentally remade by a newfound interest in questions of the global. In underscoring the "rise" of transnationalism as academic feminism's guiding principle and analytic, I want to make clear that there were *institutional* reasons for the rise of the term, including Akron and the racial violence that exploded there, *and* the efforts of nongovernmental organizations to foreground gender inequities as questions of human rights. Indeed, the early 1990s have been described as "the pinnacle of the international expression of women's rights," epitomized by the Fourth World Conference on Women in Beijing in 1995 and the UN's Decade for Women (1976–85).[32] The Beijing conference in particular led to the popularization of the slogan "women's rights are human rights," which tethered global feminist practice to a human rights framework.[33] As Jennifer Suchland notes, Beijing promised what feminists had long craved: a common vocabulary, "a unified statement for women's rights."[34] It was this particular iteration of global feminism—its promise of a feminism that could meaningfully engage geopolitical difference, a feminism that could speak in the plural but always with a singular emphasis on human rights—that captivated the NWSA in the wake of Akron. If Beijing provided a coherent framework for transnational feminist organizing, feminist theory was encountering the transnational feminist edited anthology—including *Scattered Hegemonies* (1994), *Feminist Genealogies, Colonial Legacies, Democratic Futures* (1996), and *Talking Visions: Multicultural Feminism in a Transnational Age* (1998)—and the transnational feminist documentary (most notably Alice Walker and Pratibha Parmar's collaboration *Warrior Marks*), which transformed US feminist academic practice.[35]

If transnationalism was the analytic embraced post-Akron, offering a logic of expansive global feminisms that captivated the organization, the first decade of the twenty-first century saw yet another transition in the field imaginary: an embrace of intersectionality. Crucially, intersectionality entered the discipline's professional organization—and its scholarly journals—in a different way than transnationalism. Intersectionality promised to be analytic, theory, method, framework, and politic, and it skillfully traversed the academic/activist binary that had long produced a contentious and painful fault line in the conference. Intersectionality was not, like antiracism, a labor of self-transformation that could yield better (white) feminist subjects. Rather than requiring the kind of intensive self-labor of antiracist feminism, intersectionality continued to make use of the sign "black woman" but mobilized it differently: to suggest that the fundamental questions at the heart of the discipline had to be reimagined. Intersectionality used the figure of the black woman as a metaphor for the most marginalized subject, as a way of conceptualizing how structures of domination work to wound and oppress, and suggested that feminism needed to build a theory of gender, race, sexuality, class, and nation complex enough to contend with this particular subject's distinct position. In other words, intersectionality used black woman to map what the discipline could aspire to be—a critical practice deeply attentive to complexity and particularity.

Nowhere was this engagement with intersectionality more apparent than in 2009 and 2010, two decades after the term "intersectionality" circulated in Crenshaw's canonical law review articles, when the NWSA hosted the two-year "Difficult Dialogues" conferences. The conference's idea of "difficult dialogues" borrowed from Johnnella Butler's work, which reflected on the challenges women's studies programs face precisely because they "labor under the illusion that they reflect all women's experience because they have one faculty member with expertise in some area of scholarship on women of color, offer one or two courses on the subject, or sponsor lectures or other presentations by women of color, or because they see themselves as essentially well-meaning."[36] Indeed, Butler found that women's studies faculty too often used "difficulty" as a shield, as a way of not engaging questions of so-called difference.[37] In rooting its conference in Butler's work, the NWSA crafted a *black feminist antiracism*, which abandoned the organization's earlier carefully staged difficult encounters between white and black women and replaced them with a difficult analytic that promised complex scholarship attentive to multiplicity and difference.[38] If earlier NWSA conferences presented "black woman" as a difficult figure, a disciplinarian who demanded white affective and political labor, the "Difficult Dialogues" conferences presented intersectionality as "difficult," as a disciplinary analytic that centered "black woman" in the service of transforming the field.

The call for papers for the initial "Difficult Dialogues" conference stated the conference's commitment to studying "how feminist intellectual, political, and institutional practices cannot be adequately practiced if the politics of gender are conceptualized (overtly or implicitly) as superseding or transcending the politics of race, sexuality, social class, nation, and disability."[39] Calling for scholarly conversation around difference—precisely the conversations that are "urgently needed but frequently avoided"—the 2009 NWSA call for papers *specifically* mentioned intersectionality as a challenging conversation worth having. The 2009 call noted, "Despite claims that 'everyone' now 'does' (or has always 'done') WS [women's studies] from intersectional and transnational perspectives, many of the ways in which the politics of both race and nation have been taken up in the field have been more nominal than transformative. Despite widespread changes in the WS curriculum, in feminist scholarship, and in WS institutional formations, there remains an ongoing struggle over what constitutes the legitimate terrain of feminist theory and inquiry, past and present."[40] While "difficult dialogues" seemed to suture transnationalism and intersectionality, in practice it was an embrace of an intersectional feminism, one that largely focused on the imagined difficulty of black woman, that prevailed. This was made particularly clear in the organization's selection of keynote speakers. Angela Davis, the keynote speaker in 2009, reflected on earlier NWSA conferences and noted, "There has been a long history of attempting to figure out how to think and act upon these categories as intersectional, but not always neatly intersecting, rather as overlaying and crosshatched."[41] In other words, though "difficult dialogues" promised to capture a multiplicity of difficulties, the particular challenges—and potential payoffs—of intersectionality were presented as paramount.

I linger in the NWSA's history for the purpose of telling a story different than the disciplinary common sense, and for the purpose of critically interrogating that common sense. If transnationalism "arrived" in the late 1990s, why has the field been preoccupied with insisting that this was the era of intersectionality's "arrival"? What has this preoccupation with intersectionality's emergence in the 1990s done to a consideration of intersectionality and transnationalism's intimacies, including the ways that they have been similarly institutionally constructed within US women's studies as political correctives? What might considering both as correctives do to help us collectively understand how women of color's intellectual production continues to be understood as intervention, critique, or corrective? The remainder of this chapter aspires to upend this story and to offer another narrative, one that emphasizes the particular—and similar—kinds of remedial work that both intersectionality and transnationalism have been imagined to perform.

Twin Analytics

This chapter began by closely analyzing the NWSA's engagement with antiracist feminism, transnationalism, and intersectionality as a strategy for unsettling the disciplinary common sense: that intersectionality "arrived" in the 1990s, effectively saving the discipline from its past exclusions. As I argued, this prevailing narrative forgets transnationalism, writing its centrality to the field in the 1990s out of women's studies' history. In this section, I argue that this dominant narrative obscures how both analytics have been animated as sites of racial repair for women's studies, how both analytics have been similarly situated in women's studies. In response, I attempt to suture intersectionality and transnationalism, even as I am mindful of the array of scholarly work, especially by women of color, underscoring the irreconcilability of these two terms. In suturing these terms, I want to be explicit about the university's very different investments in these analytics. Intersectionality's mobility has been made possible by the university's investment in diversity and inclusion, and by the term's imagined open-endedness, which allows it to be emptied of specific meaning. Indeed, intersectionality now appears in the strategic plans of many colleges and universities wearing the guise of diversity and inclusion in statements like "[Our] multifaceted and coordinated framework for equity and inclusion considers and affirms the role of multiple identities with relationship to various social contexts and interlocking systems of power, privilege, and oppression in shaping experiences of our community members. . . . While intentional focus on intersectionality is central to the University's framework, community- and identity-specific efforts are necessary until full equality is realized. These efforts acknowledge important nuances within diverse communities and identities and allow for strategic attention that advances the work more broadly." Universities increasingly champion "Identity and Intersectionality Education," which "provide[s] a unique setting for the encouragement of broad social, cultural, recreational, and educational programming for the . . . university and its surroundings." I pick out these statements because they reflect the institutionalization of intersectionality as an administrative ethic that shores up the notions that we are all different (and perhaps equally different from each other), that intersectionality's project is about difference recognition, and that the university is a space marked by sanctioned forms of difference celebration. Despite the celebration of the "global university" and its capacity to produce global citizens—the growth of outposts of US universities, the proliferation of study-abroad programs, and the pleas to globalize US curricula—transnational feminism has not been mobilized by the university as intersectionality has. In other words, the global university's lure and promise have not been attached to the idea of transnational feminism in the same way that ideas of diversity and inclusion have been yoked to intersectionality.

Many scholars have argued that a feminist embrace of transnationalism often masks a rejection of rigorous engagements with US racism and an unwillingness to engage US women of color, who are not imagined as global subjects, and who thus fall out of transnational feminist projects. This scholarship has revealed that, as Shireen Roshanravan writes:

> Dismissing the politics and subjects of Women of Color as US-centric in the move to a "global feminism" can easily be seen as strategic evasion of local critiques that would decenter white/Anglo perspectives and knowledges still anchoring the field. Yet this dismissal is inextricably tied to upholding Occidentalist formulations of global feminism that conceive of difference and diversification primarily as a quantitative issue measured geographically (in terms of representational samples or discrete case studies funneled through a singular epistemic framework) rather than a political issue measured through epistemic capacities (in terms of one's ability to perceive others through their own cultural logic).[42]

For Roshanravan, the shift toward the transnational is also a shift away from "local critiques" *and* a strategy for privileging geographic travel rather than the kind of "world-traveling" or epistemic movement that feminists of color, most notably Maria Lugones, have championed for decades. Similarly, Karla Holloway reveals that the transnational "manifests a profound and troubling discomfort with the local" and argues that the transnational is often a kind of permission for "local body-politics" to remain "underinterrogated"; Sandra Soto provocatively asks about the place of US women of color in the transnational turn; and Sharon Holland's recent work, which invests in the often-critiqued black/white binary, argues that attempts to destabilize this binary through transnationalism (and through ideas of

diaspora) can reify the notion of US blackness as "parochial."[43] These varied interventions mark important engagements with the racial politics of
transnationalism's institutionalization and reveal one of the key strategies
through which transnationalism and intersectionality have been kept separate: transnationalism is tethered to nation, intersectionality is tethered to
race, as if nation and race are wholly separate sites of analysis. In thinking
about intersectionality and transnationalism together, I underscore that
there is nothing *inherent* in these analytics that makes them irreconcilable;
indeed, the endeavor of this chapter is to consider how women's studies, as
a discipline, has driven a wedge between these terms. My aspiration, then,
is to insist on the intimacies between the terms, and the bodies that are
imagined to perform these terms.

This intimacy is particularly important because it both exposes and upends how intersectionality and transnationalism are regularly constructed
by the field as mutually exclusive, and even as operating in competition
for the already scarce resources allocated to women of color. The hyper-
competitive academic job market makes this abundantly clear: "intersectionality" codes as jobs focused on the United States, and particularly on
black women and black feminism, and "transnationalism" codes as jobs
focused outside the United States, and particularly on the global South.
For example, recent tenure-track job advertisements for positions in wom-
en's studies focused on "transnational feminism" call for "applicants whose
scholarly record demonstrates expertise in the study of popular culture,
media studies, political aesthetics, and feminist representations of women
and gender grounded in transnational or Global South feminisms," or for
faculty focused on the "global south" who conduct "transnational research
in such fields as critical development studies, environment and social justice, migration, indigeneity, human rights, science and technology studies,
visual cultures, and performance studies," or scholars of transnational or
indigenous feminism "whose work focuses on an innovative and rigorous
interdisciplinary approach to teaching about the Global South and/or Indigeneity." Other positions aimed at "intersectional" feminist theory emphasized an orientation toward black feminist theory, noting, "The department
is working to strengthen and deepen its commitment to intersectional feminist studies. The successful candidate will contribute to teaching Black
feminist theories and histories at the undergraduate and graduate level,
as well as other courses in the department's curriculum." Intersectionality
and transnationalism, then, are imagined as separate analytics, traditions,

methods, and modes of analysis that correspond to different geographic locations (United States vs. global South), and to differently raced bodies as object of study *and* often implicitly as the body of the researcher (black vs. nonblack person of color). I collect these advertisements much as Claire Hemmings offers excerpts from journal articles that are cited by *journal* rather than *author*; following Hemmings's lead, I seek to reveal how the job market presumes that transnational and intersectional are both analytics attached to particular identity categories (and to embodied performances by scholars) rather than to expose the idiosyncrasies of a particular institution.[44]

Intersectionality and transnationalism have entered women's studies in deeply racialized ways beyond the job market as well. If intersectionality has been a primary vehicle through which women's studies has encountered "black woman" and contended with her purported challenge to reimagine the field, M. Jacqui Alexander and Chandra Talpade Mohanty note, "the transnational has now come to occupy the place that 'race' and women of color held in women's studies syllabi in the 1990s and earlier."[45] Leela Fernandes makes similar claims, noting that transnational feminism "emerged within and is shaped in central ways by models of multicultural education that are specific to the context of the United States. . . . Dominant paradigms of multiculturalism often continue to cast transnationalism as another marker of identity so that the inclusion of transnational perspectives simply means the inclusion of one more category of the 'other.'"[46] Fernandes argues that, as practiced in institutional women's studies, transnationalism often means the "minoritization" of the world, the "transformation of the world into a minority identity."[47] Taken together, these analyses of transnational feminism suggest the analytic's deep racial politics, particularly as it is embedded and practiced in women's studies, revealing that transnationalism has been attached to ideas of so-called racial and ethnic difference, much as intersectionality has been.

One of the most glaring—and problematic—similarities between these analytics is that each has been tethered to particular racially marked bodies that are imagined *both* to perform the analytic and to be the subject of the analytic's work. In other words, intersectionality and transnationalism are imagined not merely as analytics but as racial embodiments. As Anna Carastathis notes, "The identity-based specialization of labor that these divisions imply has implications for their deployment in institutional projects of diversity management and the training of 'difference' into colonial demographic categories, which women-of-color and Indigenous scholars are then called upon to naturalize with their embodiments."[48] The notion of intersectionality's intimate relationship with black female flesh is something I have traced in my earlier works. In "Rethinking Intersectionality," for example, I argue that intersectionality theory has constructed black woman as the paradigmatic *intersectional* subject, both as the body that renders clear the importance of intersectionality as theory and practice, and as the body that is thought to be the most intersectional precisely because of its imagined multiple marginalization. Yet intersectionality is also thought to be performed by black female scholars whose very embodied presence is thought to be, in and of itself, intersectional. The continued conflation of object of study (and the collapse between black feminist theory and intersectionality) and the body of the scholar often means both that black female faculty are presumed to labor on or around intersectionality and that black female faculty are called upon to perform "intersectional" work in women's studies and allied fields.

Similarly, transnationalism has been constructed around particular racialized signs, acting as "simply another racialized marker of difference and otherness."[49] Some scholars have suggested an investigation of the racial politics of transnationalism by considering which bodies transnationalism does *not*, or even refuses to, describe. In her analysis of how postsocialism is rarely included in conceptions of "transnational feminism," Jennifer Suchland concludes that "the concept of the transnational operates as a racialized category within women's studies."[50] Suchland's point of departure is a rigorous engagement with how the "second world" remains untheorized by transnational feminism; her suggestion is that the invisibility of these locations (and these bodies) reveals transnationalism's otherwise hidden racial politics. Indeed, for Suchland, "the most common internationalizing formula is global woman = third world woman à global South = location of transnational feminist analysis."[51] In her account—one delivered in formulaic notation to underscore the reductive nature of this feminist strategy—"the transnational turn in feminist discourse was meant in part as a critique of the essentialized categories of 'other' women such as third-world women, or African women. In addition, there was an interest in decentering the West as the authority regarding research on women's global issues. . . . [Y]et, there also remained a tendency to read 'transnational' as a proxy term for 'women of color' by essentializing the teachers and areas of that subject field."[52] Suchland's cogent analysis of the racial politics of transnationalism suggests both that the term is imagined to be performed by certain bodies (and, thus, *not* performed by certain other bodies) and that the term is tethered to the global South. Like intersectionality, then, the transnational is envisioned not simply as an analytic but as something inhabited by bodies, as something worn on the flesh.

In considering how transnationalism is racialized within feminism, it is worth lingering on how "transnational" is particularly rendered synonymous with "South Asian." Though the so-called global turn in feminist theory has included, at various moments, preoccupations with "African woman" and "Muslim woman," I underscore how transnational feminism's genesis in the US academy tethered the analytic to South Asian/American women and, in the same way that intersectionality codes as "black women," became a term that signaled centering South Asian/American women in feminist scholarship. Breny Mendoza's concise history of postcolonial feminism attempts to explain this particular racialization by arguing that in the 1990s, this body of scholarship "offered an explanation not only of the distinctiveness of colonial capitalism in India, but of the operations of capitalism in other parts of the colonized world. Yet because the South Asian Subaltern Studies Group focused primarily on the colonization of India and other parts of Asia, their views about the relationship between colonialism and capitalism differed dramatically from those of the Latin American Modernity/Coloniality Group, which drew upon earlier phases of Spanish, Portuguese and French colonization and decolonization."[53] In other words, Mendoza's genealogy of transnational feminism links it both to postcolonial scholarship and to subaltern South Asian studies, suggesting that transnationalism's incorporation into women's studies has often been politically, theoretically, and even performatively linked to South Asian/American women.

If both terms have been imagined as racially marked performatives that invoke certain racially marked bodies and that are performed by certain bodies, both intersectionality and transnationalism have also, in recent years, been haunted by a "post," the promise of a beyond. In the case of intersectionality, this has largely emerged through the sign of "post-intersectionality" and the concept of assemblage. Post-intersectionality, which I referenced in the previous chapter, includes a range of questions, critical practices, and debates that have attempted to revise and rethink intersectionality. "Post-intersectionality," a term that surfaced in the legal academy and has been championed by scholars including Peter Kwan, Robert Chang, and Jerome

Culp, is an attempt to think through intersectionality's limitations and the variety of intersections it leaves untheorized, particularly sexuality/race. Thus, post-intersectional scholars have often developed new terms like "multidimensionality" and "hybrid intersectionality" to bring new forms of imagined complexity to intersectionality. Similarly, assemblage, which I discussed at length in chapter 1, endeavors to rethink intersectionality, taking as a point of departure what it considers as intersectionality's inattention to questions of movement, sensation, and affect, and intersectionality's imagined attachment to the category of identity. In both cases, intersectionality is haunted by "new" work that highlights the analytic's perceived inadequacies, and even links ideas of feminist progress and feminist complexity to newer iterations of intersectionality (or, perhaps, to leaving intersectionality behind). In the case of transnational feminism, the push toward the "beyond" has largely taken the form of the so-called decolonial turn. As Mendoza notes, decolonial scholarship, which often traces its intellectual roots to Gloria Anzaldúa and Maria Lugones, examines how the logics of colonialism, particularly in the Americas, have "established ways of thinking and modes of power that have shaped and continue to shape social and political relations that permeate all aspects of life."[54] Decolonial perspectives argue that "colonialism is what made capitalism possible" rather than considering that "capitalism is concomitant to colonialism."[55] Yet the move toward the decolonial is more than a renewed perspective on colonialism, capitalism, and imperialism; it also contains an implicit critique of postcolonial theory's influence on transnational feminism. Mendoza argues that "postcolonial feminist theory has been accused of cultural determinism and historicism. The political project of postcolonial feminists is also hard to grasp."[56] As Mendoza notes, decolonial perspectives not only challenge transnational perspectives but also are often thought to center different bodies as both the subjects of the perspective and the scholars who are thought to perform and embody the analytic. Indeed, decolonial perspectives are often linked to Native/Indigenous, Chicana, Latina, and African feminist theories, thus centering women of color bodies aside from South Asian bodies. Oftentimes, decolonial perspectives are imagined as intersectional analyses that actively describe the global workings of antiblackness. In the cases of both intersectionality and transnationalism, the emergence of the "post-" links both transnationalism and intersectionality to a kind of past tense, revealing that both have been substantially revised, or even replaced, because of significant elisions. Thus, to engage with these terms now—to link one's academic identity to either intersectionality or transnationalism—is always already to look backward, to invest in feminism's past tense.

If the past tense of these analytics is, in part, secured by "newer" work that challenges the hegemony of these terms, it is also secured through the fantasies of "political completion" that have swirled around the terms.[57] Both terms have been imagined as the tools that can enable and unleash a different kind of feminism, one that can account for myriad structures of domination. Of course, the impossibility of this demand, the impossibility that *any* analytic can perform or produce "political completion," means that both intersectionality and transnationalism have been bemoaned and criticized for what they cannot ever accomplish, and even critiqued for their imagined demands that feminism perform the impossible. I treat this particular form of frustration with analytics saddled with reparative promise, particularly the kinds of promises of freedom from racial violence that have been attached to intersectionality and transnationalism, as feminist fatigue. Rather than reading something intrinsic to either analytic as producing the kinds of exhaustion that now attach to both transnationalism and intersectionality, I foreground how analytics imaginatively attached to women of color generate feminist anxiety, discomfort, and exhaustion.

My understanding of fatigue builds on the contributions of scholars like Amber Jamilla Musser and Julie Ellison on the racial politics of feminist guilt, and the work of Sara Ahmed, who reveals that the bodies of women of color are regularly rhetorically and imaginatively linked to unhappiness (or, as Ahmed notes, the figure of the "killjoy"). In particular, I draw on Ahmed's insights that "the body of color is attributed as the cause of becoming tense, which is also the loss of a shared atmosphere (or we could say that sharing the experience of loss is how the atmosphere is shared). As a feminist of color you do not even have to say anything to cause tension. The mere proximity of some bodies involves an affective conversion."[58] Yet my understanding of fatigue is more than the "tension" or "loss of a shared atmosphere" that Ahmed argues the very presence of the woman of color is thought to produce in feminist conversation. Both transnationalism and intersectionality are often constructed as demands, as interventions that emerged through the intellectual and political labor of women of color, and thus as petitions both for the radical transformation of feminist theory and for the inclusion of myriad voices in feminist theory and politics. If each analytic is imagined narrowly as a plea, as exclusively a form of critique, once we attend to the exclusions these analytics expose, the analytics themselves are no longer useful. This is even indicative in the "stories we tell" about women's studies when we teach feminist theory, presenting transnationalism and women of color feminism as transformative forms of *critique*—of white feminism, of notions of feminist "sisterhood"—that fundamentally questioned and remade the discipline. The analytics, then, are thought to be catalysts for the discipline, as productive insofar as they called for transformation. Because both analytics have been posited as correctives, both are imagined as exhaustible or finite, precisely because the mandate of a corrective is that the discipline adjust itself in relationship to what has been demanded by the analytic (here, again, the labor of intersectionality and transnationalism is to make a demand, and this demand is embodied by symbols—women of color—that are always already imagined as demanding).

Of course, this conception of these analytics is at odds with the analytics themselves, both of which call for ongoing feminist engagements with questions of power, dominance, and subordination. For Inderpal Grewal and Caren Kaplan, for example, transnationalism allows for a feminist practice that theorizes power—or what they term "scattered hegemonies"—in more complex ways, a strategy that could "articulate the relationship of gender to scattered hegemonies such as global economic structures, patriarchal nationalisms, 'authentic' forms of tradition, local structures of domination, and legal-juridical oppression on multiple levels."[59] Similarly for Crenshaw, intersectionality as an analytic spotlighted antidiscrimination law's continued inattention to black women, its failure to attend to the particular raced and gendered forms of violence black women endured, forms of invisibility that feminism and antiracism only replicated. Intersectionality unraveled conventional legal doctrine revealing the limitations of prevailing conceptions of discrimination and harm. Both analytics, then, continue to offer strategies for theorizing the state, power, and ongoing violence with an attention to inequity and harm.

Fatigue also emerges from the rhetoric that intersectionality and transnationalism have been linked to: difficulty. These analytics exhaust us because they are thought to be difficult and because they demand so much complexity. This grievance has been performed in both scholarly and popular venues. Heather Hillsburg, for example, argues, "It is impossible to account for all possible intersections, and, given time constraints and funding limitations, researchers cannot pose unending questions."[60] Underpinning these well-rehearsed refrains is the idea that intersectionality's (and transnationalism's) imagined plea to account for everything is an impossibility. Here, these analytics' status as something that disciplines feminism, as something complicated, is precisely what makes them exhausting, even as that complexity and difficulty is how their value has been articulated.

Thus, if both are imagined as exhaustible, they are also imagined as exhausting. Indeed, what interests me about the debates swirling around both terms, and particularly intersectionality, is the sense that everything that needs to be said already has, a sense that the analytic itself is tiring, repetitive, or already all too familiar. Tiffany Lethabo King, for example, describes how "the neoliberal corporate university produces intersectionality as a passé analytic and 'risky' space destined for relegation to the anachronistic time-space of the *post*."[61] Her ethnographic work on the production of intersectionality as "passé" reveals that "intersectionality indexes a space of risk and danger that one must get over or avoid entirely as it has no future or speculative value in the neoliberal university."[62] The idea of intersectionality as something "one must get over," as an analytic that must simply be left behind, reveals that intersectionality is imagined not only as finite in scope but as something that drains feminism of its current vitality. Ultimately, the promise invested in these analytics is always already tinged with failure, with incompletion. These analytics, then, enter the feminist imagination as tools that are designed to exhaust. As Jigna Desai describes in her engagement with how fatigue operates, "Clearly, 'race, class, and gender' has become a theoretical and methodological cliché in U.S.-based feminist studies. The mantra associated with a 'been there, done that' exasperation by many feminists does not address the ways in which contemporary feminist scholarship has barely begun to understand how an analytic based on multiple and simultaneous contextual differences might affect feminist theories."[63] It is this idea of a "'been there, done that' exasperation" which Desai captures that I argue is a racialized affective formation within women's studies, and an affect that binds intersectionality and transnationalism.

In capturing how both intersectionality and transnationalism have been posited as correctives, as analytics deployed by aggrieved subjects to demand that the discipline take account of them, I aspire to show how both have similar intellectual, institutional, and affective trajectories within US academic feminism *despite* the fact that they have so often been constructed as mutually exclusive, and even as competing (as I argued earlier, some of this has come from the fact that each analytic has been imagined to be animated by a particular key figure or symbol, and the bodies of these symbols have been treated as irreconcilable). Reading these analytics together, though, resists the symbolic work to which both black woman and South Asian woman have been put, insisting that the discipline contend with the host of racial politics that produce the cycle of promise/peril and that imagine and reimagine women of color's bodies as demanding disciplinarians. Moreover, this kind of reading practices a different kind of feminist "storytelling," to borrow Hemmings's term, one that resist the impulse to reduce either analytic to corrective, and that insists instead on seeing both as intellectually and politically transformative interventions *and* rich, vibrant sites of debate.

Intimacies, or Thinking Otherwise

This chapter has argued that women's studies has imagined intersectionality and transnationalism as mutually exclusive, largely ignoring how both have been similarly constructed as remedial regimes that are embodied and performed by particular racialized bodies. I conclude by asking how the similar construction of these analytics might provide fertile ground for black feminists to embrace the intimacies of these analytics, and even the intimacies of the figures that stand as the key symbols of both of these traditions. In other words, I ask what it might mean for black feminism to insist on telling other stories about intersectionality, stories that suture intersectionality to transnationalism. I ask: How might black feminists despecify intersectionality both to interrupt the incessant demand that black women perform and embody the analytic and to require women's studies to tell its histories otherwise, in ways that recognize and reckon with the similar construction of these analytics? What I am advocating is a conception of intersectionality expansive, broad, and deterritorialized enough to move with figures beyond "black woman." This is an intersectionality that surrenders its exclusive investment in black woman and emphasizes the analytic's capacity to speak to "women of color" broadly. Ultimately, surrendering the notion that intersectionality must be the terrain for speaking about black women, and that deployments of the term beyond black women are violent acts of misuse, would be an act of radical antiterritoriality, a refusal of the proprietary relationship that marks black feminist engagement with intersectionality. This is an intellectual move that eschews defensiveness and replaces it with a radical embrace of the political potentiality of intimacy.

My attempts to suture these analytics draws on other scholarly attempts to think through intersectionality and transnationalism together. Yet often these attempts have been fraught, approached with anxiety, insisting on a kind of fundamental respect for the differences between these traditions. At times, these cautionary notes have emphasized the urgency of not conflating "black woman" and "woman of color," and, at times, these cautions have sought to guard against the impulse to ignore the specific intellectual labor of black woman and woman of color and the particular genealogies (and political contexts) out of which intersectionality and transnationalism emerged. For example, Mendoza notes, "Postcolonial theory entails a unique theoretical and political program that should not be confused with other theoretical approaches. Important differences exist among black feminist, Chicana feminist, and postcolonial feminist theory and practice."[64] For Mendoza, the distinct intellectual and political questions that underpin the analytics require feminist treatment of them separately. Of course, this perspective emerges in part because of the myriad ways that the intellectual production of both black women and women of color has been effaced, conflated, or wholly ignored. An insistence on honoring the particular and specific traditions out of which intersectionality and transnationalism emerge recognizes the intellectual production of both black feminist and woman of color feminist scholars. Other scholars suggest that the two analytics might be placed in conversation to render one or the other more robust or more complex. Here, placing them in conversation serves to either strengthen or reveal the weaknesses of one analytic. For example, the Santa Cruz Feminist of Color Collective argues that "anticolonial feminist theory moves intersectionality beyond critiques of state based legal practice to 'glocalizing' dynamics, and so uses transnationalism to expand and reconfigure intersectionality."[65] In other words, transnationalism effectively reimagines intersectionality and expands its imagined "critiques of state based legal practice." Similarly, Mendoza suggests that intersectionality is "amenable to a liberal politics of inclusion" which necessarily puts it against decolonial politics which refuses notions of inclusion. In these cases, the impulse to think about these analytics together is imagined to provide a crucial repair, to assist one of the analytics in moving beyond a weakness.

Other attempts to think through these analytics together have often done so around the framework of *coalition*, considering how each analytic—and arguably both—can circumvent the imagined problems of identitarianism by acting as a coalition that unites heterogeneous subjects. Part of this impulse toward thinking coalitionally is to resuscitate analytics often linked with identity politics from relegation to feminist history. If identity is feminism's past tense, coalition remains a celebrated portion of the field's present tense. For example, Carastathis reminds readers that "identity remains a useful basis for political organizing, as long as identity categories are conceptualized as coalitions," as "internally heterogeneous, complex unities constituted by their internal differences and dissonances and by internal as well as external relations of power."[66] In other work, she notes, "If we grapple with intersectionality as a provisional concept that enables us to live our struggle identities [sic] in a radically different way, eschewing the categorical, representational and political violence in and through which they have been forged to fragment, marginalize, and silence some subjects while exalting and empowering others, can we envision, on the horizon, an intersectional politics of coalition which intimates the decolonial 'elsewheres' that all of us—on all sides of colonial divides—urgently need to imagine?"[67] Here, intersectionality is freed from the imagined pitfalls of identity politics through unleashing its investment in fluidity; it is a tool that brings together marginal subjects or, to borrow from Cathy Cohen, that can unify "punks, bulldaggers, and welfare queens."[68] Similarly, "coalition" has long been a critical keyword for transnational feminists who have advocated for laboring in coalition and solidarity as a way of circumventing the pitfalls and elisions of sisterhood. The logic of "coalition" is a way of describing "the cross-cultural commonality of struggles" and the politics of what Chandra Talpade Mohanty identifies simply as "survival" rather than the always-problematic "shared oppression."[69] The guiding principle of transnational feminism, then, became the possibilities of "women of different communities and identities build[ing] coalitions and solidarities across borders."[70] Coalition has become envisioned as a strategy that can allow intersectionality and transnationalism to redeem themselves from their association with identity politics, which continues to be coded as passé and problematic.

I do not advocate reading these analytics together because of the possibility of coalition-building as a redemptive route out of identity politics. Instead, I am invested in the possibilities of reading these analytics together to unleash *intimacies* among women of color, and *intimacies* between analytics that have been wedged apart. In shifting from *coalition* to *intimacy*, I argue that the ongoing battle over identity politics in the field—one that requires us again and again to insist on identity's productivity, or on intersectionality's capacity to move apart from identity—is another manifestation of the intersectionality wars. I am invested in what it means to blur the boundaries of who these analytics "belong" to, who they can—or should—describe. I use the term "intimacy" precisely because of the ways it suggests the permeability between concepts and their imagined "origins," and between bodies (a concept I will return to in the next chapter when I take up vulnerability), including the possibility of being done and undone through relationality. I am inspired by Sylvanna Falcón's conception of transnational feminism as "an anti-subordination logic that is mutually constructive or overlapping with intersectionality."[71] While Falcón's analysis of transnational feminism is deeply attentive to the particular intellectual genealogies of transnationalism, and the debates and historical context in which transnationalism emerged, it is committed to construing the analytic broadly to be an anti-subordination tool, much like intersectionality, suggesting that it is "women of color," broadly speaking, who are the subjects of both terms. As Falcón reminds us, thinking about intersectionality and transnationalism side by side, as analytics that touch, upends the logic of a "setting that wants us to avoid working collaboratively or in solidarity."[72] Considering *both* analytics as "anti-subordination logics" that stage their political work in distinctive *and* overlapping ways reveals the fundamental intimacy between the terms' political aspirations, and between the gendered and raced bodies who are often re-presented as the subjects and embodiments of these analytics. In other words, transnationalism can be mobilized to theorize the global *and* local migrations of gendered and sexualized discourses of antiblackness, and intersectionality can be mobilized to theorize the global *and* local articulations of interlocking structures of domination that conscript bodies to the metaphorical basement Crenshaw describes. Intersectionality can also attend to the variety of ways—globally—that the state's antidiscrimination apparatus becomes a critical tool in entrenching and reproducing violent harm against marginalized bodies.

In thinking of intersectionality and transnationalism's intimacies, I think of June Jordan's "Report from the Bahamas," a critical memoir that details her trip to the Bahamas, a trip she makes with her "consciousness of race and class and gender identity." Jordan's "consciousness," though, is always shaped by her sense of her shifting and complicated position as an American traveler, a black woman traveler, a black woman traveler seeking solace in the Sheraton British Colonial even as "a Black woman seeking refuge in a multinational corporation may seem like a contradiction to some, but there you are."[73]

Jordan's piece is an interrogation of how categories like race, gender, class, and sexuality fail to provide a ground for commonality, even as she imagines they will. She writes, "Yes; race and class and gender remain as real as the weather. But what they must mean about the contact between two individuals is less obvious and, like the weather, not predictable. . . . I am saying the ultimate connection cannot be the enemy. The ultimate connection must be the need that we find between us."[74] Jordan's "report" tracks both the persistence of structures of domination and their shifting meanings across national borders, their salience for producing conditions of subordination, and their insufficiency for producing intimacies and connections. It is an account that sits at the intersections of transnationalism and intersectionality, reflecting both on the interlocking nature of structures of domination *and* on their shifting meanings across national borders. It asks what, for example, black womanhood means when we inhabit it in the context of US global supremacy. For me, Jordan's account is an example of the analytical, theoretical, and political possibilities of putting intersectionality and transnationalism side by side, mobilizing both analytics to think in supple ways about structures of domination and their deeply contingent meanings. Indeed, in Jordan's hands, a consideration of interlocking structures of domination enables robust considerations of the distinct positions of various bodies, including but not exclusively black women's bodies.

A rigorous consideration of the intimacy between these analytics also aspires to reanimate alternate genealogies of intersectionality, linking intersectionality's advent to multiple women of color feminist scholar-activists including Kimberlé Crenshaw, Audre Lorde, the Combahee River Collective, Gloria Anzaldúa, Cherríe Moraga, Mari Matsuda, Leslie Marmon Silko, and Yuri Kochiyama, rather than claiming that one of these scholar-activists produced, authored, or invented the term's core ideas and commitments. My impulse toward emphasizing multiple genealogies does not seek to efface the very specific black feminist juridical tradition that Crenshaw was invested in when she coined the term "intersectionality," or to signify that she gave a name to a practice that scholars were involved in for decades. Rather, I ask what it might mean to read different intersectional articulations simultaneously, to consider Crenshaw's legal intervention alongside Anzaldúa's work on *mestizaje*, to consider Collins's conception of the "matrix of domination" alongside Matsuda's work on accent discrimination. In short, I advocate for embracing the promise that underscored volumes like *This Bridge Called My Back*—the promise of considering "third world women" or "women of color" as an analytic not to efface variety and heterogeneity but to engender generative feminist connections that consider questions of both place and race as fundamentally made through each other, and that center multiple and crosscutting projects of domination, including race, gender, sexuality, class, accent, and ability.

While I am inspired by the women of color intimacies that animated *Bridge*, intimacies that were both sites of collaboration and, at times, productive frictions, I am also inspired by Shireen Roshanravan's critical methodology of the "plurilogue," which "pursues dissimilarities to clarify the conceptual interventions made within Women of Color theorizing and the relationship among the different patterns of oppression that each intervention exposes."[75] Roshanravan interrupts the idea of "woman of color" as a unified space, instead calling attention to the variety of strategies for "resisting racialized, heteropatriarchal oppressions of global capitalism and colonialism" that various women of color feminists have pursued. Thinking about intersectionality and transnationalism together pursues what Roshanravan calls for, disrupting women of color feminism as a monologue, and attending to the "polyphonic" ways women of color feminism has theorized, and debated, our survival, needs, and political desires. Roshanravan underscores that an attention to the intimacy between women of color need not obscure or elide the debates that have long circulated *within* women of color, including debates about the meanings of the analytics intersectionality and transnationalism. Indeed, a celebration of the intimacy among women of color, a politics of surrender that allows intersectionality and transnationalism the breathing room to describe and attach to a variety of kinds of bodies opens up space for new debates about the analytic's utility far beyond questioning who owns intersectionality.

THIS CHAPTER HAS SOUGHT to treat surrender as what Gayle Wald terms a practice of "un-forgetting," a way of considering how intersectionality's histories, as retold in women's studies, have hinged on a forgetting of transnationalism. This institutionalized forgetting obscures the racial politics that again and again constructs these analytics as both similar and mutually exclusive precisely because each is imagined to be embodied by a particular and distinctive woman of color.[76] I argue for a black feminist narrative that emphatically places pressure on women's studies' dominant story, revealing how transnationalism and intersectionality have been treated as in competition for scarce resources—jobs, time, funding—allocated to women of color's intellectual contributions. In particular, I suggest that black feminists can perform a radical surrender, upending their long-standing investment in black woman as intersectionality's key sign. In its place, I argue for a black feminist theoretical and affective stance that thinks expansively about who intersectionality can describe and analyze, and generously about the overlaps between black woman and woman of color. Indeed, I suggest that black feminist theorists treat intersectionality, like transnationalism, as an antisubordination project even as it is one with a specific genealogy. This practice of surrender necessarily upends the institutional women's studies project that presumes that intersectionality is performed and embodied by black women who stage their grievances to repair the field (or, perhaps, to exhaust the field). Surrender also opens up—theoretically, politically, creatively, and affectively—new intimacies between bodies of thought, and material bodies, that are so often kept separate in women's studies, namely, between black woman and woman of color. Ultimately, surrender locates political promise in a revitalized intimacy and even promiscuity among the intellectual and political work of black woman and woman of color, of intersectionality and transnationalism. It is this radical intimacy, a letting go of what we think intersectionality must do, that will compel women's studies to tell a different story about what black feminist theory can do.

FOUR. love in the time of death

Black feminism is preoccupied with death. In many ways, this is unsurprising. We live in a moment where afropessimism has made black death the centerpiece of US black studies, where social movements like Black Lives Matter and Say Her Name have rendered visible the continued invisibility of black deaths, and where black feminists have continued to name mourning as "the condition of black life."[1] In the midst of an unrelenting list of black deaths—Trayvon Martin, Jordan Davis, Tamir Rice, Philando Castile, Renisha McBride—black feminist theorists, including Christina Sharpe, Saidiya Hartman, and Simone Brown, have emphatically underscored that black death has long been the state's project. This iteration of black feminist theory views the state as deeply antiblack, as a project that relies on the continued violent subordination of black flesh, and particularly the continued invisibility of violence inflicted on black women. In this sense, black feminist scholarship has been at the vanguard of now widely circulating critiques of "governance feminism" and "carceral feminism" and the host of ways that feminism has problematically found itself "at home with the law."[2] In its contemporary form, black feminist theory often performs its imaginative "freedom dreaming" and world-making work apart from, and even against, law precisely because law is imagined to be the paradigmatic space of antiblack violence.[3]

This attention to black death is not only an investment in exposing spectacular and quotidian antiblack violence that produces and reinforces the noncitizen (and arguably, at least for some scholars, the nonhuman) status of black bodies; it is also a way of talking about intellectual production. It has become commonplace for black feminists to proclaim the death of black feminism itself, to announce that the field's future is in peril because its visionary work has been stymied. Brittney Cooper, for example, writes: "It is not at all clear to me that Black feminism has a future. Despite the 'citational ubiquity' of intersectionality in fields and disciplines across the humanities and social sciences and despite the proliferation of vibrant cultures of Black feminisms on the interwebs, academic Black feminisms still confront a 'culture of justification,' in which one is always asked to prove that the study of Black women's lives, histories, literature, cultural production, and theory is sufficiently academic, and sufficiently 'rigorous' to merit academic resources."[4] In Cooper's analysis, black feminism is without "a future" because of the neoliberal university's investment in ideas of theory-making that police black feminist intellectual production out of the conception of theory.[5] It is precisely because black feminism—and black feminists—face a "culture of justification" that the field itself is in jeopardy.

If the neoliberal university's selective incorporation of difference endangers black feminism, some of the field's precarity comes from black feminist theory itself. Indeed, Cooper notes that we have "fallen into a state of deep inertia around critical political and philosophical questions."[6] Black feminists have neglected to develop "our conceptions of freedom and justice" and have "failed to fully lay out our own accounts of race and gender, of blackness and womanhood."[7] This notion of the field's theoretical impoverishment has proliferated in contemporary black feminist work. Joan Morgan asserts that the field has become "overly reliant on . . . [its] most trenchant theories—specifically Kimberlé Crenshaw's 'intersectionality,' Patricia Collins' 'controlling images,' Audre Lorde's deployment of the erotic, Higginbotham's 'respectability politics,' Hine's 'cultural dissemblance.' Bequeathing them the sanctity of dogma and rendering them impervious to the changes of time, we've often failed to re-interrogate these venerated interventions with the temporal, cultural specificity reflected in contemporary US black women's ethnic heterogeneity, queerness, and the advent of digital technologies and social media."[8] For Morgan, it is the field's investment in making theory into "dogma," into rendering certain concepts transhistorical truths, that has brought the field to the brink of its own demise.

Intersectionality plays a central role in black feminists' projection of the field's imminent death. As Morgan suggests, intersectionality has become an analytic on which black feminists are "overly reliant," something that has become "dogma" rather than productive analytic. Other scholars assert that the field is dying because of what has happened to intersectionality, namely, its appropriation, institutionalization, and misuse. In other words, intersectionality has been depoliticized and rendered "ornamental" in ways that effectively steal black feminism's creative energies.[9] Collins and Bilge argue that "intersectionality stands at the crossroads. In order to remain a vibrant, growing endeavor, intersectionality must cast a self-reflexive eye on its own truths and practices."[10] This diagnosis suggests that intersectionality is on the brink of losing its "vibrancy," that this is a critical moment that will determine the fate of the analytic. Indeed, what Robyn Wiegman has termed the "apocalyptic" mode has come to mark black feminist thought, with intersectionality holding a privileged place in black feminist musings about the death of the field.[11] This chapter takes this near-death diagnosis as a point of departure; to name black feminism as dead or dying is to reveal the necessity of resuscitating the field's key analytics, and the necessity of black feminist rescue efforts geared toward reviving the analytic.

Rather than ruminate on death and its attendant affects of grief and loss—whether the relentless killing labor of the state or the imagined demise of the field and its key analytics—this chapter proposes love as a way forward, as another way of feeling black feminism in the context of the US academy. I turn toward love with both excitement and trepidation. It has become a kind of contemporary black feminist aesthetic to champion love's radical potentiality, and so I seek to engage love's potential with a kind of specificity that I find often lacking from the turn toward love as utopian site of black feminist possibility. My turn to love is also mindful of how the beginning portion of this book tracked the proprietary impulse that can undergird care. In thinking about loving engagement with intersectionality as a way of feeling black feminism differently, my intention is not to set care and love against each other or to suggest that love inherently escapes mobilizations that are violent, proprietary, or territorial. Both love and care can clearly be called upon to perform a variety of forms of problematic labor, including holding on. If the second chapter sought to trace how care can be enlisted to engage in pernicious territorial labor, here I aspire to think about love's radical potentiality alongside an archive that contemporary black feminist theorists have largely disavowed: law. I ask, what if the disavowed deathly archive of law is reimagined as a home for black feminism's loving practice? How might we reimagine black feminist feelings toward intersectionality by actively reengaging its largely forgotten connections with law, and its fundamental commitment to remaking law in unfamiliar and productive ways? How might remembering intersectionality's juridical work produce space for new black feminist feelings, including an embrace of the ethic of radical vulnerability that intersectionality has demanded law champion?

In this chapter, I think about love in two ways. First, I argue that black feminism's long practice of love-politics centers on two key ideas: vulnerability and witnessing. I carefully trace how black feminist theorists have elaborated these twin concepts and their crucial linkages to love. Second, I argue that we can imagine intersectionality's juridical work as part of—rather than separate from—black feminism's longer tradition of love-politics, as a radical attempt to reorient law around vulnerability and witnessing, effectively demanding that law exceed the limits of what it imagines as possible (or even desirable). While the previous chapter advocated surrender as a critical practice of letting go, this chapter imagines letting go otherwise. I invite a black feminist letting go of presumptions about the state, about law as *the* location of black death, and about radical politics as necessarily requiring an antistate vision. I also encourage a black feminist letting go of the notion that certain practices of intersectionality—namely legal ones—should be avoided, downplayed, or ignored. This form of letting go actually enables different and potentially surprising kinds of attachments to intersectionality, particularly the analytic's juridical life. Treating intersectionality as an analytic that mandates a different way of engaging the state offers black feminism—and black feminists—the chance to cultivate new affective engagements with the state and the chance to ask (or even demand) that the state feel and act differently toward black women.

My interest in thinking about intersectionality alongside love is motivated, at least in part, by Wiegman's claim that "intersectionality is a critical practice motivated by love."[12] For Wiegman, the attachments that undergird feminist engagement with intersectionality are evidence of a feminist affection for the term and its politics. Though I do not view feminist engagements with intersectionality as motivated by love—indeed, much of my inquiry in this book aspires to reveal the complex affects that underpin feminist engagement with intersectionality—I endeavor to explore what it might mean for black feminists to treat intersectional theoretical work *as* loving practice, and to consider intersectionality's loving work as staged in and through law. My turn to love is also inspired by Tiffany Lethabo King's critical call for "loving" engagement with intersectionality. King writes, "Seeing intersectionality differently or lovingly could begin with a focus on it as a flexible mode of critique that also runs along anti-identitarian and subjectless axes. In other words, how might one think about intersectionality functioning as a method/mode/way of conceptualizing movement, time, space, and effects of power? As a mode of critique, how does it, in fact, destabilize the individual and the subject?"[13] For King, a "long and loving look at intersectionality" reveals that the term "responds to the precarious and violent ecology of neoliberal institutions like the university" and shows that intersectionality is a deeply "flexible" analytic that can perform a variety of forms of theoretical work.[14] Finally, various scholars (including me) have written about black feminism's long engagement with love as a mode of self-transformation *and* political transformation and have cast black feminism's rich love-politics tradition as an alternative to intersectionality's imagined identity politics. In my earlier work, I situated intersectionality's presumed identity politics and black feminist love-politics as wholly separate. In this chapter, I return to the questions I posed in previous work but answer them differently (or anew), suggesting that we need not consider love-politics and intersectionality as in opposition, that intersectionality is itself a black feminist articulation of love, and that law can be a(nother) site of black feminism's love-politics. Ultimately, against the grain of the moment, I suggest that the juridical might be precisely where black feminists need to root our loving practice, and a site where we can unleash new ways of feeling black feminist.

Loving Feminism

Black feminism is distinctive in its commitment to love as a political practice. From Alice Walker's definition of womanism that places self-love at the center of black feminist subjectivity to the Combahee River Collective's statement that its political work emerged from "a healthy love for ourselves, our sisters, and our community," black feminists have long emphasized the importance of love as a form of collectivity, a way of feeling, and a practice of ordering the self.[15] In other words, love operates as a principle of vulnerability and accountability, of solidarity and transformation, that has organized and undergirded black feminist practice. In my earlier work, I developed the idea of *love-politics* to describe black feminism as "a tradition marked by transforming love from the personal . . . into a theory of justice. . . . I analyze 'second-wave' black feminism's pleas for love as a significant call for ordering the self *and* transcending the self, a strategy for remaking the self *and* for moving beyond the limitations of selfhood."[16] In this section of the chapter, I build on that earlier work and inflect it differently, emphasizing the notion of black feminist love-politics as undergirded by a dual commitment to *mutual vulnerability* and *witnessing*.

Mutual vulnerability is marked by a commitment to unleashing the "sacred possibilities" between us, to emphasizing that "nobody means more to me than you."[17] Indeed, this perspective recognizes that my survival and thriving depend on yours. If our survivals are mutually dependent, we are, then, mutually vulnerable, as our thriving requires our coexistence. To act in love, *with* love, is to recognize this mutual vulnerability as something that must be not eschewed but rather embraced, as a necessary positionality to the project of social justice. Put differently, a commitment to mutual vulnerability constitutes a commitment to be intimately bound to the other (or to others), to refuse boundaries between self and other. Witnessing describes black feminist theory's investment in a rich and political counterhistory, one that draws on memory—personal, collective, or embodied—to demand an ethical reckoning with past and present.

Vulnerability and love are often imaginatively tethered, though in the prevailing account, the vulnerability that emerges from love is described in either the romantic or the familial domain. In this commonly rehearsed narrative, love renders us uniquely open and capable of being wounded, because the object of our affection has the capacity to wound us, or to disappoint us. That love brings about a potentially radical openness—even an openness to pain—is precisely what makes it an affect that critical theorists have invested in. Indeed, it is our willingness to be open to myriad forms of being known *and* potential alienation that makes love a site of tremendous self-transformation, a place that is, in Lauren Berlant's words, "one of the few places where people actually admit they want to become different."[18] In Berlant's account, love is potentially transformative because of the "non-sovereignty" that its particular relationality makes possible. Christine Straehle echoes this view of the radical possibility of love, noting that "many would agree that we are vulnerable in parental, romantic, and filial love. We might say that in such relationships, we are emotionally and psychologically vulnerable. Yet we not only accept this vulnerability because of the emotional and psychological gains that also come from living relationships but also because this kind of vulnerability helps us constitute ourselves as agents in the world."[19] Love, she argues, "brings about emotional and psychological vulnerability. . . . We have to trust those whom we love to recognize us as those we propose to be. To be sure, if such recognition by the beloved is not forthcoming, then vulnerability in love may turn into self-negating vulnerability and become morally problematic. In the first instance, however, love allows us to conceive of ourselves as a specific person who adopts love as a principle of her will."[20] For Straehle, love's promise is the distinct vulnerability it makes possible.

I am drawn to the vision of love as a space of vulnerability, nonsovereignty, and radical relationality. Yet my interest in vulnerability is not simply that it is a space in which we allow the potential to be wounded. Drawing on Judith Butler's work, I argue that "vulnerability is [not] reducible to its injurability."[21] Instead, I embrace her broad view of vulnerability as the experience of "coming up against" the bodies of others, as a practice of intimate proximity to others.[22] In other words, my vision of black feminist politics is not that love's vulnerability is merely a way of insisting that we are all susceptible to injury; instead vulnerability requires us to embrace the fact that we can be—and often are—"undone" by each other. As Butler notes, being "undone" can happen "in the face of the other, by the touch, by the scent, by the feel, by the prospect of the touch, by the memory of the feel."[23] It can take the form of grief and mourning, desire and ecstasy, solidarity and empathy, and mutual regard. In other words, to be undone is not synonymous with to be wounded, though it can take that form. The realization of our capacity to be "undone," of the way others can "undo" us, and the decision to embrace rather than retreat from the possibility of our potential undoing, is the logic of black feminist love-politics.

Moreover, while I am drawn to Straehle's emphasis on the transformative capacity of love, and the myriad ways that love produces multiple forms of vulnerability, I upend an emphasis on "parental, romantic, and filial love" as the locations of love's radical potential. Instead, I emphasize how black feminists have advocated expansive conceptions of relationality, encouraging us to view ourselves as deeply embedded in the world, and thus as deeply connected to others, effectively exploding the hold romantic and familial have had on conceptions of intimacy, vulnerability, and relatedness. Black feminist conceptions of love as a unifying political principle encourage us to ask about our deep responsibilities to each other, and our enduring connections to each other, by virtue of our collective inhabitation of the social world. This view, of course, entails risk. It is risky to view one's self as bound up with others and to fully accept the responsibility and potential peril that are entailed in embracing and practicing a worldview of linked fate. But this is the visionary call of black feminist love-politics—a radical embrace of connectedness.

June Jordan's "Poem about My Rights," for example, illuminates this conception of love as a collective project of vulnerability. It begins as a rumination on experiences of disenfranchisement. Jordan describes the need to

> take a walk and clear
> my head . . . about why I can't
> go out without changing my clothes my shoes
> my body posture my gender identity my age.[24]

What does it *feel* like, Jordan asks, to experience disenfranchisement and vulnerability? Indeed, Jordan's poem suggests the myriad ways that forms of oppression are layered on each other; body, posture, gender identity, and age bleed into each other and become indistinguishable, each one lending meaning to the others. Jordan writes,

> I can't do what I want
> to do with my own body because I am the wrong
> sex the wrong age the wrong skin.

But as the poem unfolds, it becomes not a rumination on individual experiences of marginalization, but an analysis of collective subordination. Jordan continues,

> We are the wrong people of
> the wrong skin on the wrong continent . . .
> I am the history of rape
> I am the history of the rejection of who I am
> I am the history of the terrorized incarceration of myself
> I am the history of battery assault and limitless
> armies against whatever I want do with my mind
> and my body and my soul.[25]

It is this movement between "I" and "we" that marks the kinds of vulnerability that are at the heart of black feminist love-practice, an insistence that the recognition that "I can't do what I want" depends on an analysis of how "we are the wrong people of the wrong skin on the wrong continent." For Jordan, an account of individual marginalization hinges on a recognition of collective marginalization and depends on an analysis of how "we" become constructed and imagined as "the wrong people." It is this recognition of how "I" and "we" are mutually constituted that lends a particular force to the final lines of Jordan's poem:

> but I can tell you that from now on my resistance
> my simple and daily and nightly self-determination
> may very well cost you your life.

For Jordan, the possibility of "my resistance," one born of "determination," emerges from the realization of collectivity and mutual regard. Indeed, the poem ends by reminding the reader that the "I" and the collective "we" are opposed to an imagined hegemonic and oppressive "you." It is a vision of collectivity and mutuality that permits Jordan to imagine a forceful "resistance" and "self-determination."

If vulnerability is a recognition that we are undone by each other, and an invitation to embrace rather than retreat from that fact, it is also a testament to how we are witnesses to moments when we are subjected to violence, particularly by social structures that have been constructed to discipline and surveil. Black feminism's long-standing investment in both the experiential as a rich episteme and the particular standpoint of black women reveals that the tradition has long treated black women as subjects who witness what is meant to be kept invisible, unnamed, unseen. In other words, black feminism has positioned and imagined black women as "outsiders-within" who have a particular vantage point on how structures of domination operate to marginalize, constrain, and injure certain bodies.[26] Black women are, then, witnesses who can see and even name forms of violence that other subjects cannot see, or simply refuse to see. This willingness to name, to make visible, to again and again describe and analyze structures of domination is a laborious act for black women, one that can be emotionally and politically taxing. Yet this act of witnessing, for self and for others, for naming what others seek to ignore or normalize, is, black feminists assert, a practice of love, of tenderness, and of political world-making. The black feminist archive of what is witnessed often takes on forms that challenge or upend the neutral and detached demands of academic writing, including forms like memoir, narrative, autobiography, and "alchemical" writing that make visible (and palpable) black women's embodied experiences (often while carving out space for the privacy and sanctity of black women's interiority).[27] Witnessing is often performed through strategic self-disclosures that enable black women to bear witness to their own (and each other's) "complex personhood," to experiences of violence, and to black women's rich interiority.[28]

Witnessing, then, is a practice of calculated self-disclosure that puts political pressure on the host of ways that violence inflicted on black women's bodies is rendered normative or invisible. For example, legal scholar Patricia Williams recounts her experience shopping at Benetton—a store famous for its "united colors" multiculturalism campaign—two weeks before Christmas. As Williams recounts, buzzers were "big" at the entrances to stores in New York City then, a technology that allowed storekeepers to quickly assess the perceived dangerousness of a shopper and to grant or refuse entry accordingly. When the white shopkeeper refused to grant Williams entry, despite the fact that the store was open—"there were several white people in the store who appeared to be shopping for things for their mothers"—Williams channeled her "admittedly diffuse" and "symmetrical" rage to ask others to bear witness to the racial profiling she experienced. In her various retellings of her experience—in a sign she hung outside of Benetton, in a law review essay, in a speech—Williams encounters the challenges of being a black woman witness, the presumption of her dishonesty (shouldn't she consider the perspective of the white shopkeeper who refused her entry, some urged?), the presumption that her account failed to be sufficiently neutral or objective. The essay, an engagement with the experience of racial profiling and exclusion, is also an investigation of what it means when black women's experiences are treated as "unverifiable," as outside the "genre of legal writing," as lacking substantial "evidence." And, Williams necessarily asks, what would it take for her experience of violence and exclusion to be verifiable? Is it ever possible for a black woman to own her account of what happened to her, in a world that is structured by the presumption of her dishonesty and unreliability? What would it mean for Williams to be regarded as the expert on her own experience, as a reliable narrator recounting what unfolded? Ultimately, Williams's memoir is a commentary (or critique) of the "genre of legal writing" that devalues the "evidence of experience," which establishes categories like verifiability that foreclose naming experiences like Williams's as racial profiling and violent exclusion.[29] Williams, then, proffers her experience as a witness, one who challenges the very legal conception of witnessing and its fetishization of certain forms of evidence and certain bodies as sites of reliable evidence. Her form of witnessing is a radical counterarchive that puts analytical and political pressure on the categories and ideologies that law fetishizes.

My conception of witnessing is also resonant with Sharpe's notion of "wake work," an insistence that black subjects live *in the midst of* ordinary daily violence, but that we live nonetheless. Here, Sharpe builds on the long black feminist engagement with survival as a radical form of politics, a tradition that emphasizes black creativity, black thriving, and black life in the midst of overwhelming violence. For Sharpe, "wake work" refers to how black subjects "resist, rupture, and disrupt that immanence and imminence [death] aesthetically and materially."[30] It is an analytic, a critical practice, a mode of living, and a form of witnessing that names the ecology of relentless antiblack violence and the acts of black world-making that unfold nonetheless. It is, then, a form of witnessing that attends to black life in "the wake."

This section has endeavored to reanimate some of my earlier work on love-politics by centering vulnerability and witnessing as crucial to black feminism's long labor of investing in love as a political practice. In so doing, I aspire to theorize love's meanings more robustly than has been done in black feminist scholarship, which simply claims love as a terrain of hope, potentiality, or promise. Instead, I aim to think through the underpinnings of love, carefully tracing the analytics that undergird black feminism's investment in loving practices as political work. In the next section, I consider how, surprisingly, intersectionality's juridical iterations make visible and possible black feminism's long-standing investment in these dual ethics.

Returning to the State

This book began with substantial engagement with intersectionality's origin stories, examining how the question of where the analytic came from, who coined it, and who deserves "credit" for its rise and circulation have come to predominate in black feminist scholarship. Curiously, though, none of these widely circulating origin stories contend with intersectionality's connections to the juridical, or think deeply about intersectionality as a legal project. Though this book eschews simple origin stories that presume that intersectionality has a singular history, in this section, I advocate for remembering intersectionality's connections to critical race theory, and thus its intimate relationship with remaking law. I invest in this project because intersectionality has been swept into a larger black feminist conversation that presumes the violence of the juridical, ignoring *both* intersectionality's loving investment in the juridical and the juridical as a potential site of loving practice. Put differently, in this section, I emphasize intersectionality's location in critical race theory, in Left legal projects, to move beyond the now knee-jerk Left (and black feminist) sense that radical and transgressive projects are necessarily antistate. In place of this now familiar political terrain, I seek to ask different questions: Is it simply collusion or "cruel optimism" for black feminists to seek engagement with the state?[31] Can we imagine black feminist engagements with the state as taking forms other than seeking redress and demanding visibility? Are there ways to imagine black feminist legal engagement that circumvent the uncomfortable and problematic position of being "at home with the law"? How can black feminists reimagine law as a site for staging productive intimacies and enacting radical vulnerabilities?

In its juridical iteration, intersectionality emerged in a moment where critical race theorists offered analytical tools to upend prevailing fictions of law's objectivity, to reveal the quotidian nature of racism and sexism, and to argue for fundamental transformations in legal pedagogy. Critical race theory, then, was born of a sustained attention to law's failures, even as it contained—at times—certain kinds of faith in law's potentiality and promise. Critical race scholars were a post–*Brown v. Board of Education* generation who witnessed the end of the Warren court's promises of integration and inclusion. They saw affirmative action rolled back, transformed from a substantive remedy for past and ongoing discrimination to a promise of "diversity" to benefit white students who would be changed into global citizens ready for corporate employment thanks to their "exposure" to so-called racial difference.[32] They witnessed the ratcheting up of standards for proving employment discrimination from racially disparate effects to discriminatory intent, effectively making it harder for minoritarian plaintiffs to prevail in discrimination suits. They emphatically asked, then, whether the goal of antiracist legal scholars *should* be inclusion in white institutions or whether it should be, for example, the creation of robustly funded and supported black institutions. They interrogated whether the Warren court's landmark decision in *Brown* would have better served its black plaintiffs if it equally funded black schools, rather than championing desegregation and then mandating integration at "all deliberate speed." They debated whether affirmative action should be supported if the only logic to support it is "diversity," where students of color provide a pedagogical value for white students. Critical race theory, then, was never an embrace of an ethic of inclusion, or even a form of advocacy for new forms of redress. Instead, it was undergirded by an investment in revealing that racial progress was the result of "interest convergence" rather than a genuine investment in antisubordination, and by a fundamental belief that law would look and *feel* different if it "looked to the bottom."[33]

While critical race theorists offered critical interrogations of law's imagined progress, treating it as evidence of US self-interest rather than a genuine investment in racial redress, they also routinely offered ways of imagining law otherwise, refashioning antidiscrimination law, conceptions of evidence, property, and contract. They imagined a form of law that eschewed color blindness and argued that any legal regime that sought to contend with American racial violence had to be deeply color-conscious to exact meaningful remedies. They advanced new methods — narrative, parable, allegory, speculative fiction, storytelling — in an effort to jam the fictions of objectivity and neutrality and to expose that law is itself a racial project, never removed from the racial regimes it purports to disrupt. In other words, they sought to use their locations in the legal academy and in the legal profession to radically remake law, to push the boundaries of how legal doctrine could be written, imagined, and enacted. They aspired to make law into something unrecognizable and unimaginable, to push at its very parameters in the pursuit of a "jurisprudence of generosity."[34]

My entry point for thinking through law as a site of black feminist love-politics is through the work of Patricia J. Williams. Her book *The Alchemy of Race and Rights* is complex in its form and its argument — it is memoir, "diary," legal treatise, and critical theory at once. Williams presents herself as professor, consumer, daughter, granddaughter, train rider, and "crazy" black woman exhausted from the ordinary and spectacular raced and gendered brutalities of American life and the project of teaching law at a historically white law school. The project, then, is a rumination on the felt life of racial and gendered violence, and a critical analysis of the myriad spaces where this violence unfolds, from the media onslaught against Tawana Brawley to the experiences of being a black female faculty member at a law school.

Williams's inquiry, though, is not simply about documenting the ubiquity of racial and gendered violence but also about engaging and describing the lived experience of racialized and gendered vulnerability, what she terms "spirit murder." For Williams, "spirit murder" is the psychic and spiritual wounding that unfolds as a result of racial violence. "Spirit murder" describes the wounds left on the flesh, psyche, and even soul of those who experience violence *and* the wounds, often invisible, that haunt perpetrators of violence, including a willingness to accept, and to render *unseen*, those who are dispossessed. Williams's task, then, is to imagine what law could look and feel like if it accounted for "spirit murder," a form of violence that she argues includes "cultural obliteration, prostitution, abandonment of the elderly and the homeless, and genocide. . . . What I call spirit murder—disregard for others whose lives qualitatively depend on our regard—is that it produces a system of formalized distortions of thought."[35] Williams argues that "we need to elevate spirit murder to the conceptual—if not punitive—level of a capital moral offense. . . . We need to eradicate its numbing pathology before it wipes out what precious little humanity we have left."[36] Williams's conception of "spirit murder" imagines law's capacity to remedy forms of violence against the psyche and soul, a terrain that has been unimaginable to law precisely because of its commitment to remedying only visible and legible harms, and law's ability to be mobilized "conceptually"—but not punitively—to respond to violence. In other words, the endeavor of the text is to imagine a legal project capacious and creative enough to attend to what it has always ignored: the violence inflicted on the psyche. Williams effectively invites us to imagine how we might feel differently toward each other, and toward law itself, if we had *legal* obligations toward mutual regard, if we knew that law took seriously spirit murder.

If Williams seeks to use law to exceed what it aspires to do, to respond to the "cultural cancer" of spirit murder, her book also contains a resounding, and even surprising, redemption of rights as a key strategy for reforming law. An embrace of rights might sound like a deeply conventional strategy, mobilizing law to do what it has long claimed to do on behalf of racialized and gendered minorities: confer rights. Despite her lengthy engagement with state violence, her exacting critique of how law permits rather than redresses spirit murder, Williams ends not with an abandonment of the state but with a deep affection for what rights could accomplish. She writes:

> The task is to expand private property rights into a conception of civil rights, into the right to expect civility from others. . . . Instead, society must *give* them [rights] away. Unlock them from reification by giving them to slaves. Give them to trees. Give them to cows. Give them to history. Give them to rivers and rocks. Give to all of society's objects and untouchables the rights of privacy, integrity and self-assertion; give them distance and respect. Flood them with the animating spirit that rights mythology fires in this country's most oppressed psyches,

and wash away the shroud of inanimate-object-status, so that we may say not that we own gold but that a luminous golden spirit owns us.[37]

If critical legal studies called for the abandonment of investment in rights, treating rights as relatively unsuccessful in securing social change and as promoting problematic conceptions of individualism, Williams makes a plea for a dramatic expansion of rights and a surprising reconceptualization of the labor of rights. Rights, she argues, should not be the purview of those who can explicitly and legibly name harm. Cows, history, and rocks should have rights, including rights to "privacy, integrity and self-assertion." Rights should not be "reified" but generously bestowed upon everyone and everything; rights should not be used to shore up ideas of property and ownership, to allow us to claim that "we own gold," but instead to ensure a deep spiritual connection between us. In so doing, law could remake "society," transforming its investments in rights as something that protects property holders into rights as something that can ensure our mutual accountability, and reminds us of the "luminous golden spirit [that] owns us" all.

It is easy to read Williams as optimistically rehabilitating rights from the critical legal studies' critique of rights, and problematically investing in precisely the doctrinal formulation that has consistently failed minoritarian subjects. In this reading, Williams is imagined as paradoxically investing in precisely the site of violence she carefully documents with far too little explanation for how rights can circumvent the problems of racism and sexism she delineates. Yet I read Williams's visionary account of rights differently. For her, law can be mobilized not to produce new causes of action, to simply make visible new wounded subjects who can make appeals to redress, but to imagine new and radical vulnerabilities. As it is currently structured, property deeply organizes sociality, and law operates to protect property from trespass and theft. Thus, law operates to create categories like property holder (owner) and trespasser (thief), and to organize the social world around proximities to ownership. Williams uses her capacious conception of rights to imagine another way of organizing sociality: around vulnerability. Indeed, Williams asks: How are we bound up with others? What is our responsibility to ensuring the vital "spirit" of others, and to demanding the protection of our own "spirits"? What happens when we harm things that can't articulate injuries (trees, rocks, rivers) but can only make that injury visible and oftentimes in ways that we refuse to recognize, or that might even make that injury visible in another time, in decades or centuries when we are not even here to be accountable? What happens when we take responsibility for our capacity to wound and for the histories of wounding and violence that have unfolded, often in our names? And what happens when law becomes a critical tool in making visible mutual vulnerability, in insisting that we recognize that we can "undo each other," and in demanding that we take seriously our indebtedness to each other? For Williams, then, expanding rights becomes a strategy for transforming law to be a space that enshrines a vision of interdependence and shared vulnerability.

I begin my investigation of the possibility of rooting black feminist love-politics in law with Williams's visionary work because it reveals the potential of black feminist legal scholarship that fundamentally reorients law around ethics of vulnerability. This is work that expresses a fundamental faith in law's capacity to perform different kinds of justice work, even as it recognizes how law is often mobilized as an agent of inequality and injustice. Like Williams's radical remaking of rights, Crenshaw's conception of intersectionality tugs at the seams of law, working within its confines to radically unleash its transformative capacity. As I explained earlier in the book, intersectionality is primarily remembered for its now widely circulating accident metaphor, where discrimination is imagined as traffic flowing through an intersection. It can move in one direction, another direction, or both, and an "accident" can occur on either street *or* in the intersection. According to this logic, discrimination can be race-based, gender-based, or race-*and*-gender-based, yet the possibility of raced and gendered discrimination is rendered impossible by antidiscrimination law that actively refuses to account for this form of violence. As Crenshaw notes, "Judicial decisions which premise intersectional relief on a showing that Black women are specifically recognized as a class are analogous to a doctor's decision at the scene of an accident to treat an accident victim only if the injury is recognized by medical insurance."[38] Intersectionality, then, spotlights law's refusal to see black women's race- and gender-based injuries.

Many have envisioned intersectionality's mandate as the insertion of black women into existing antidiscrimination law, as a call for antidiscrimination law to abandon its race *or* gender logic and instead embrace a race *and* gender logic. Yet, as Crenshaw's second metaphor reveals, antidiscrimination law is constructed around leaving the multiply marginalized in the proverbial basement. Put differently, antidiscrimination law itself is constructed around remedying only certain forms of discriminatory activity and is designed to refuse to recognize and redress discrimination against the most vulnerable. Intersectionality, then, is not a call for inserting black women into a preexisting legal regime, precisely because that regime is designed to refuse to see black women. Instead, it is a tactic of making visible black women's status as witnesses who can name and describe the basement, which is not merely a social location but a space produced by law's doctrinal failures.

If intersectionality embraces black women's social location as a juridical starting point, it also advocates for tailoring law to address injuries in *particular* ways. In other words, it offers a vision of law that is rooted in flexibility and customization, in responding to particular lived experience. In her second article on intersectionality, "Mapping the Margins," Crenshaw reveals not only that law ignores black women's experiences of injury but also that intersectionality compels state interventions that more appropriately respond to black women's particular experiences of injury. In the context of domestic violence, for example, Crenshaw shows that meaningful legal intervention requires an attention to race, gender, class, and immigration status, and thus state intervention might need to take different and multiple forms to produce substantive justice. Intersectionality, then, requires a commitment to witnessing, to empathic looking, that responds not with the messy bluntness that law so often deploys in the name of fairness and uniformity. Instead, intersectionality calls for imagining legal action that can be individualized, intimate, and rooted in lived experience. This work has been expanded by other scholars, especially those working in the context of domestic violence law, including Linda Mills and Elizabeth Schneider, who have considered how mandatory arrest/no-drop policies ignore the particular experiences of women of color who may have to weigh their own distrust of the state, the necessity of a partner's income to survive, and the potential stigma, shame, or violence of calling law enforcement against a desire for bodily integrity and safety. As Mills suggests, a vision of legal intervention that is survivor-centered and survivor-guided, that recognizes the differently situatedness of each subject who engages with the state, is the only way to ensure justice, particularly in the context of intimate life. Similarly, Crenshaw's work asks for law to witness violence as it unfolds and to respond contextually, to recognize that uniformity might not be the hallmark of fairness and equity. Ultimately, Crenshaw's vision of the demands of intersectionality in the context of violence has underscored the importance of law as a tool that sees, witnesses, and even willingly inhabits the social locations of the multiply marginalized.

If it is easy to dismiss Williams's embrace of rights as overly optimistic in the face of ample description of law's failures, it is all too easy to treat Crenshaw as an inclusionist, one who imagines intersectionality as a strategy that grants black women entry into the problematic logics of antidiscrimination law. Yet in my reading of intersectionality, Crenshaw's vision is not one of including black women in existing legal doctrine, or simply expanding legal doctrine to make space for black women's particular experiences of discrimination. Indeed, Crenshaw ends "Demarginalizing the Intersection" with a personal account that underscores her deep commitment to unsettling inclusionary politics. She describes an experience in which, as a law school student, she was invited to a prestigious Harvard men's club, one that was formerly all white, to celebrate the end of first-year exams. Upon her arrival, her friend—a member of the club—quietly mentioned that he had forgotten to share an important detail: Crenshaw would have to enter the club through the back door because she was a woman. She and her friends had long assumed that it was their blackness that would bar them from the club, but it was her womanhood that required her to use the back door if she wanted entry into the club. Crenshaw ruminates on this experience as emblematic of the importance of intersectional analysis, noting that "this story does reflect a markedly decreased political and emotional vigilance toward barriers to Black women's enjoyment of privileges that have been won on the basis of race but continue to be denied on the basis of sex."[39] Yet what interests me about this account, and how it animates the end of the article, which borrows from Paula Giddings's work to conclude "when they enter, we all enter," is that intersectionality is not a tool Crenshaw uses to advocate access and entry. In other words, she does not suggest that an intersectional analysis demands her inclusion—and all black women's inclusion—in a structure constructed around black women's exclusion. Instead, the story reveals that battles for entry are always imperfect, exclusionary, and problematic. To be granted entry to a space because of blackness and to be barred entry to that same space because of womanhood speaks to the flimsiness of entry as a form of politics, precisely because inclusion *always* hinges on a system of exclusion, hierarchy, and valuation. Ultimately, intersectionality reveals both the limits of juridical projects *and* the possibility of mobilizing law to exceed law's own critical desires. In Crenshaw's hands, intersectionality invites a legal project that takes seriously black women's witnessing (and black women as witnesses, something crucial in a juridical system that continues to disbelieve black women), that invites an attention to a literal, material space—the intersection, the basement—that black women know, experience, and inhabit.

In this section, I ask what might happen if black feminists treated intersectionality's legal roots not as an embarrassment but as a crucial site of the analytic's transformative potential. Indeed, in reading Crenshaw's conception of intersectionality alongside Williams's work on rights, and in emphasizing intersectionality's roots in critical race theory, I treat intersectionality as an analytic that radically *occupies* law, takes hold of legal doctrine and refuses its conceptions of neutrality and uniformity as performance of justice. It is, then, a strategy of demanding that law move otherwise, that it center witnessing and vulnerability, that it encourage forms of relationality and accountability that jettison logics of contract and property. My reading insists that black feminists refuse well-rehearsed dismissals of intersectionality as an inclusionary project (dismissals that are all the more possible to rehearse because this is how intersectionality so often circulates in the university) that seeks to insert black women's bodies into otherwise problematic structures, and instead advocates treating intersectionality's juridical project as the very heart of its radical political agenda. It is intersectionality's capacity to index vulnerability and witnessing, to imagine legal doctrine as centering those ethics (even as law might refuse those efforts), that makes intersectionality a space that resonates deeply with black feminism's ongoing efforts to construct a political agenda rooted in love.

Risk and Promise

What if we refused the lure of negative affects, the tendency to grieve and mourn black feminism and its analytics? What if we rejected both the notion that blackness is synonymous with death and the idea that black feminism is dead or dying? My call for this rejection is not meant as a wholesale rejection of afropessimism, and its attendant affects of grief, loss, mourning, and despair. Nor is my plea here rooted in a sense that negative affects are per se problematic; indeed, the work of a host of scholars including Ann Cvetkovich, Heather Love, and Sianne Ngai has been to reclaim negative affects and to mine these feelings for their productive, world-making potential. Instead, my call is for us to consider why the position of death has become so alluring in this moment, particularly for black feminists who have made a practice of lamenting the slow and steady demise of our tradition. This chapter, then, aspires to perform letting go by suggesting another way to feel black feminism, one rooted in love rather than territoriality and defensiveness. Indeed, I argue that remembering intersectionality's juridical orientations, and recovering them rather than eschewing them (even in a moment where law is treated as the paradigmatic site of antiblack violence), might allow black feminists to encounter the broad sweep of our transformative call for love-politics. In so doing, I emphasize that law might be a space of black women's survival rather than simply the site of black women's wounding. Moreover, I underscore that a space that black women did not author, and that was created largely with the interest in enshrining black women as property rather than as subjects, might become a site that allows us to imagine other ways of being and feeling black feminist. As I argue, black feminism's long-standing commitment to love-politics, to ethics of mutual vulnerability and witnessing, is echoed by critical race feminist legal practices, including Williams's expansive investment in rights and Crenshaw's engagement with intersectionality as a critique of inclusionary politics. What both share are demands that law imagine itself *otherwise*, that it unfold and move in ways that might seem contrary to its fundamental project. These are demands that law acknowledge the failures and short-sightedness of inclusion and redress projects, and that law instead imagine its radical work to be an embrace of ideas of intimacy, proximity, vulnerability, and mutual regard. Reanimating black feminist engagement with law is particularly important because it upends the long-standing tenet that black women's freedom comes exclusively through spaces that we self-authored, and, correlatively, that sites historically constructed to secure our status as property can never become locations where we stage our liberation. My inquiry shows otherwise and argues that freedom and radical black feminist politics can be rooted in myriad sites, including spaces that have been rife with our own subordination. Indeed, my engagement with law seeks to rescue law's status of death in black studies, tracing how it can be a location of radical freedom-dreaming and visionary world-making rather than simply a deathworld and *the* paradigmatic site of antiblackness.

This and the preceding chapter are about feeling apart from defensiveness, about allowing black feminism—and black feminists—to refuse the lure of territoriality, a form of agency that always brings us back to an impasse rather than liberating us from the destructive intersectionality wars. Letting go is, though, a risky proposition. To speak on behalf of intersectionality, on behalf of black feminism, on behalf of black women, is politically powerful, a seemingly virtuous form of agency. And yet, as I have argued in this book, it locks us into feelings of defensiveness, and perhaps most problematically, into making intersectionality into property to be defended and guarded despite black feminism's long-standing anticaptivity orientation, and the tradition's deep critiques of how logics of property enshrine boundaries and ensure that value is communicated exclusively through ownership. The book traces two ways of letting go — reanimating the notion of "women of color," reinvigorating connections between transnationalism and intersectionality, and unleashing radical intimacies among women of color *and* a deep embrace and return to intersectionality's juridical orientations. Yet these two practices of letting go are not meant to capture the totality of what letting go might look like. Indeed, there are myriad ways to practice this radical form of relating to intersectionality, endless ways to undo the treatment of intersectionality as property, and endless ways to imagine feeling black feminist otherwise. While the risks of letting go are indeed high, requiring us to dream of different ways of being and feeling black feminist, envisioning black feminist identities untethered to territoriality, the benefits are even greater, giving black feminists the opportunity to envision new forms of agency and relationality, and to reenvision our relationship to academic women's studies, feminist theory, and the corporate university.

CODA. **some of us are tired**

I finish this book in the midst of Donald Trump's presidency, an era marked by rapidly proliferating forms of racist, Islamophobic, misogynist, homophobic, and transphobic terror. While this project has focused on intersectionality's complicated and contested lives in US academic feminism, I feel compelled to speak about the analytic's political purchase for feminism in a moment marked by deep insecurity. Indeed, in the midst of the uncertainties of the everyday, the promise of intersectionality has become even more significant to feminist practice. For example, the days following Trump's Electoral College victory were marked by the mainstream media struggling to make sense of their incorrect predictions of Clinton's triumph. How had they so spectacularly failed to predict the outcome of the election? In posing this question, the media often turned to voter data: 53 percent of white female voters had cast their ballots for Trump, and 94 percent of black female voters had selected Clinton. These figures were quickly taken up as evidence of black women's consistent and ethical political labor. Brittney Cooper captured this sentiment: "We have a vision for the kind of future we want to build, but also an acute sense of taking care of the least of these, such as protecting funding for schools for our kids and benefits like Medicare and Social Security for the elderly. We always vote with those things in mind."[1] In another forum, Cooper noted, "It is women of color, and black women in particular, who keep on saving democracy. We have been most deeply committed to a progressive agenda that moves the nation forward inch by inch in a way that includes vulnerable populations like children, the elderly, those with disabilities, immigrants, and queer communities."[2] In the years since Trump's election, the notion of black women as the Left's political consciousness has been repeatedly rehearsed. For example, in December 2017, two-thirds of Alabama's white female voters cast their votes in the Senate special election for Roy Moore, a "man accused of sexually assaulting teenagers and one with a dismal record on civil rights who was on tape saying the country was last 'great' during slavery."[3] It was black women voters who secured the election for Democratic candidate Doug Jones: 98 percent of black women who voted cast their votes for Jones. In the days after the election, the Internet was flooded with Left "gratitude" for black women (indeed, the hashtag #blackwomen developed to collectively amplify this so-called appreciation) who were cast as the saviors of Democratic politics. Some black feminists used the Jones election to again emphasize that black women have long been the political conscience of the nation. Ashley Nkadi, for example, noted, "Every time there is something good in this world—know that black women probably did it first, said it first. . . . Conversely, most negative things in this world, black women tried to save you from."[4] Other black feminists, like Angela Peoples, critiqued this outpouring of gratitude, noting, "Black women are being widely credited for saving the day in Alabama, and that credit is one small step in the right direction. But we don't need thanks—we need you to get out of the way and follow our lead."[5]

The vision of black women as the saviors of American political life, as the heart of the Left, was echoed by US women's studies programs and departments as they reached out to their constituents in the wake of the presidential election. One women's studies program sent an e-mail announcing that Trump's election "marks a profound failure of mainstream feminism" and noted that "Clinton's stunning loss underscores that without intersectional analysis, feminism remains unable to dismantle the patriarchal American political system." Another women's studies department noted that the election results revealed that "black women again did the heavy lifting for women." In the hands of academic feminism, the election was taken as evidence of both the long-standing ethical labor of black women—the notion that it would behoove so-called white feminism to follow black feminists' political leadership—and the urgency of intersectionality, an analytic that could help explain Trump's appeal, especially to white women voters.

If intersectionality could explain the election's results, it could also reorient feminism, holding white women responsible for their "failures" to recognize and respond to Trump's misogyny and racism.[6] The weeks after Trump's election were marked by calls for "intersectional resistance." Of course, unpacking the meaning of intersectional resistance proved challenging. The global women's marches in January 2017, a critical feminist response to Trump's election, were marked by contentious debates about diversity, inclusion, and intersectionality's mandates (the Tennessee's women's march, for example, was renamed "Power Together Tennessee, in Solidarity with Women's March on Washington" to gesture to its investment in intersectional politics), and over the political demands that would animate the protests. Would the women's march really be a march *for* women? A protest centered on gendered issues? Or was it a collective action marked by antiracist, queer, feminist, Marxist, and radical politics? Feminists actively debated if the conception of the march was adequately intersectional and asked what would make the marches sufficiently "intersectional." Was this a question of leadership, of numbers, of representation, of the nature of the demands amplified? Intersectionality could be, at times, deeply frustrating, it seemed, as feminists asked if the energy that gave rise to the women's marches would yield to feminist fractiousness. A widely circulating image of black feminist Angela Peoples holding a handmade sign that read "Don't Forget: White Women Voted for TRUMP" standing next to three white women wearing "pussy hats" and taking pictures with their phones suggested the historical labor of black women, the failure of white women to act as "allies" (to use the language of the day), and the ways in which black women remain the conscience of feminism. Yet that very same image seemed to also stand for the imagined unrelenting political unhappiness of black women. Black women, it seems, were the figures that would again and again point out white women's political failures, *even in the context* of a presumably feminist women's march. Here, at its most explicit, on its largest political stage to date, intersectionality was the medicine required to fix the ailments of the present, *and* the toxic dose that could fatally kill feminism.

While this project has focused on the place of intersectionality in US academic feminism, I end with our current political climate because it has made hypervisible what has long been a prevailing account in academic feminism: black women are the beginning and end of politics, the figures that will salvage feminism, even as that salvation might rupture the project of feminism altogether. Indeed, in the Trump era, the stakes of the intersectionality wars have never been higher, as intersectionality is increasingly hailed as the tool that will "save" the Left and "save" feminism even as it can fracture political movements like the women's march. Academic feminism has found itself mired in these political debates, increasingly hailing intersectionality as precisely the analytic required to make sense of the conditions of the present, and black women as the very figures who must be "listened" to in order to respond to Trump's election. And the contentious debates that have circulated in academic feminism about intersectionality—the intersectionality wars—have become increasingly public and political in the wake of the new presidential regime. In other words, academic debates about intersectionality acted as a laboratory for the debates that now circulate outside of academic feminism, in popular feminism practiced on Twitter and Facebook, at protests and rallies.

Black Feminism Reimagined has argued against treating intersectionality, and black women, as so-called white feminism's salvific figures because of what this narrative has done to black feminism and to black feminists. This narrative—one where black feminism's primary task is to discipline so-called white feminism and women's studies—has produced defensiveness as the hallmark of the felt life of US academic black feminism. In other words, the deeply narrow role that women's studies has allocated to black feminist theory, which includes the presumption that the exclusive labor of black feminist theory is intersectionality, has produced a black feminist proprietary relationship to intersectionality. When intersectionality is women's studies' most valued currency (currency that can be hypervalued and devalued simultaneously), black feminists emphatically reiterate "correct" usages of the term and insist on "correct" histories and genealogies of the analytic. These "correct" deployments of intersectionality incessantly return the analytic to its imagined true origins in black feminism, and its imagined true intimacy with black women. And when intersectionality is figured as the site of the field's imagined undoing, as the field-ending demand for endless complexity, black feminists insistently argue in favor of the analytic, emphasizing that intersectionality's analytic power has yet to be unleashed because it is not used correctly, in ways that are faithful to the term's foundational texts and original scholars. In both cases, the labor of black feminism is to treat intersectionality as territory under siege, and to protect and safeguard it from violent "appropriations," "commodifications," and critiques. Black Feminism Reimagined argues that the prevailing feeling of defensiveness and its attendant performances of holding on are deeply alluring precisely because they appear to be assertions of agency exerted on behalf of black women's intellectual production. Yet, as I have argued throughout this book, defensiveness conscripts black feminism into participation in the intersectionality wars and shores up black feminists' territorial hold on intersectionality. Defensiveness is a form of obstructed agency, something that hinders black feminism's theoretical and political imagination rather than unleashing it.

Indeed, I have emphasized that the defensive position finds black feminists making intersectionality into *property*, turf that must be carefully guarded and even policed to ensure that it is not traversed by outsiders. It is, of course, deeply ironic that an intellectual and political tradition that has been at the vanguard of revealing the racialized and gendered underpinnings of property—from theorizing "whiteness as property" to radically exposing how conceptions of property make possible forms of racially violent vigilantism—would find itself making property of intersectionality.[7] Black feminism, then, has mirrored a larger US tradition in which to care for something is to assert ownership over it, and thus to protect it from imagined threat of trespass. Yet black feminist theory has long been an anticaptivity project, one fundamentally invested in radical conceptions of freedom. Thus, underpinning my investment in letting go is reanimating black feminism's radical imagination, its capacity to continue to ask: What if we imagined relationships with what we cherish beyond the racially saturated conceptions of property and ownership? Can we untether care and love from ownership? Can we express our deepest and most cherished investments otherwise?

My endeavor in this book is to show that this proprietary relationship with intersectionality—these practices of holding on—actually constrains black feminist theory and black feminists. The defensive affect makes black feminism a critical interlocutor in the intersectionality wars rather than a tradition that can crucially explore and expose the racial politics of intersectionality's circulation in women's studies. In theorizing how black feminism has become constrained, I am not arguing that black feminism is dead or dying; indeed, I am deeply suspicious of the allure of death rhetorics. Instead, I insist that black feminism—theory, politics, and praxis—is alive and vibrant, containing rich new debates about eroticism, reproduction, visual culture, maternity, and surveillance. But this vibrancy has not been captured in debates around intersectionality, where too often black feminists devote intellectual and political energy to calling out misuses of intersectionality rather than interrogating the lure of intersectionality and the analytic's racial politics, or exposing how and why correct usage of intersectionality has become a prevailing feminist preoccupation. Ultimately, the defensive position is an exhausting one for black feminists, who are both shielding themselves from attack and relentlessly guarding imagined territory. It is tiring precisely because of the radical dreaming it forecloses, and because it relentlessly reduces rich debates to accusations of trespass and practices of recovery. It is also tiring because of what it does to black feminist bodies. While black feminist theory has brilliantly captured the ways that the US academy has been a killing machine that cannibalizes black women, violently extracting our knowledge and diversity service, it has yet to fully capture the toxicity of defensiveness, and how exhausting—physically, spiritually, psychically—the defensive posture can be.

If my book is an inquiry into black feminist feelings, and the particular kinds of black feminist feelings US women's studies has produced, I should be clear that the affective attachments underpinning my inquiry are an enduring wish for a black feminist theory that refuses to participate in the intersectionality wars, and that insists that women's studies move away from its insistent use of black woman as the field's key sign. My wish is for black feminist theory that can name the fatigue, the tiredness, and even the violence that comes with always being made a symbol, even if that symbol is seemingly a productive one—a figure that can save the field of women's studies from its history, its ongoing violence, effectively rescuing it from itself. I dream of black feminist theory that puts pressure on women's studies to recognize the utopian world-making work of our still unfolding political dreaming, which *includes* but also *exceeds* intersectionality. My wish is for black feminist theory that refuses to perform service work for women's studies, and that instead compels the field to reckon with its own racially saturated fantasies and attachments. I want this reckoning *not* to take the form of gratitude, appreciation, or apology, the primary forms that circulate in both popular and academic feminisms, but to instead include a deep historical engagement with the labor that black women, black feminists, and black feminist theories are regularly called upon to perform for women's studies, effectively shoring up women's studies' own claims to virtue. Letting go untethers black feminism from the endless fighting over intersectionality, the elaborate choreography of rescuing the analytic from misuses, the endless corrections of the analytic's usage. Letting go allows us to put the visionary genius of black feminism to work *otherwise*. It is, thus, a practice of freedom.

INTRODUCTION

1. Nathan Heller, "The Big Uneasy," *New Yorker*, May 30, 2016, www.newyorker.com /magazine/2016/05/30/the-new-activism-of-liberal-arts-colleges.

2. Andrew Sullivan, "Is Intersectionality a Religion?," *New York Magazine*, March 10, 2017, http://nymag.com/daily/intelligencer/2017/03/is-intersectionality-a-religion.html.

3. Sullivan, "Is Intersectionality a Religion?"

4. See, for example, Sunnivie Brydym and Evan Derkacz, "Andrew Sullivan Really Took This Opportunity to Misread Intersectionality?," *Religion Dispatches*, March 23, 2017, http://religiondispatches.org/andrew-sullivan-really-took-this-opportunity-to-misread -intersectionality/; Laura Nelson, "No, Andrew Sullivan, Intersectionality Is Not a Re- ligion," *Patheos*, March 14, 2017, www.patheos.com/blogs/friendlyatheist/2017/03/14/no -andrew-sullivan-intersectionality-is-not-a-religion/.

5. Tom Bartlett, "When a Theory Goes Viral," *Chronicle of Higher Education*, May 21, 2017.

6. I map black feminism's relationship to feminism's past and future in my earlier work. See Jennifer C. Nash, "Institutionalizing the Margins," *Social Text* 32.1 (2014): 45–65.

7. It is worth noting that intersectionality's varied meanings have also been animated outside of academic feminism, namely, in the context of feminist politics, and femi- nist scholars have recently debated whether intersectionality was born in the university, through political activism, or both. While this book only touches upon the term's political life outside of the university, the kind of expansive labor intersectionality is currently called upon to perform in feminism's political life and the debates that swirl around the term's political promise (and imagined danger) have long animated debates about intersectionality in US women's studies.

8. Robyn Wiegman, *Object Lessons* (Durham, NC: Duke University Press, 2012), 240.

9. Patricia Hill Collins described intersectionality as "gentrified" in her keynote ad- dress at the Social Theory Forum in 2015. The speech is available online at www.youtube

.com/watch?v=pqToqQCZtvg (accessed March 4, 2016). For more on "stewardship," see Ange-Marie Hancock, *Intersectionality: An Intellectual History* (New York: Oxford University Press, 2016), and chapter 4 of this book.

10. For more on black female faculty and service work, see Amber Jamilla Musser, "Specimen Days: Diversity, Labor, and the University," *Feminist Formations* 27.3 (2015): 1–20; Rachel Lee, "Notes from the (Non)Field: Teaching and Theorizing Women of Color," *Meridians* 1.1 (2000): 85–109.

11. Lee, "Notes from the (Non)Field," 91.

12. See Claire Hemmings, *Why Stories Matter* (Durham, NC: Duke University Press, 2010).

13. Robin D. G. Kelley, *Freedom Dreams: The Black Radical Imagination* (Boston: Beacon Press, 2003).

14. See Nikol G. Alexander-Floyd, "Disappearing Acts: Reclaiming Intersectionality in the Social Sciences in a Post–Black Feminist Era," *Feminist Formations* 24.1 (2012): 1–25.

15. Ange-Marie Hancock, "Intersectionality as a Normative and Empirical Paradigm," *Politics and Gender* 3.2 (2007): 249.

16. Jennifer C. Nash, "Intersectionality and Its Discontents," *American Quarterly* 69.1 (2017): 126.

17. Deborah K. King, "Multiple Jeopardy, Multiple Consciousness: The Context of a Black Feminist Ideology," *Signs* 14.1 (1988): 43.

18. See Brittney Cooper, *Beyond Respectability: The Intellectual Thought of Race Women* (Urbana-Champaign: University of Illinois Press, 2017).

19. Vivian May, "Intellectual Genealogies, Intersectionality, and Anna Julia Cooper," in *Feminist Solidarity at the Crossroads: Intersectional Women's Studies for Transracial Alliance*, ed. Kim Marie Vaz and Gary L. Lemons (New York: Routledge, 2012), 61.

20. May, "Intellectual Genealogies," 61.

21. Vivian May, "Intersectionality," in *Rethinking Women's and Gender Studies*, ed. Catherine M. Orr and Ann Braithwaite (New York: Routledge, 2011), 157.

22. Combahee River Collective, "A Black Feminist Statement," in *All the Women Are White, All the Men Are Men, But Some of Us Are Brave: Black Women's Studies*, ed. Gloria T. Hull, Patricia Bell Scott, and Barbara Smith (New York: Feminist Press, 1982), 16.

23. Evelyn Brooks Higginbotham, "African American Women's History and the Metalanguage of Race," *Signs* 17.2 (1992): 255.

24. Frances Beal, "Double Jeopardy: To Be Black and Female," qtd. in King, "Multiple Jeopardy, Multiple Consciousness," 46.

25. King, "Multiple Jeopardy, Multiple Consciousness," 43.

26. King, "Multiple Jeopardy, Multiple Consciousness," 47.

27. Brittney Cooper, "Intersectionality," in *The Oxford Handbook of Feminist Theory*, ed. Lisa Jane Disch and M. E. Hawkesworth (New York: Oxford University Press, 2016), 386.

28. Kimberlé Crenshaw, "Demarginalizing the Intersection of Race and Sex: A Black Feminist Critique of Antidiscrimination Doctrine, Feminist Theory and Antiracist Politics," *University of Chicago Legal Forum* 1 (1989): 139–40.

29. Anna Carastathis explores why only one of these metaphors has been taken up. See Anna Carastathis, "Basements and Intersections," *Hypatia* 28.4 (2013): 698–715.

30. Crenshaw, "Demarginalizing the Intersection of Race and Sex," 149.

31. Crenshaw, "Demarginalizing the Intersection of Race and Sex," 151–52.

32. In my earlier work, I examine how Crenshaw and Collins were laboring in the same historical moment. See Jennifer C. Nash, "'Home Truths' on Intersectionality," *Yale Journal of Law and Feminism* 23.2 (2011): 445–70.

33. Patricia Hill Collins, *Black Feminist Thought*, 2nd ed. (New York: Routledge, 2000), 18.

34. Collins, *Black Feminist Thought*, 287.

35. Kathy Davis, "Intersectionality as Buzzword: A Sociology of Science Perspective on What Makes a Feminist Theory Successful," *Feminist Theory* 9.1 (2008): 68; Leslie McCall, "The Complexity of Intersectionality," *Signs* 30.3 (2005): 1771.

36. Wiegman, *Object Lessons*, 240. The term "corporate university" (and other terms like "neoliberal university") is often used as a shorthand for a range of practices, including the rise of student debt; the proliferation of precarious adjunct faculty labor; the seemingly endless expansion of the job responsibilities of tenure-track and tenured faculty; the increasing demands for affective faculty labor; the deployment of rubrics, assessments, and other measurement tools to determine the value of courses and disciplines; the university's strategic deployment of signifiers of difference, including the uses of terms like "intersectionality," "diversity," and "globalization" to signal an investment in producing "global citizens" and diverse "learning communities." Robert McRuer notes, "Inside and outside the university, corporate elites demand that composition courses focus on demonstrable professional-managerial skills rather than critical thought—or, more insidiously, 'critical thought' is reconceptualized through a skills-based mode ultimately grounded in measurement and marketability, or measurement for marketability. The most troubling feature of our current corpo-reality is that composition at most institutions is routinely taught by adjunct or graduate student employees who receive low pay and few (if any) benefits: the composition work force, at the corporate university, is highly contingent and replaceable, and instructors are thus often forced to piece together multiple appointments at various schools in a region." Robert McRuer, *Crip Theory: Cultural Signs of Queerness and Disability* (New York: NYU Press, 2006), 148. Matthew Frye Jacobson echoes this in his 2012 ASA presidential address: "As bastions of military research and as traditional purveyors of legitimizing imperialist narratives, universities are implicated in imperialist aggrandizement, but universities also find themselves imperiled under the neoliberal regime of privatization, enforced public austerity, market orientation, and atomized notions of civic collectivity and destiny. Yet, we must insist, university communities remain potentially important voices—as yet unvanquished—in defense of democratic ideals and of 'the civic.'"

See, for example, Naomi Greyser and Margot Weiss, "Left Intellectuals and the Neoliberal University," *American Quarterly* 64.4 (2012): 787–93; Purnima Bose, "Faculty Activism and the Corporatization of the University," *American Quarterly* 64.4 (2012): 815–18; Jeffrey R. DiLeo, *Corporate Humanities in Higher Education: Moving beyond the Neoliberal Academy* (New York: Palgrave Macmillan, 2013); Robert McRuer, "Composing Bodies; or, De-composition: Queer Theory, Disability Studies, and Alternative Corporealities," *jac* 24.1 (2004): 47–78; Samantha King, "Nike U: Full Program Athletics Contracts and the Corporate University," in *Sports and Neoliberalism: Politics, Consumption, and Culture*, ed. David L. Andrews and Michael L. Silk (Philadelphia: Temple University Press, 2012);

Thorstein Veblen, *The Higher Learning in America* (New York: B. W. Huebsch, 1918); Marc Bousquet, *How the University Works: Higher Education and the Low-Wage Nation* (New York: NYU Press, 2008); Christopher Newfield, *Unmaking the Public University: The Forty-Year Assault on the Middle Class* (Cambridge, MA: Harvard University Press, 2008); Sheila Slaughter and Larry L. Leslie, *Academic Capitalism: Politics, Policies, and the Entrepreneurial University* (Baltimore: Johns Hopkins University Press, 1997); Gregory Jay, "Hire Ed! Deconstructing the Crises in Academe," *American Quarterly* 63.1 (2011): 163–78; Henry A. Giroux, *Neoliberalism's War on Higher Education* (New York: Haymarket Books, 2014); Piya Chatterjee and Sunaina Maira, eds., *The Imperial University: Academic Repression and Scholarly Dissent* (Minneapolis: University of Minnesota Press, 2014); Joyce E. Canaan and Wesley Shumar, *Structure and Agency in the Neoliberal University* (London: Routledge, 2011); Eric Cheyfitz, "The Corporate University, Academic Freedom, and American Exceptionalism," *South Atlantic Quarterly* 108.4 (2009): 701–22; Andrew Ross, "The Corporate Analogy Unravels," *Chronicle of Higher Education*, October 17, 2010, http://chronicle .com/article/Farewell-to-the-Corporate/124919/.

37. Robyn Wiegman, ed., *Women's Studies on Its Own* (Durham, NC: Duke University Press, 2002), 3; Joan Wallach Scott, *Women's Studies on the Edge* (Durham, NC: Duke University Press, 2008), 13.

38. Scott, *Women's Studies on Its Own*, 3.

39. Wendy Brown, "The Impossibility of Women's Studies," in *Edgework: Critical Essays on Knowledge and Politics* (Princeton, NJ: Princeton University Press, 2005), 120.

40. Hemmings, *Why Stories Matter*, 45.

41. Lee, "Notes from the (Non)Field," 86.

42. Lee, "Notes from the (Non)Field," 91.

43. Brown, "The Impossibility of Women's Studies," 130.

44. My thinking on "white feminism" is informed and inspired by Samantha Pinto's talk "The Uses of (White Feminist) Guilt and the Production of Black Feminist Fatigue" at the American Studies Association 2017 conference, Chicago, November 9–12.

45. Brown, "The Impossibility of Women's Studies," 123.

46. Brittney Cooper, "Love No Limit: Towards a Black Feminist Future (in Theory)," *Black Scholar* 45.4 (2015): 15.

47. Wiegman, *Object Lessons*, 240 (emphasis in original); Maxine Baca Zinn, "Patricia Hill Collins: Past and Future Innovations," *Gender and Society* 26 (2012): 31; Davis, "Intersectionality as Buzzword," 72; Ange-Marie Hancock, *Solidarity Politics for Millennials: A Guide to Ending the Oppression Olympics* (New York: Palgrave, 2011), 3.

48. Flavia Dzodan, "My Feminism Will Be Intersectional or It Will Be Bullshit," *Tiger Beatdown*, October 10, 2011, http://tigerbeatdown.com/2011/10/10/my-feminism-will-be -intersectional-or-it-will-be-bullshit/.

49. Svati Shah, panel conversation "Reading Intersectionality's Genealogy for Strategy: Reflections on an Intervention," University of Massachusetts Amherst, April 2012.

50. Syracuse University Women's and Gender Studies Objectives, http://wgs.syr.edu /About/WGS_Objective.html (accessed July 14, 2016).

51. Ohio State University Women's, Gender, and Sexuality Studies Department website, https://wgss.osu.edu/ (accessed July 14, 2016).

52. University of California, Berkeley, Department of Gender and Women's Studies website, http://womensstudies.berkeley.edu/ (accessed July 14, 2016).

53. Denison University Women's and Gender Studies Program website, http://denison .edu/academics/womens-gender-studies/about/about (accessed July 14, 2016).

54. I have decided not to cite the institutions that circulated these advertisements precisely because my interest is less in the specific institutional setting that produced the advertisement than in what these advertisements represent about the field and its investments.

55. Grace Hong, "'The Future of Our Worlds': Black Feminism and the Politics of Knowledge in the University under Globalization," *Meridians* 8.2 (2008): 96.

56. Ann duCille, "The Occult of True Black Womanhood: Critical Demeanor and Black Feminist Studies," in *Female Subjects in Black and White: Race, Psychoanalysis, Feminism*, ed. Elizabeth Abel, Barbara Christian, and Helen Moglen (Berkeley: University of California Press, 1997), 31.

57. Barbara Christian, "Diminishing Returns: Can Black Feminism(s) Survive the Academy," in *New Black Feminist Criticism, 1985–2000*, ed. Gloria Bowles, M. Giulia Fabi, and Arlene Keizer (Urbana-Champaign: University of Illinois Press, 2007), 214.

58. Samantha Pinto, "Black Feminist Literacies: Ungendering, Flesh, and Post-Spillers Epistemologies of Embodied and Emotional Justice," *Journal of Black Sexuality and Relationships* 4.1 (2017): 40.

59. Patrice D. Douglass, "Black Feminist Theory for the Dead and Dying," *Theory & Event* 21.1 (2018): 106–23.

60. Douglass, "Black Feminist Theory," 119.

61. Calvin Warren, "Onticide: Afro-pessimism, Gay Nigger #1, and Surplus Violence," GLQ 23.3 (2017): 409.

62. Douglass, "Black Feminist Theory," 115.

63. I trace some of this in my earlier work. See Jennifer C. Nash, "Unwidowing: Rachel Jeantel, Black Death, and the 'Problem' of Black Intimacy," *Signs* 41.4 (2016): 751–74.

64. See LaMonda Horton Stallings, *Funk the Erotic: Transaesthetics and Black Sexual Culture* (Urbana-Champaign: University of Illinois Press, 2016).

65. On the emergence of intersectionality centers at colleges and universities, see, for example, Columbia University's Center for Intersectionality and Social Policy Studies, or the University of Tennessee's Intersectionality Community of Scholars.

66. Rachel E. Luft and Jane Ward, "Toward an Intersectionality Just Out of Reach: Confronting Challenges to Intersectional Practice," in *Perceiving Gender Locally, Globally, and Internationally*, ed. Vasilikie Demos and Marcia Texler Segal (Bingley, UK: Emerald, 2009), 14; Sara Ahmed, *On Being Included: Racism and Diversity in Institutional Life* (Durham, NC: Duke University Press, 2012), 14.

67. Roderick Ferguson, "Administering Sexuality; or, the Will to Institutionality," *Radical History Review* 100 (2008): 162–63.

68. *Grutter v. Bollinger*, 539 U.S. 306 (2003).

69. Ahmed, *On Being Included*, 52.

70. Ahmed, *On Being Included*, 52.

71. Chandra Mohanty, *Feminism without Borders: Decolonizing Theory, Practicing Solidarity* (Durham, NC: Duke University Press, 2003), 193.

72. Banu Subramaniam, *Ghost Stories for Darwin: The Science of Variation and the Politics of Diversity* (Urbana-Champaign: University of Illinois Press, 2014), 15.

73. Subramaniam, *Ghost Stories for Darwin*, 15.

74. Mohanty, *Feminism without Borders*, 193; Ahmed, *On Being Included*, 1.

75. May, *Pursuing Intersectionality*, 90.

76. May, *Pursuing Intersectionality*, 66.

77. Sara Ahmed, "Women of Colour as Diversity Workers," *feministkilljoys*, November 26, 2015, https://feministkilljoys.com/2015/11/26/women-of-colour-as-diversity-workers/.

78. See, for example, Jennifer C. Nash, "Pedagogies of Desire," *differences* (forthcoming).

79. Ntozake Shange, *For Colored Girls Who Have Considered Suicide / When the Rainbow Is Enuf* (New York: Scribner, 1977), 49.

These lines are recited by the lady in green:

somebody almost walked off wid alla my stuff
not my poems or a dance i gave up in the street
but somebody almost walked off wid alla my stuff
like a kleptomaniac workin hard & forgettin while stealin
this is mine / this aint yr stuff /
now why don't you put me back & let me hang out in my own self

80. Lauren Berlant, *Cruel Optimism* (Durham, NC: Duke University Press, 2011), 5.

81. See Christian, "Diminishing Returns."

82. Sianne Ngai, *Ugly Feelings* (Cambridge, MA: Harvard University Press, 2005), 3.

83. Cooper, "Love No Limit," 7.

84. Ann duCille, *Skin Trade* (Cambridge, MA: Harvard University Press, 1996), 81–82.

85. Ann Cvetkovich, "Public Feelings," *South Atlantic Quarterly* 106.3 (2007): 461.

86. Ann Cvetkovich, *Depression: A Public Feeling* (Durham, NC: Duke University Press, 2012), 17.

87. Gabriella Gutiérrez y Muhs, Yolanda Flores Niemann, Carmen G. González, and Angela P. Harris, eds., *Presumed Incompetent: The Intersections of Race and Class for Women in Academia* (Boulder: University Press of Colorado, 2012); Deborah Gray White, ed., *Telling Histories: Black Women Historians in the Ivory Tower* (Chapel Hill: University of North Carolina Press, 2008). See also Moya Bailey and Shannon J. Miller, "When Margins Become Centered: Black Queer Women in Front and Outside of the Classroom," *Feminist Formations* 27.3 (2015): 168–88.

88. Paulette M. Caldwell, "A Hair Piece: Perspectives on the Intersection of Race and Gender," *Duke Law Journal* 40.2 (1991): 366.

89. Caldwell, "A Hair Piece," 368.

90. Patricia Williams, *The Alchemy of Race and Rights* (Cambridge, MA: Harvard University Press, 1992), 95–96.

ONE. a love letter from a critic

1. Patrick Grzanka, ed., *Intersectionality: A Foundations and Frontiers Reader* (Boulder, CO: Westview Press, 2014), 301.

2. Jasbir Puar, "'I Would Rather Be a Cyborg Than a Goddess': Intersectionality, Assemblage, and Affective Politics," European Institute for Progressive Cultural Politics, http://eipcp.net/transversal/0811/puar/en (accessed May 3, 2016).

3. Vivian May, *Pursuing Intersectionality, Unsettling Dominant Imaginaries* (New York: Routledge, 2015), 6, 8.

4. I am grateful to Sarah Jane Cervenak for this tremendously useful phrasing.

5. See 2014 American Studies Association Conference Program. Though it is beyond the scope of this project, I do think it is worth at least posing the question of the place of feminism in American studies, and the relationship of women's studies to American studies. In posing this question, I think alongside Samantha Pinto, James Bliss, Emily Owens, Mairead Sullivan, and Sara Matthiesen. Together, we were part of a panel at the 2017 American Studies Association conference, "Untimely Objects: Feminism and/in/ Eclipsed by the ASA." The description (authored by Pinto) noted,

> At first, it may sound ridiculous to bring up feminism in antagonism to the present day ASA. One might argue that nearly every member would identify themselves as feminist scholars, even, especially a series of the organization's top officers— many of whom have positions in Women's and Gender Studies departments. But is "feminism" claimed as a central intellectual and disciplinary project of the ASA? In particular, how might the ASA's intellectual projects reproduce some of the object wars of women's and gender studies of the past 25 years—conversations that frequently reproduce "women," "lesbian," and even "feminism" as passé subjects of study, ones that the most politically radical scholars are already "over" or "beyond." Feminism may not be denied, so much as it appears always already eclipsed, and hence incorporated into the assumed history of the field but not prominent at its center as such, which focuses on theories of queer, post-humanist, transnational, and ethnic studies of the neoliberal state/order. In this roundtable panel, several scholars of feminist, women's, gender, and sexuality studies reflect on the field's engagement with ASA, as well as the differential development of the space of the annual conference in each field. What are the different protocols of these fields, and how do they (over)determine the intellectual and academic subjects that seem to define their discrete intellectual projects?

6. Sharon Holland notes, "Intersectionality has become something that black feminists 'do' by default. For a time in the 1980s, it didn't matter if you were working on 'intersectionality' directly or not; if you appeared to be a black feminist, you were assumed to be working on it. By the same token, a nod to intersectionality in any feminist conference paper was assumed to represent a whole host of theorists in exchange for actual engagement." Sharon Holland, *The Erotic Life of Racism* (Durham, NC: Duke University Press, 2013), 123.

7. See Lisa Duggan and Nan D. Hunter, *Sex Wars: Sexual Dissent and Political Culture* (New York: Routledge, 1996).

8. Robyn Wiegman, *Object Lessons* (Durham, NC: Duke University Press, 2012), 240.

9. Janet Halley, *Split Decisions: How and Why to Take a Break from Feminism* (Princeton, NJ: Princeton University Press, 2006), 192.

10. Brittney Cooper, "Intersectionality," in *The Oxford Handbook of Feminist Theory*, ed. Lisa Disch and Mary Hawkesworth (New York: Oxford University Press, 2016), 395.

11. Nikol G. Alexander-Floyd, "Disappearing Acts: Reclaiming Intersectionality in the Social Sciences in a Post–Black Feminist Era," *Feminist Formations* 24.1 (2012): 11.

12. Alexander-Floyd, "Disappearing Acts," 2.

13. Bilge, "Whitening Intersectionality: Evanescence of Race in Intersectionality Scholarship," https://www.academia.edu/11805835/Whitening_Intersectionality._Evanescence_of_Race_in_Intersectionality_Scholarship (accessed March 1, 2017) (emphasis added).

14. Crunk Feminist Collective, "The R-Word: Why 'Rigorous' Is the New Black," *Crunk Feminist Collective*, November 17, 2010, https://crunkfeministcollective.wordpress.com/2010/11/17/the-r-word-why-rigorous-is-the-new-black/.

15. Bilge, "Whitening Intersectionality."

16. Bilge, "Whitening Intersectionality."

17. Bilge, "Whitening Intersectionality."

18. Bilge, "Whitening Intersectionality."

19. Anna Carastathis, "The Concept of Intersectionality in Feminist Theory," *Philosophy Compass* 9.5 (2014): 304.

20. Jean Ait Belkhir, "The 'Johnny's Story': Founder of the Race, Gender, and Class Journal," in *The Intersectional Approach: Transforming the Academy through Race, Class, and Gender*, ed. Michele Tracy Berger and Kathleen Guidroz (Chapel Hill: University of North Carolina Press, 2009), 303.

21. Rachel E. Luft and Jane Ward, "Toward an Intersectionality Just Out of Reach: Confronting Challenges to Intersectional Practice," in *Perceiving Gender Locally, Globally, and Intersectionally*, ed. Vasilikie Demos and Marcia Texler Segal (Bingley, UK: Emerald, 2009), 12.

22. See Ange-Marie Hancock, "Empirical Intersectionality: A Tale of Two Approaches," *UC Irvine Law Review* 3.2 (2010): 259–96.

23. May, *Pursuing Intersectionality*, 11.

24. Carastathis, "The Concept of Intersectionality in Feminist Theory," 305.

25. Devon Carbado, "Colorblind Intersectionality," *Signs* 38.4 (2013): 811; Vrushali Patil, "From Patriarchy to Intersectionality: A Transnational Feminist Assessment of How Far We've Really Come," *Signs* 38.4 (2013): 852; Barbara Tomlinson, "To Tell the Truth and Not Get Trapped: Desire, Distance, and Intersectionality at the Scene of Argument," *Signs* 38.4 (2013): 993.

26. Patricia Hill Collins, "Sharpening Intersectionality's Critical Edge," Social Theory Forum keynote address, www.youtube.com/watch?v=pqToqQCZtvg&feature=youtu.be (accessed June 24, 2015).

27. Wiegman, *Object Lessons*, 244.

28. Wiegman, *Object Lessons*, 244.

29. Alexander-Floyd, "Disappearing Acts," 2.

30. Rachel Lee, "Notes from the (Non)Field: Teaching and Theorizing Women of Color," *Meridians* 1.1 (2000): 91.

31. Luft and Ward, "Toward an Intersectionality Just Out of Reach," 17.

32. Carastathis, "The Concept of Intersectionality in Feminist Theory," 304.

33. Bilge, "Whitening Intersectionality" (emphasis added).

34. On intersectionality's "success," Brittney Cooper notes, "As a conceptual and analytic tool for thinking about operations of power, intersectionality remains one of the most useful and expansive paradigms we have" (Cooper, "Intersectionality," 405). Kathy Davis's widely cited article "Intersectionality as Buzzword" also attempts to explore intersectionality's "success."

35. See, for example, the "post-intersectionality" scholarship emerging out of the legal academy, including Robert S. Chang and Jerome McCristal Culp Jr., "After Intersectionality," *UMKC Law Review* 71.2 (2002): 485–91; Peter Kwan, "Intersections of Race, Ethnicity, Class, Gender and Sexual Orientation: Jeffrey Dahmer and the Cosynthesis of Categories," *Hastings Law Journal* 48 (1997): 1257–92; Darren Lenard Hutchinson, "Out Yet Unseen: A Racial Critique of Gay and Lesbian Legal Theory and Political Discourse," *Connecticut Law Review* 29 (1997): 561–645.

36. Moreover, a number of scholars—including most notably Tiffany Lethabo King—have persuasively revealed the ways that intersectionality gets tethered to the past, so that to invest in the analytic is to invest in something seen as identitarian and thus as always already passé. King's analysis of the way this circulates in an academic milieu that privileges and fetishizes the new suggests that critiques of intersectionality are fundamentally rooted in a university that privileges newness and that presumes that black female bodies are historical—or, perhaps more aptly, old-fashioned, and wedded to a concept of injury that always offers up black female flesh as evidence of a kind of wound.

37. Maria Carbin and Sara Edenheim, "The Intersectional Turn: A Dream of a Common Language?," *European Journal of Women's Studies* 20.3 (2013): 234.

38. May, *Pursuing Intersectionality*, 107; Tomlinson, "To Tell the Truth and Not Get Trapped," 993.

39. May, *Pursuing Intersectionality*, 112.

40. May, *Pursuing Intersectionality*, 98.

41. May, *Pursuing Intersectionality*, 98.

42. Tomlinson, "To Tell the Truth and Not Get Trapped," 997.

43. James Bliss, "Black Feminism Out of Place," *Signs* 41.4 (2016): 731.

44. Tomlinson, "To Tell the Truth and Not Get Trapped," 999.

45. May, *Pursuing Intersectionality*, 101.

46. May, *Pursuing Intersectionality*, 103.

47. May, *Pursuing Intersectionality*, 106.

48. Carbado, "Colorblind Intersectionality," 812.

49. Carbado, "Colorblind Intersectionality," 815.

50. The notion of Jasbir Puar as intersectionality's key critic is not only articulated in academic circles. A recent *New Yorker* article on the politics of campus life also treated Puar as critic. Nathan Heller writes, "The Rutgers scholar Jasbir K. Puar charges that intersectionality posits people whose attributes—race, class, gender, etc.—are 'separable analytics,' like Legos that can be snapped apart, when in truth most identities operate more like the night sky: we see meaningful shapes by picking out some stars and ignoring others, and these imagined pictures can change all the time." See Nathan Heller, "The Big Uneasy," *New Yorker*, May 30, 2016.

51. Carastathis, "The Concept of Intersectionality in Feminist Theory," 149; Grzanka, *Intersectionality*, xvii.

52. Bliss, "Black Feminism Out of Place," 734.

53. Tiffany Lethabo King, "Post-identitarian and Post-intersectional Anxiety in the Neoliberal Corporate University," *Feminist Formations* 27.3 (2015): 119.

54. Amy L. Brandzel, *Against Citizenship: The Violence of the Normative* (Urbana-Champaign: University of Illinois Press, 2016), 22.

55. Jasbir K. Puar, *Terrorist Assemblages: Homonationalism in Queer Times* (Durham, NC: Duke University Press, 2007), 212.

56. Puar, "'I Would Rather Be a Cyborg Than a Goddess.'"

57. See Cooper, referring to my work, for example, as "the work of *black feminist theorist* Jennifer Nash" (emphasis added). Cooper, "Intersectionality," 391.

58. See Egbert Alejandro Martina, "More on Puar and Intersectionality," *Processed Lives*, http://processedlives.tumblr.com/post/84342486940/more-on-puar-and-intersectionality (accessed March 1, 2017).

59. Lynn Huffer, *Are the Lips a Grave?* (New York: Columbia University Press, 2013), 17.

60. Roderick Ferguson, *Aberrations in Black: Toward a Queer of Color Critique* (Minneapolis: University of Minnesota Press, 2003), 149.

61. Jafari S. Allen, "Black/Queer/Diaspora at the Current Conjuncture," GLQ 18.2–3 (2012): 230.

62. Roderick Ferguson and Grace Hong, eds., *Strange Affinities: The Gender and Sexual Politics of Comparative Racialization* (Durham, NC: Duke University Press, 2011), 2.

63. Ferguson, *Aberrations in Black*, 52.

64. Alison Peipmeier, "Besiegement," in *Rethinking Women's and Gender Studies*, ed. Catherine M. Orr and Ann Braithwaite (New York: Routledge, 2011), 119.

65. Lauren Berlant and Michael Hardt, "No One Is Sovereign in Love: A Conversation between Lauren Berlant and Michael Hardt," *No More Potlucks*, http://nomorepotlucks.org/site/no-one-is-sovereign-in-love-a-conversation-between-lauren-berlant-and-michael-hardt/ (accessed March 31, 2017).

TWO. the politics of reading

1. Ange-Marie Hancock, *Intersectionality: An Intellectual History* (New York: Oxford University Press, 2016), 201.

2. See Jennifer C. Nash, "Feminist Originalism: Intersectionality and the Politics of Reading," *Feminist Theory* 17.1 (2016): 3–20.

3. Jennifer C. Nash, "Intersectionality and Its Discontents," *American Quarterly* 69.1 (2017): 119.

4. Anna Carastathis, "Basements and Intersections," *Hypatia* 28.4 (2013): 699.

5. Sumi Cho, Kimberlé Williams Crenshaw, and Leslie McCall, "Toward a Field of Intersectionality Studies: Theory, Applications, and Praxis," *Signs* 38.4 (2013): 807.

6. Barbara Tomlinson, "To Tell the Truth and Not Get Trapped: Desire, Distance, and Intersectionality at the Scene of the Argument," *Signs* 38.4 (2013): 993–1017.

7. Vivian May, *Pursuing Intersectionality, Unsettling Dominant Imaginaries* (New York: Routledge, 2015), 18.

8. Cho, Crenshaw, and McCall, "Toward a Field of Intersectionality Studies," 788.

9. Tomlinson, "To Tell the Truth and Not Get Trapped," 996 (emphasis in original). The critique of critiques circulate outside of the special issues I describe here as well. For example, Vivian May writes, "Nonetheless, it is important to consider how critique narratives may be framed within (and reinforce) accepted ways of thinking (about gender, feminism, politics, research, policy, and so on), even when these same paradigms (for example, 'pop-bead' approaches to identity or gender-universal notions of equity) are at the center of what intersectionality has consistently sought to challenge and transform throughout its various iterations and histories." See May, *Pursuing Intersectionality*, 95.

10. Sirma Bilge, "Intersectionality Undone: Saving Intersectionality from Feminist Intersectionality Studies," *Du Bois Review* 10.2 (2013): 411.

11. Bilge, "Intersectionality Undone," 411.

12. Tomlinson, "To Tell the Truth and Not Get Trapped," 993.

13. Bilge, "Intersectionality Undone," 411.

14. Devon Carbado, "Colorblind Intersectionality," *Signs* 38.4 (2013): 812.

15. Carbado, "Colorblind Intersectionality," 812.

16. Carbado, "Colorblind Intersectionality," 817.

17. Sumi Cho, "Post-intersectionality," *Du Bois Review* 10.2 (2013): 386.

18. Cho, "Post-intersectionality," 387.

19. Cho, "Post-intersectionality," 399.

20. See Sara Ahmed, *On Being Included: Racism and Diversity in Institutional Life* (Durham, NC: Duke University Press, 2012), 14.

21. Cho, Crenshaw, and McCall, "Toward a Field of Intersectionality Studies," 785, 787 (emphasis added).

22. Tomlinson, "To Tell the Truth and Not Get Trapped," 993 (emphasis added).

23. Carbado, "Colorblind Intersectionality," 812 (emphasis added). The abundant references to intersectionality's "travels" borrow from Edward Said's work on "travelling theory," which emphasized that as theory traverses borders—geographic, disciplinary, and political—it is altered and remade. See Edward Said, *The World, the Text, and the Critic* (Cambridge, MA: Harvard University Press, 1993).

24. Nivedita Menon, "Is Feminism about 'Women'? A Critical View on Intersectionality from India," *International Viewpoint*, May 18, 2015, http://www.internationalviewpoint.org/spip.php?page=imprimir_articulo&id_article=4038.

25. Menon, "Is Feminism about 'Women'?"

26. Vrushali Patil, "From Patriarchy to Intersectionality: A Transnational Feminist Assessment of How Far We've Really Come," *Signs* 38.4 (2013): 853.

27. Jennifer C. Nash, "Re-thinking Intersectionality," *Feminist Review* 89.1 (2008): 8.

28. Nikol G. Alexander-Floyd, "Disappearing Acts: Reclaiming Intersectionality in the Social Sciences in a Post–Black Feminist Era," *Feminist Formations* 24.1 (2012): 4.

29. Nancy Ehrenreich, "Subordination and Symbiosis: Mechanisms of Mutual Support between Subordinating Systems," *UMKC Law Review* 71.2 (2002): 290 (emphasis in original).

30. Ange-Marie Hancock, "Intersectionality as a Normative and Empirical Paradigm," *Politics and Gender* 2 (2007): 251.

31. Carbado, "Colorblind Intersectionality," 812.

32. Carbado, "Colorblind Intersectionality," 812.

33. Carbado, "Colorblind Intersectionality," 813.

34. Tomlinson, "To Tell the Truth and Not Get Trapped," 993.

35. Devon W. Carbado, Kimberlé Williams Crenshaw, Vickie M. Mays, and Barbara Tomlinson, "Intersectionality: Mapping the Movements of a Theory," *Du Bois Review* 10.2 (2013): 304.

36. Devon Carbado and Mitu Gulati, "The Intersectional Fifth Black Women," *Du Bois Review* 10.2 (2013): 531.

37. Kathy Davis, "Intersectionality as Buzzword: A Sociology of Science Perspective on What Makes a Feminist Theory Successful," *Feminist Theory* 9.1 (2008): 68.

38. Cho, Crenshaw, and McCall, "Toward a Field of Intersectionality Studies," 797.

39. Tomlinson, "To Tell the Truth and Not Get Trapped," 1012.

40. Jennifer Jihye Chun, George Lipsitz, and Young Shin, "Intersectionality as a Social Movement Strategy: Asian Immigrant Women Advocates," *Signs* 38.4 (2013): 923.

41. Carbado, "Colorblind Intersectionality," 817.

42. Carbado, "Colorblind Intersectionality," 814.

43. Hancock, *Intersectionality*, 23.

44. Hancock, *Intersectionality*, 23.

45. Hancock, *Intersectionality*, 26.

46. Hancock, *Intersectionality*, 27.

47. Audre Lorde, *Burst of Light* (New York: Ixia Press, 2017), 130. See also Jordan Kisner, "The Politics of Conspicuous Displays of Self Care," *New Yorker*, March 14, 2017, www.newyorker.com/culture/culture-desk/the-politics-of-selfcare.

48. Kai M. Green and Marquis Bey, "Self-Love," in *Gender: Love*, ed. Jennifer C. Nash (New York: Macmillan, 2016), 108.

49. Green and Bey, "Self-Love," 108.

50. Evette Dionne, "For Black Women, Self-Care Is a Radical Act," *Ravishly*, March 9, 2015, www.ravishly.com/2015/03/06/radical-act-self-care-black-women-feminism.

51. Christina Sharpe, *In the Wake: On Blackness and Being* (Durham, NC: Duke University Press, 2016), 22.

52. Sharpe, *In the Wake*, 5.

53. Sharpe, *In the Wake*, 10.

54. Patricia J. Williams, *The Alchemy of Race and Rights* (Cambridge, MA: Harvard University Press, 1992); see chapter 4, this volume.

55. May, *Pursuing Intersectionality*, xi.

THREE. surrender

1. NWSA Call for Papers, 1994 Annual Conference Box (University of Maryland).

2. Bethania Maria, qtd. in Marilyn Jacoby Boxer and Catherine R. Stimpson, *When Women Ask the Questions: Creating Women's Studies in America* (Baltimore: Johns Hopkins University Press, 2001), 115.

3. The call for papers in 1997 noted: "As feminist educators, we would transform this historical gateway of western expansion into a contemporary one of a crossroads bringing together all streams of our rich native and immigrant traditions. Themes of migration, immigration, exploration, and an inclusive 'gateway' become linked with the city in which we celebrate."

The call for papers in 1998 explained: "'Women's Rights Around the World: Past, Present, and Future' is the title of the embedded conference, cosponsored with Women's Rights National Historical Park in Seneca Falls, New York. Questions to be explored include: What theoretical perspectives inform rights language(s)? How do languages of rights translate in various cultures? Can an international community create a common language? What has been/is the role of international organizations like the United Nations in expanding, protecting, and defining women's rights? What are the costs of women's rights activism? How can/does an international community of women's rights activists support and encourage each other? To observe the 150th anniversary of the Seneca Falls convention, theorists, scholars, and activists are invited to explore the legacy, advance the agenda, and create the networks to sustain women's rights activism into the twenty-first century."

4. Garcia-Pinto Presidential Address, NWSA 2003 Conference, NWSA Archives (University of Maryland).

5. Colette Morrow Presidential Address, NWSA 2004 Conference, NWSA Archives (University of Maryland).

6. Nikol G. Alexander-Floyd, "Disappearing Acts: Reclaiming Intersectionality in the Social Sciences in a Post–Black Feminist Era," *Feminist Formations* 24.1 (2012), 1; Carolyn Pedwell, *Feminism, Culture, and Embodied Practice: The Rhetorics of Comparison* (New York: Routledge, 2010), 34; Jasbir Puar, "I Would Rather Be a Cyborg Than a Goddess," European Institute for Progressive Cultural Politics, http://eipcp.net/transversal/0811 /puar/en/print (accessed May 24, 2015); Roderick A. Ferguson, "Reading Intersectionality," *Trans-Scripts* 2 (2012): 91; Leslie McCall, "The Complexity of Intersectionality," *Signs* 30.3 (2005): 1776.

7. Robyn Wiegman, *Object Lessons* (Durham, NC: Duke University Press, 2012), 240.

8. Kevin Quashie, *The Sovereignty of Quiet: Beyond Resistance in Black Culture* (New Brunswick, NJ: Rutgers University Press, 2012), 27.

9. Quashie, *The Sovereignty of Quiet*, 28.

10. Audre Lorde, *Sister Outsider: Essays and Speeches* (Berkeley: Crossing Press, 1984), 113.

11. Much of this history is traced in an issue of *Women's Studies Quarterly* (Spring–Summer 1997). The NWSA archive also captures this shift. For example, a 1978 letter from Eleanor Smith to Elaine Reuben, the national coordinator of NWSA, notes, "Up to this point, it seems to me that women's studies has strictly been about and for white women. The networking, materials, resources have been kept strictly among white women. . . . One thing that might be done is some honesty [sic] dialogue where we do away with the games and false liberalism and deal with the gut level issues."

12. Barbara Smith, "Racism and Women's Studies," *Frontiers: A Journal of Women's Studies* 5.1 (1980): 48.

13. Smith, "Racism and Women's Studies," 48.

14. Becky W. Thompson, *A Promise and a Way of Life: White Antiracist Activism* (Minneapolis: University of Minnesota Press, 2001), 199.

15. Thompson details that "women of color" responded by "turning the ghettoizing structure around to one in which they could, as Chela Sandoval noted, collectively see differences among women of color as the 'source of a new kind of political movement.' This new group of women was able to exert political pressure on NWSA" (Thompson, *A Promise and a Way of Life*, 200).

16. See NWSA 2014 Program, www.nwsa.org/Files/2014/2014ProgramFINAL.pdf (accessed September 19, 2016).

17. Adrienne Rich, *Blood, Bread, and Poetry: Selected Prose* (New York: Norton, 1994), 80.

18. It is worth noting that this conception of labor of self as political was circulating within feminist theory in this moment. For more on this, see my analysis of Alice Walker's notion of womanism. Jennifer C. Nash, "Practicing Love: Black Feminism, Love-Politics, and Post-intersectionality," *Meridians* 11.2 (2011): 1–24.

19. 1985 Conference Box, NWSA Archives (University of Maryland).

20. 1990 Conference Box, NWSA Archives (University of Maryland).

21. The debate about Sales was covered in *The Black Explosion*, December 11, 1990, which, in an article entitled "Ruby Sales Fired from NWSA," reported that "Caryn Musil, NWSA's ED [executive director], said that Sales was fired because of poor job performance and not because of racism."

22. Open Letter to the Lesbian Caucus, 1990, NWSA Archives (University of Maryland).

23. NWSA Steering Committee, 1990, NWSA Archives (University of Maryland).

24. NWSA Women of Color Caucus, 1990, NWSA Archives (University of Maryland).

25. NWSA Women of Color Caucus, 1990, NWSA Archives (University of Maryland).

26. Ruby Sales, "A Letter from Ruby N. Sales," *Off Our Backs* 20.8 (August/September 1990): 25.

27. Sara Evans, *Tidal Wave: How Women Changed America at Century's End* (New York: Free Press, 2004), 222.

28. Maria C. Gonzalez, "This Bridge Called NWSA," *NWSA Journal* 14.1 (2002): 77.

29. Barbara Scott, qtd. in Evans, *Tidal Wave*, 223.

30. Robin Leidner, "Constituency, Accountability, and Deliberation Reshaping Democracy in the National Women's Studies Association," *NWSA Journal* 5.1 (Spring 1993): 5.

31. The NWSA continues to narrate it this way, describing 1990 as one where "women of color and their allies walked out to protest the Association's entrenched racism" and to celebrate the "healing presidencies" of Vivien Ng and Betty Harris (1994 and 1997). See NWSA's 2014 Program, particularly "A Brief (and Incomplete) History of the NWSA Women of Color Caucus," www.nwsa.org/Files/Program%20PDFs/2014ProgramFINAL .pdf (accessed March 14, 2017).

32. Jennifer Suchland, "Is Postsocialism Transnational?," *Signs* 36.4 (2011): 837.

33. There have been myriad critiques of the rhetoric of "women's rights are human rights." See, for example, Leela Fernandes, *Transnational Feminism in the United States: Knowledge, Ethics, Power* (New York: NYU Press, 2013), 33.

34. Jennifer Suchland, *Economies of Violence: Transnational Feminism, Postsocialism, and the Politics of Sex Trafficking* (Durham, NC: Duke University Press, 2015), 105.

35. Samantha Pinto's forthcoming work on the "transnational feminist anthology" has influenced my thinking.

36. Johnnella Butler, "Difficult Dialogues," *Women's Review of Books* 6.5 (1989): 16.

37. Butler, "Difficult Dialogues," 16.

38. I take up the ideas of difficulty and complexity in more detail in my earlier work. See Jennifer C. Nash, "On Difficulty: Intersectionality as Feminist Labor," *Scholar and Feminist* 8.3 (2010), http://sfonline.barnard.edu/polyphonic/nash_01.htm.

39. NWSA Call for Papers, 2009 Annual Meeting, NWSA Archives (University of Maryland).

40. NWSA Call for Papers, 2009 Annual Meeting, NWSA Archives (University of Maryland).

41. Angela Y. Davis, "Difficult Dialogues: NWSA Conference, Atlanta," in *The Meaning of Freedom: And Other Difficult Dialogues* (San Francisco: City Light Books, 2012), 191.

42. Shireen Roshanravan, "Staying Home While Studying Abroad: Anti-imperial Praxis for Globalizing Feminist Visions," *Journal of Feminist Scholarship* 2 (Spring 2012), www.jfsonline.org/issue2/articles/roshanravan/.

43. Karla F. C. Holloway, "'Cruel Enough to Stop the Blood': Global Feminisms and the US Body Politic, or 'They Done Taken My Blues and Gone,'" *Meridians* 7.1 (2006): 2; Sandra K. Soto, "Where in the Transnational World Are US Women of Color?," in *Women's Studies for the Future: Foundations, Interrogations, Politics*, ed. Elizabeth Lapovsky Kennedy and Agatha Beins (New Brunswick, NJ: Rutgers University Press, 2005), 114; Sharon Patricia Holland, *The Erotic Life of Racism* (Durham, NC: Duke University Press, 2012).

44. See Claire Hemmings, *Why Stories Matter: The Political Grammar of Feminist Theory* (Durham, NC: Duke University Press, 2011).

45. M. Jacqui Alexander and Chandra Talpade Mohanty, "Cartographies of Knowledge and Power: Transnational Feminism as Radical Praxis," in *Critical Transnational Feminist Praxis*, ed. Amanda Lock Swarr and Richa Nagar (Albany: SUNY Press, 2010), 35.

46. Fernandes, *Transnational Feminism in the United States*, 168.

47. Fernandes, *Transnational Feminism in the United States*, 168.

48. Anna Carastathis, *Intersectionality: Origins, Contestations, Horizons* (Lincoln: University of Nebraska Press, 2016), 199.

49. Fernandes, *Transnational Feminism in the United States*, 166.

50. Suchland, "Is Postsocialism Transnational?," 852.

51. Suchland, "Is Postsocialism Transnational?," 838.

52. Suchland, "Is Postsocialism Transnational?," 851.

53. Breny Mendoza, "Coloniality of Gender and Power: From Postcoloniality to Decoloniality," in *The Oxford Handbook of Feminist Theory*, ed. Lisa Jane Disch and M. E. Hawkesworth (New York: Oxford University Press, 2016), 107.

54. Mendoza, "Coloniality of Gender and Power," 119.

55. Mendoza, "Coloniality of Gender and Power," 112.

56. Mendoza, "Coloniality of Gender and Power," 114.

57. Wiegman, *Object Lessons*, 240.

58. Sara Ahmed, *The Promise of Happiness* (Durham, NC: Duke University Press, 2010), 67.

59. Inderpal Grewal and Caren Kaplan, *Scattered Hegemonies: Postmodernity and Transnational Feminist Practices* (Minneapolis: University of Minnesota Press, 1994), 17–18.

60. Heather Hillsburg, "Towards a Methodology of Intersectionality: An Axiom-Based Approach," *Atlantis* 36.1 (2013): 7.

61. Tiffany Lethabo King, "Post-identitarian and Post-intersectional Anxiety in the Neoliberal Corporate University," *Feminist Formations* 27.3 (2015): 118.

62. King, "Post-identitarian and Post-intersectional Anxiety," 118.

63. Jigna Desai, *Beyond Bollywood: The Cultural Politics of South Asian Diasporic Film* (New York: Routledge, 2004), 25.

64. Mendoza, "Coloniality of Gender and Power," 105.

65. Santa Cruz Feminist of Color Collective, "Building on 'the Edge of Each Other's Battles': A Feminist of Color Multidimensional Lens," *Hypatia* 29.1 (2014): 33.

66. Anna Carastathis, "Identity Categories as Potential Coalitions," *Signs* 38.4 (2013): 942.

67. Carastathis, *Intersectionality*, 232.

68. See Cathy Cohen, "Punks, Bulldaggers, and Welfare Queens: The Radical Potential of Queer Politics?," GLQ 3.4 (1997): 437–65.

69. Chandra Mohanty, *Feminism without Borders* (Durham, NC: Duke University Press, 2003), 117.

70. Mohanty, *Feminism without Borders*, 226.

71. Sylvanna M. Falcón, *Power Interrupted: Antiracist and Feminist Activism inside the United Nations* (Seattle: University of Washington Press, 2016), 21.

72. Sylvanna M. Falcón and Jennifer C. Nash, "Shifting Analytics and Linking Theories: A Conversation about the 'Meaning Making' of Intersectionality and Transnational Feminism," *Women's Studies International Forum* 50 (2015): 6.

73. June Jordan, "Report from the Bahamas," in *Feminist Theory Reader: Local and Global Perspectives*, ed. Carole R. McCann and Seung-kyung Kim (New York: Routledge, 2017), 305.

74. Jordan, "Report from the Bahamas," 310.

75. Shireen Roshanravan, "Motivating Coalition: Women of Color and Epistemic Disobedience," *Hypatia* 29.1 (2014): 41.

76. Gayle Wald, "Rosetta Tharpe and Feminist 'Un-forgetting,'" *Journal of Women's History* 21.4 (2009): 157–60.

FOUR. love in the time of death

1. Claudia Rankine, "The Condition of Black Life Is One of Mourning," *New York Times*, June 22, 2015.

2. On "governance feminism," see Janet Halley, *Split Decisions: How and Why to Take a Break from Feminism* (Princeton, NJ: Princeton University Press, 2006); on "carceral feminism," see Elizabeth Bernstein, "Militarized Humanitarianism Meets Carceral Feminism: The Politics of Sex, Rights, and Freedom in Contemporary Antitrafficking Campaigns," *Signs* 36.1 (2010): 45–72; on "at home with the law," see Jeannie Suk, *At Home with the Law: How the Domestic Violence Revolution Is Transforming Privacy* (New Haven, CT: Yale University Press, 2009).

3. I borrow the idea of "freedom dreaming" from Robin D. G. Kelley's *Freedom Dreams*.

4. Brittney Cooper, "Love No Limit: Towards a Black Feminist Future (in Theory)," *Black Scholar* 45.4 (2015): 7.

5. For more on black feminist critiques of theory and its exclusion of women of color, see Barbara Christian, "The Race for Theory," *Cultural Critique* 6 (1987): 51–63.

6. Cooper, "Love No Limit," 7.

7. Cooper, "Love No Limit," 8.

8. Joan Morgan, "Why We Get Off: Moving towards a Black Feminist Politics of Pleasure," *Black Scholar* 45.4 (2015): 38.

9. See Sirma Bilge, "Intersectionality Undone: Saving Intersectionality from Intersectionality Studies," *Du Bois Review* 10.2 (2013): 405–24.

10. Patricia Hill Collins and Sirma Bilge, *Intersectionality (Key Concepts)* (New York: Polity, 2016), 191.

11. See Robyn Wiegman, "Feminism's Apocalyptic Futures," *New Literary History* 31.4 (2000): 805–25.

12. Robyn Wiegman, *Object Lessons* (Durham, NC: Duke University Press, 2012), 250.

13. Tiffany Lethabo King, "Post-identitarian and Post-intersectional Anxiety in the Neoliberal Corporate University," *Feminist Formations* 27.3 (2015): 132.

14. King, "Post-identitarian and Post-intersectional Anxiety," 135.

15. See Alice Walker, *In Search of Our Mothers' Gardens* (New York: Harcourt, 1983); Combahee River Collective, "Combahee River Collective Statement," in *Home Girls: A Black Feminist Anthology*, ed. Barbara Smith (New York: Kitchen Table Press, 1983), 287.

16. Jennifer C. Nash, "Practicing Love: Black Feminism, Love-Politics, and Post-intersectionality," *Meridians* 11.2 (2011): 3.

17. June Jordan, *Some of Us Did Not Die* (New York: Basic Books, 2003), 270; June Jordan, "Nobody Mean More to Me Than You and the Future Life of Willie Jordan," in *Some of Us Did Not Die* (New York: Basic Books, 2003), 157–73.

18. Lauren Berlant and Michael Hardt, "No One Is Sovereign in Love: A Conversation between Lauren Berlant and Michael Hardt," *No More Potlucks*, http://nomorepotlucks .org/site/no-one-is-sovereign-in-love-a-conversation-between-lauren-berlant-and-michael -hardt/ (accessed March 31, 2017).

19. Christine Straehle, "Introduction: Vulnerability, Autonomy, and Self-Respect," in *Vulnerability, Autonomy, and Applied Ethics*, ed. Christine Straehle (New York: Routledge, 2017), 34.

20. Straehle, "Introduction," 34.

21. Judith Butler, *Frames of War: When Is Life Grievable?* (London: Verso, 2016), 34.

22. Butler, *Frames of War*, 34.

23. Judith Butler, *Undoing Gender* (New York: Routledge, 2004), 19.

24. June Jordan, "Poem about My Rights," in *Directed by Desire*, ed. Jan Heller Levi and Sara Miles (Port Townsend, WA: Copper Canyon, 2007), 309.

25. Jordan, "Poem about My Rights," 309.

26. See Patricia Hill Collins, "Learning from the Outsider Within: The Sociological Significance of Black Feminist Thought," *Social Problems* 33.6 (1986): s14–s32.

27. In other work, I describe this as "beautiful" black feminist writing. See Jennifer C. Nash, "Writing Black Beauty," *Signs* (forthcoming).

28. Avery Gordon develops the concept of "complex personhood." See Avery Gordon, *Ghostly Matters: Haunting and the Sociological Imagination* (Minneapolis: University of Minnesota Press, 1997).

29. See Joan Wallach Scott, "The Evidence of Experience," *Critical Inquiry* 17.4 (1991): 773–97.

30. Christina Sharpe, *In the Wake: On Blackness and Being* (Durham, NC: Duke University Press, 2016), 13.

31. See Lauren Berlant, *Cruel Optimism* (Durham, NC: Duke University Press, 2011).

32. See, for example, *Grutter v. Bollinger*, 539 U.S. 306 (2003).

33. See Derrick Bell, "*Brown v. Board of Education* and the Interest-Convergence Dilemma," *Harvard Law Review* 93 (1980): 518–33; see Mari Matsuda, "Looking to the Bottom: Critical Legal Studies and Reparations," *Harvard Civil Rights–Civil Liberties Law Review* 22 (1987): 323–99.

34. Patricia J. Williams, *The Alchemy of Race and Rights* (Cambridge, MA: Harvard University Press, 1992), 8.

35. Williams, *The Alchemy of Race and Rights*, 73.

36. Williams, *The Alchemy of Race and Rights*, 78.

37. Williams, *The Alchemy of Race and Rights*, 165.

38. Kimberlé Crenshaw, "Demarginalizing the Intersection of Race and Sex: A Black Feminist Critique of Antidiscrimination Doctrine, Feminist Theory, and Antiracist Politics," *University of Chicago Legal Forum* 1 (1989): 149.

39. Crenshaw, "Demarginalizing the Intersection of Race and Sex," 161.

CODA

1. Brittney Cooper, qtd. in Vanessa Williams, "Black Women—Hillary Clinton's Most Reliable Voting Bloc—Look beyond Defeat," *Washington Post*, November 12, 2016, www.washingtonpost.com/politics/black-women—hillary-clintons-most-reliable-voting-bloc—look-beyond-defeat/2016/11/12/86d9182a-a845–11e6-ba59-a7d93165c6d4_story.html?utm_term=.550a5f4618ce.

2. Brittney Cooper, "Donald Trump's Triumph Is a Victory for White Supremacy," *Cosmopolitan*, November 9, 2016, www.cosmopolitan.com/politics/a8262379/donald-trump-white-supremacy/.

3. Angela Peoples, "Don't Just Thank Black Women. Follow Us," *New York Times*, December 16, 2017, www.nytimes.com/2017/12/16/opinion/sunday/black-women-leadership.html?_r=0.

4. Ashley Nkadi, "Y'All Don't Deserve Black Women," *The Root*, December 13, 2017, www.theroot.com/yall-dont-deserve-black-women-1821255162.

5. Peoples, "Don't Just Thank Black Women."

6. This was captured by a *McSweeney's* parody. See Catie Hogan, "I Googled 'Intersectionality' So Now I'm Totally Woke," *McSweeney's*, March 7, 2017, www.mcsweeneys.net/articles/i-googled-intersectionality-so-now-im-totally-woke.

7. See Cheryl Harris, "Whiteness as Property," *Harvard Law Review* 106.8 (1993): 1707–91.

Ahmed, Sara. *On Being Included: Racism and Diversity in Institutional Life*. Durham, NC: Duke University Press, 2012.

Ahmed, Sara. *The Promise of Happiness*. Durham, NC: Duke University Press, 2010.

Ahmed, Sara. "Women of Colour as Diversity Workers." *feministkilljoys*, November 26, 2015. https://feministkilljoys.com/2015/11/26/women-of-colour-as-diversity-workers/.

Alexander, M. Jacqui, and Chandra Talpade Mohanty. "Cartographies of Knowledge and Power: Transnational Feminism as Radical Praxis." In *Critical Transnational Feminist Praxis*, edited by Amanda Lock Swarr and Richa Nagar, 23–45. Albany: SUNY Press, 2010.

Alexander, M. Jacqui, and Chandra Talpade Mohanty, eds. *Feminist Genealogies, Colonial Legacies, Democratic Futures*. New York: Routledge, 1996.

Alexander-Floyd, Nikol G. "Disappearing Acts: Reclaiming Intersectionality in the Social Sciences in a Post–Black Feminist Era." *Feminist Formations* 24.1 (2012): 1–25.

Allen, Jafari S. "Black/Queer/Diaspora at the Current Conjuncture." GLQ 18.2–3 (2012): 211–48.

Baca Zinn, Maxine. "Patricia Hill Collins: Past and Future Innovations." *Gender and Society* 26 (2012): 28–32.

Bartlett, Tom. "When a Theory Goes Viral." *Chronicle of Higher Education*, May 21, 2017.

Beal, Frances. "Double Jeopardy: To Be Black and Female." In *Words of Fire: An Anthology of African-American Feminist Thought*, edited by Beverly Guy-Sheftall, 146–56. New York: New Press, 1995.

Belkhir, Jean Ait. "The 'Johnny's Story': Founder of the Race, Gender, and Class Journal." In *The Intersectional Approach: Transforming the Academy through Race, Class, and Gender*, edited by Michele Tracy Berger and Kathleen Guidroz, 300–308. Chapel Hill: University of North Carolina Press, 2009.

Bell, Derrick. "*Brown v. Board of Education* and the Interest-Convergence Dilemma." *Harvard Law Review* 93 (1980): 518–33.

Berlant, Lauren. *Cruel Optimism.* Durham, NC: Duke University Press, 2011.

Berlant, Lauren, and Michael Hardt. "No One Is Sovereign in Love." *No More Pot Lucks.* http://nomorepotlucks.org/site/no-one-is-sovereign-in-love-a-conversation-between -lauren-berlant-and-michael-hardt/. Accessed March 31, 2017.

Bernstein, Elizabeth. "Militarized Humanitarianism Meets Carceral Feminism: The Politics of Sex, Rights, and Freedom in Contemporary Antitrafficking Campaigns." *Signs* 36.1 (2010): 45–72.

Bilge, Sirma. "Intersectionality Undone: Saving Intersectionality from Intersectionality Studies." *Du Bois Review* 10.2 (2013): 405–24.

Bilge, Sirma. "Whitening Intersectionality: Evanescence of Race in Intersectionality Scholarship." https://www.academia.edu/11805835/Whitening_Intersectionality._Evanescence _of_Race_in_Intersectionality_Scholarship. Accessed March 1, 2017.

Bliss, James. "Black Feminism Out of Place." *Signs* 41.4 (2016): 727–49.

Boxer, Marilyn Jacoby, and Catherine R. Stimpson. *When Women Ask the Questions: Creating Women's Studies in America.* Baltimore: Johns Hopkins University Press, 2001.

Brandzel, Amy L. *Against Citizenship: The Violence of the Normative.* Urbana-Champaign: University of Illinois Press, 2016.

Brown, Wendy. *Edgework: Critical Essays on Knowledge and Politics.* Princeton, NJ: Princeton University Press, 2005.

Browne, Simone. *Dark Matters: On the Surveillance of Blackness.* Durham, NC: Duke University Press, 2015.

Butler, Johnnella. "Difficult Dialogues." *Women's Review of Books* 6.5 (1989): 16.

Butler, Judith. *Frames of War: When Is Life Grievable?* London: Verso, 2016.

Butler, Judith. *Undoing Gender.* New York: Routledge, 2004.

Caldwell, Paulette M. "A Hair Piece: Perspectives on the Intersection of Race and Gender." *Duke Law Journal* 40.2 (1991): 365–96.

Carastathis, Anna. "Basements and Intersections." *Hypatia* 28.4 (2013): 698–715.

Carastathis, Anna. "The Concept of Intersectionality in Feminist Theory." *Philosophy Compass* 9.5 (2014): 304–14.

Carastathis, Anna. "Identity Categories as Potential Coalitions." *Signs* 38.4 (2013): 941–65.

Carastathis, Anna. *Intersectionality: Origins, Contestations, Horizons.* Lincoln: University of Nebraska Press, 2016.

Carbado, Devon W. "Colorblind Intersectionality." *Signs* 38.4 (2013): 811–45.

Carbado, Devon W. "Race to the Bottom." UCLA *Law Review* 49 (2001): 1283–313.

Carbado, Devon W., Kimberlé Williams Crenshaw, Vickie M. Mays, and Barbara Tomlinson. "Intersectionality: Mapping the Movements of a Theory." *Du Bois Review* 10.2 (2013): 303–12.

Carbado, Devon W., and Mitu Gulati. "The Intersectional Fifth Black Women." *Du Bois Review* 10.2 (2013): 527–40.

Carbin, Maria, and Sara Edenheim. "The Intersectional Turn: A Dream of a Common Language?" *European Journal of Women's Studies* 20.3 (2013): 233–48.

Chang, Robert S., and Jerome McCristal Culp Jr. "After Intersectionality." UMKC *Law Review* 71.2 (2002): 485–92.

Cho, Sumi. "Post-intersectionality." *Du Bois Review* 10.2 (2013): 385–404.

Cho, Sumi, Kimberlé Williams Crenshaw, and Leslie McCall. "Toward a Field of Intersectionality Studies: Theory, Applications, and Praxis." *Signs* 38.4 (2013): 785–810.

Choo, Hae Yeon, and Myra Marx Ferree. "Practicing Intersectionality in Sociological
Research: A Critical Analysis of Inclusions, Interactions, and Institutions in the Study
of Inequalities." *Sociological Theory* 28.2 (2010): 129–49.

Christian, Barbara. "Diminishing Returns: Can Black Feminism(s) Survive the Academy?"
In *New Black Feminist Criticism, 1985–2000*, edited by Gloria Bowles, M. Giulia Fabi, and
Arlene Keizer, 204–15. Urbana-Champaign: University of Illinois Press, 2007.

Christian, Barbara. "The Race for Theory." *Cultural Critique* 6 (1987): 51–63.

Chun, Jennifer Jihye, George Lipsitz, and Young Shin. "Intersectionality as a Social Movement Strategy: Asian Immigrant Women Advocates." *Signs* 38.4 (2013): 917–40.

Cohen, Cathy J. 1997. "Punks, Bulldaggers, and Welfare Queens: The Radical Potential of
Queer Politics?" GLQ 3.4 (1997): 437–65.

Collins, Patricia Hill. *Black Feminist Thought*. 2nd ed. New York: Routledge, 2000.

Collins, Patricia Hill. "Learning from the Outsider Within: The Sociological Significance
of Black Feminist Thought." *Social Problems* 33.6 (1986): s14–s32.

Collins, Patricia Hill, and Sirma Bilge. *Intersectionality (Key Concepts)*. New York: Polity, 2016.

Combahee River Collective. "A Black Feminist Statement." In *All the Women Are White, All
the Men Are Men, But Some of Us Are Brave: Black Women's Studies*, edited by Gloria T.
Hull, Patricia Bell Scott, and Barbara Smith, 13–22. New York: Feminist Press, 1982.

Combahee River Collective. "Combahee River Collective Statement." In *Home Girls: A
Black Feminist Anthology*, edited by Barbara Smith, 272–82. New York: Kitchen Table
Press, 1983.

Cooper, Brittney. *Beyond Respectability: The Intellectual Thought of Race Women*. Urbana-
Champaign: University of Illinois Press, 2017.

Cooper, Brittney. "Intersectionality." In *The Oxford Handbook of Feminist Theory*, edited
by Lisa Jane Disch and M. E. Hawkesworth, 385–406. New York: Oxford University
Press, 2016.

Cooper, Brittney. "Love No Limit: Towards a Black Feminist Future (in Theory)." *Black
Scholar* 45.4 (2015): 7–21.

Crenshaw, Kimberlé. "Demarginalizing the Intersection of Race and Sex: A Black Feminist Critique of Antidiscrimination Doctrine, Feminist Theory and Antiracist Politics."
University of Chicago Legal Forum 140 (1989): 139–68.

Crenshaw, Kimberlé. "Mapping the Margins: Intersectionality, Identity Politics, and Violence against Women of Color." *Stanford Law Review* 43.6 (1991): 1241–99.

Crunk Feminist Collective. "The R-Word: Why 'Rigorous' Is the New Black." *Crunk Feminist Collective*, November 17, 2010. https://crunkfeministcollective.wordpress.com/2010
/11/17/the-r-word-why-rigorous-is-the-new-black/.

Cvetkovich, Ann. *Depression: A Public Feeling*. Durham, NC: Duke University Press, 2012.

Cvetkovich, Ann. "Public Feelings." *South Atlantic Quarterly* 106.3 (2007): 459–68.

Davis, Angela Y. "Difficult Dialogues: NWSA Conference, Atlanta." In *The Meaning of
Freedom: And Other Difficult Dialogues*. San Francisco: City Light Books, 2012.

Davis, Kathy. "Intersectionality as Buzzword: A Sociology of Science Perspective on What
Makes a Feminist Theory Successful." *Feminist Theory* 9.1 (2008): 67–85.

Desai, Jigna. *Beyond Bollywood: The Cultural Politics of South Asian Diasporic Film*. New York: Routledge, 2004.

Dionne, Evette. "For Black Women, Self-Care Is a Radical Act." *Ravishly*, March 9, 2015. www.ravishly.com/2015/03/06/radical-act-self-care-black-women-feminism.

Douglass, Patrice D. "Black Feminist Theory for the Dead and Dying." *Theory & Event* 21.1 (2018): 106–23.

duCille, Ann. "The Occult of True Black Womanhood: Critical Demeanor and Black Feminist Studies." In *Female Subjects in Black and White: Race, Psychoanalysis, Feminism*, edited by Elizabeth Abel, Barbara Christian, and Helen Moglen, 21–56. Berkeley: University of California Press, 1997.

duCille, Ann. *Skin Trade*. Cambridge, MA: Harvard University Press, 1996.

Duggan, Lisa, and Nan D. Hunter. *Sex Wars: Sexual Dissent and Political Culture*. New York: Routledge, 1996.

Ehrenreich, Nancy. "Subordination and Symbiosis: Mechanisms of Mutual Support between Subordinating Systems." *UMKC Law Review* 71.2 (2002): 251–324.

Evans, Sara. *Tidal Wave: How Women Changed America at Century's End*. New York: Free Press, 2004.

Falcón, Sylvanna M. *Power Interrupted: Antiracist and Feminist Activism inside the United Nations*. Seattle: University of Washington Press, 2016.

Falcón, Sylvanna M., and Jennifer C. Nash. "Shifting Analytics and Linking Theories: A Conversation about the 'Meaning Making' of Intersectionality and Transnational Feminism." *Women's Studies International Forum* 50 (2015): 1–10.

Ferguson, Roderick. *Aberrations in Black: Toward a Queer of Color Critique*. Minneapolis: University of Minnesota Press, 2003.

Ferguson, Roderick. "Administering Sexuality; or, the Will to Institutionality." *Radical History Review* 100 (2008): 158–69.

Ferguson, Roderick. "Reading Intersectionality." *Trans-Scripts* 2 (2012): 91–99.

Ferguson, Roderick, and Grace Hong, eds. *Strange Affinities: The Gender and Sexual Politics of Comparative Racialization*. Durham, NC: Duke University Press, 2011.

Fernandes, Leela. *Transnational Feminism in the United States: Knowledge, Ethics, Power*. New York: NYU Press, 2013.

Gonzalez, Maria C. "This Bridge Called NWSA." *NWSA Journal* 14.1 (2002): 77.

Gordon, Avery. *Ghostly Matters: Haunting and the Sociological Imagination*. Minneapolis: University of Minnesota Press, 1997.

Green, Kai M., and Marquis Bey. "Self-Love." In *Gender: Love*, edited by Jennifer C. Nash, 107–20. New York: Macmillan, 2016.

Grewal, Inderpal, and Caren Kaplan. *Scattered Hegemonies: Postmodernity and Transnational Feminist Practices*. Minneapolis: University of Minnesota Press, 1994.

Grzanka, Patrick, ed. *Intersectionality: A Foundations and Frontiers Reader*. Boulder, CO: Westview Press, 2014.

Gutiérrez y Muhs, Gabriella, Yolanda Flores Niemann, Carmen G. González, and Angela P. Harris, eds. *Presumed Incompetent: The Intersections of Race and Class for Women in Academia*. Boulder: University Press of Colorado, 2012.

Halley, Janet. *Split Decisions: How and Why to Take a Break from Feminism*. Princeton, NJ: Princeton University Press, 2006.

Hancock, Ange-Marie. "Empirical Intersectionality: A Tale of Two Approaches." *UC Irvine Law Review* 3.2 (2010): 259–96.

Hancock, Ange-Marie. *Intersectionality: An Intellectual History*. New York: Oxford University Press, 2016.

Hancock, Ange-Marie. "Intersectionality as a Normative and Empirical Paradigm." *Politics and Gender* 3.2 (2007): 248–54.

Hancock, Ange-Marie. *Solidarity Politics for Millennials: A Guide to Ending the Oppression Olympics*. New York: Palgrave, 2011.

Hancock, Ange-Marie. "When Multiplication Doesn't Equal Quick Addition: Examining Intersectionality as a Research Paradigm." *Perspectives on Politics* 5.1 (2007): 63–79.

Harris, Cheryl. "Whiteness as Property." *Harvard Law Review* 106.8 (1993): 1707–91.

Heller, Nathan. "The Big Uneasy." *New Yorker*, May 30, 2016.

Hemmings, Claire. *Why Stories Matter*. Durham, NC: Duke University Press, 2010.

Higginbotham, Evelyn Brooks. "African American Women's History and the Metalanguage of Race." *Signs* 17.2 (1992): 251–74.

Hillsburg, Heather. "Towards a Methodology of Intersectionality: An Axiom-Based Approach." *Atlantis* 36.1 (2013): 3–11.

Holland, Sharon Patricia. *The Erotic Life of Racism*. Durham, NC: Duke University Press, 2013.

Holloway, Karla F. C. "'Cruel Enough to Stop the Blood': Global Feminisms and the US Body Politic, or 'They Done Taken My Blues and Gone.'" *Meridians* 7.1 (2006): 1–18.

Hong, Grace. "'The Future of Our Worlds': Black Feminism and the Politics of Knowledge in the University under Globalization." *Meridians* 8.2 (2008): 95–115.

Huffer, Lynn. *Are the Lips a Grave?* New York: Columbia University Press, 2013.

Hutchinson, Darren Lenard. "Identity Crisis: Intersectionality, Multidimensionality, and the Development of an Adequate Theory of Subordination." *Michigan Journal of Race and Law* 6 (2000): 285–318.

Hutchinson, Darren Lenard. "Ignoring the Sexualization of Race: Heteronormativity, Critical Race Theory, and Anti-racist Politics." *Buffalo Law Review* 47.1 (1999): 1–116.

Hutchinson, Darren Lenard. "New Complexity Theories: From Theoretical Innovation to Doctrinal Reform." *UMKC Law Review* 71.2 (2002): 431–46.

Hutchinson, Darren Lenard. "Out Yet Unseen: A Racial Critique of Gay and Lesbian Legal Theory and Political Discourse." *Connecticut Law Review* 29.2 (1997): 561–645.

Jordan, June. "Poem about My Rights." In *Directed by Desire*, edited by Jan Heller Levi and Sara Miles, 309. Port Townsend, WA: Copper Canyon, 2007.

Jordan, June. "Report from the Bahamas." In *Feminist Theory Reader: Local and Global Perspectives*, edited by Carole R. McCann and Seung-kyung Kim, 304–12. New York: Routledge, 2017.

Jordan, June. *Some of Us Did Not Die*. New York: Basic Books, 2003.

Kelley, Robin D. G. *Freedom Dreams: The Black Radical Imagination*. Boston: Beacon Press, 2003.

King, Deborah K. "Multiple Jeopardy, Multiple Consciousness: The Context of a Black Feminist Ideology." *Signs* 14.1 (1988): 42–72.

King, Tiffany Lethabo. "Post-identitarian and Post-intersectional Anxiety in the Neoliberal Corporate University." *Feminist Formations* 27.3 (2015): 114–38.

Kwan, Peter. "Complicity and Complexity: Cosynthesis and Praxis." *DePaul Law Review* 49 (1999): 673–90.

Kwan, Peter. "Intersections of Race, Ethnicity, Class, Gender and Sexual Orientation: Jeffrey Dahmer and the Cosynthesis of Categories." *Hastings Law Journal* 48 (1997): 1257–92.

Lee, Rachel. "Notes from the (Non)Field: Teaching and Theorizing Women of Color." *Meridians* 1.1 (2000): 85–109.

Leidner, Robin. "Constituency, Accountability, and Deliberation Reshaping Democracy in the National Women's Studies Association." *NWSA Journal* 5.1 (1993): 4–27.

Lorde, Audre. *Burst of Light*. New York: Ixia Press, 2017.

Lorde, Audre. *Sister Outsider: Essays and Speeches*. Berkeley: Crossing Press, 1984.

Luft, Rachel E., and Jane Ward. "Toward an Intersectionality Just Out of Reach: Confronting Challenges to Intersectional Practice." In *Perceiving Gender Locally, Globally, and Intersectionally*, edited by Vasilikie Demos and Marcia Texler Segal, 9–37. Bingley, UK: Emerald, 2009.

Matsuda, Mari. "Looking to the Bottom: Critical Legal Studies and Reparations." *Harvard Civil Rights–Civil Liberties Law Review* 22 (1987): 323–99.

May, Vivian. "Intellectual Genealogies, Intersectionality, and Anna Julia Cooper." In *Feminist Solidarity at the Crossroads: Intersectional Women's Studies for Transracial Alliance*, edited by Kim Marie Vaz and Gary L. Lemons, 59–71. New York: Routledge, 2012.

May, Vivian. "Intersectionality." In *Rethinking Women's and Gender Studies*, edited by Catherine M. Orr and Ann Braithwaite, 155–72. New York: Routledge, 2011.

May, Vivian. *Pursuing Intersectionality, Unsettling Dominant Imaginaries*. New York: Routledge, 2015.

McCall, Leslie. "The Complexity of Intersectionality." *Signs* 30.3 (2005): 1771–800.

McKittrick, Katherine, ed. *Sylvia Wynter: On Being Human as Praxis*. Durham, NC: Duke University Press, 2015.

McRuer, Robert. *Crip Theory: Cultural Signs of Queerness and Disability*. New York: NYU Press, 2006.

Mendoza, Breny. "Coloniality of Gender and Power: From Postcoloniality to Decoloniality." In *The Oxford Handbook of Feminist Theory*, edited by Lisa Jane Disch and M. E. Hawkesworth, 100–121. New York: Oxford University Press, 2016.

Menon, Nivedita. "Is Feminism about 'Women'? A Critical View on Intersectionality from India." *International Viewpoint*, May 18, 2015. http://www.internationalviewpoint.org/spip.php?page=imprimir_articulo&id_article=4038.

Mohanty, Chandra. *Feminism without Borders: Decolonizing Theory, Practicing Solidarity*. Durham, NC: Duke University Press, 2003.

Morgan, Joan. "Why We Get Off: Moving towards a Black Feminist Politics of Pleasure." *Black Scholar* 45.4 (2015): 36–46.

Musser, Amber Jamilla. *Sensational Flesh*. New York: NYU Press, 2014.

Musser, Amber Jamilla. "Specimen Days: Diversity, Labor, and the University." *Feminist Formations* 27.3 (2015): 1–20.

Nash, Jennifer C. "Feminist Originalism: Intersectionality and the Politics of Reading." *Feminist Theory* 17.1 (2016): 3–20.

Nash, Jennifer C. "'Home Truths' on Intersectionality." *Yale Journal of Law and Feminism* 23.2 (2011): 445–70.

Nash, Jennifer C. "Institutionalizing the Margins." *Social Text* 32.1 (2014): 45–65.

Nash, Jennifer C. "Intersectionality and Its Discontents." *American Quarterly* 69.1 (2017): 117–29.

Nash, Jennifer C. "On Difficulty: Intersectionality as Feminist Labor." *Scholar and Feminist* 8.3 (2010). http://sfonline.barnard.edu/polyphonic/nash_01.htm—text5.

Nash, Jennifer C. "Practicing Love: Black Feminism, Love-Politics, and Post-intersectionality." *Meridians* 11.2 (2011): 1–24.

Nash, Jennifer C. "Re-thinking Intersectionality." *Feminist Review* 89.1 (2008): 1–15.

Nash, Jennifer C. "Unwidowing: Rachel Jeantel, Black Death, and the 'Problem' of Black Intimacy." *Signs* 41.4 (2016): 751–74.

Nash, Jennifer C. "Writing Black Beauty." *Signs* (forthcoming).

Ngai, Sianne. *Ugly Feelings*. Cambridge, MA: Harvard University Press, 2005.

Patil, Vrushali. "From Patriarchy to Intersectionality: A Transnational Feminist Assessment of How Far We've Really Come." *Signs* 38.4 (2013): 847–67.

Pedwell, Carolyn. *Feminism, Culture, and Embodied Practice: The Rhetorics of Comparison*. New York: Routledge, 2010.

Peipmeier, Alison. "Besiegement." In *Rethinking Women's and Gender Studies*, edited by Catherine M. Orr and Ann Braithwaite, 119–34. New York: Routledge, 2011.

Pinto, Samantha. "Black Feminist Literacies: Ungendering, Flesh, and Post-Spillers Epistemologies of Embodied and Emotional Justice." *Journal of Black Sexuality and Relationships* 4.1 (2017): 40.

Puar, Jasbir K. "'I Would Rather Be a Cyborg Than a Goddess': Intersectionality, Assemblage, and Affective Politics." European Institute for Progressive Cultural Politics. http://eipcp.net/transversal/0811/puar/en. Accessed May 3, 2016.

Puar, Jasbir K. "Queer Times, Queer Assemblages." *Social Text* 23.3–4 (2005): 121–39.

Puar, Jasbir K. *Terrorist Assemblages: Homonationalism in Queer Times*. Durham, NC: Duke University Press, 2007.

Quashie, Kevin. *The Sovereignty of Quiet: Beyond Resistance in Black Culture*. New Brunswick, NJ: Rutgers University Press, 2012.

Rankine, Claudia. "The Condition of Black Life Is One of Mourning." *New York Times*, June 22, 2015.

Rich, Adrienne. *Blood, Bread, and Poetry: Selected Prose*. New York: Norton, 1994.

Roshanravan, Shireen. "Motivating Coalition: Women of Color and Epistemic Disobedience." *Hypatia* 29.1 (2014): 41–58.

Roshanravan, Shireen. "Staying Home While Studying Abroad: Anti-imperial Praxis for Globalizing Feminist Visions." *Journal of Feminist Scholarship* 2 (Spring 2012). http://www.jfsonline.org/issue2/articles/roshanravan/.

Sales, Ruby. "A Letter from Ruby N. Sales." *Off Our Backs* 20.8 (August/September 1990): 25.

Scott, Joan Wallach. "The Evidence of Experience." *Critical Inquiry* 17.4 (1991): 773–97.

Scott, Joan Wallach. *Women's Studies on the Edge*. Durham, NC: Duke University Press, 2008.

Shange, Ntozake. *For Colored Girls Who Have Considered Suicide / When the Rainbow Is Enuf*. New York: Scribner, 1977.

Sharpe, Christina. *In the Wake: On Blackness and Being*. Durham, NC: Duke University Press, 2016.

Shohat, Ella, ed. *Talking Visions: Multicultural Feminism in a Transnational Age*. Cambridge, MA: MIT Press, 2001.

Smith, Barbara. "Racism and Women's Studies." *Frontiers: A Journal of Women's Studies* (1980): 48–49.

Soto, Sandra K. "Where in the Transnational World Are US Women of Color?" In *Women's Studies for the Future: Foundations, Interrogations, Politics*, edited by Elizabeth Lapovsky Kennedy and Agatha Beins, 111–24. New Brunswick, NJ: Rutgers University Press, 2005.

Spillers, Hortense. *Black, White, and in Color: Essays on American Literature and Culture*. Chicago: University of Chicago Press, 2003.

Stallings, LaMonda Horton. *Funk the Erotic: Transaesthetics and Black Sexual Culture*. Urbana-Champaign: University of Illinois Press, 2016.

Straehle, Christine, ed. *Vulnerability, Autonomy, and Applied Ethics*. New York: Routledge, 2017.

Subramaniam, Banu. *Ghost Stories for Darwin: The Science of Variation and the Politics of Diversity*. Urbana-Champaign: University of Illinois Press, 2014.

Suchland, Jennifer. *Economies of Violence: Transnational Feminism, Postsocialism, and the Politics of Sex Trafficking*. Durham, NC: Duke University Press, 2015.

Suchland, Jennifer. "Is Postsocialism Transnational?" *Signs* 36.4 (2011): 837–62.

Suk, Jeannie. *At Home with the Law: How the Domestic Violence Revolution Is Transforming Privacy*. New Haven, CT: Yale University Press, 2009.

Sullivan, Andrew. "Is Intersectionality a Religion?" *New York Magazine*, March 10, 2017.

Thompson, Becky W. *A Promise and a Way of Life: White Antiracist Activism*. Minneapolis: University of Minnesota Press, 2001.

Tomlinson, Barbara. "To Tell the Truth and Not Get Trapped: Desire, Distance, and Intersectionality at the Scene of Argument." *Signs* 38.4 (2013): 993–1017.

Wald, Gayle. "Rosetta Tharpe and Feminist 'Un-forgetting.'" *Journal of Women's History* 21.4 (2009): 157–60.

Walker, Alice. *In Search of Our Mothers' Gardens*. New York: Harcourt, 1983.

Warren, Calvin. "Onticide: Afro-pessimism, Gay Nigger #1, and Surplus Violence." GLQ 23.3 (2017): 391–418.

White, Deborah Gray, ed. *Telling Histories: Black Women Historians in the Ivory Tower*. Chapel Hill: University of North Carolina Press, 2008.

Wiegman, Robyn. "Feminism's Apocalyptic Futures." *New Literary History* 31.4 (2000): 805–25.

Wiegman, Robyn. *Object Lessons*. Durham, NC: Duke University Press, 2012.

Wiegman, Robyn, ed. *Women's Studies on Its Own*. Durham, NC: Duke University Press, 2002.

Williams, Patricia J. *The Alchemy of Race and Rights*. Cambridge, MA: Harvard University Press, 1992.

academic feminism: American studies and,
145n5; disciplinary, 64; intersectionality
and, 2, 12, 16, 82–85, 103–4, 133, 135–36,
138, 139n7; orthodoxy of, 12; postcolonial,
100; transnationalism in, 91, 99. *See also*
black feminism

academy: diversity/inclusion complex in,
22–26, 94; invisible labor of black women
in, 3, 5; racism/sexism of, 66; scrutiny on
black feminism, 29; violence toward black
feminism, 3–5, 19, 27, 63–64, 123, 138

affect theory, 29–30

affirmative action, 23–24, 122. *See also* diver-
sity/inclusion complex

afropessimism, 20, 21, 111, 129

Ahmed, Sara, 24, 25, 66–67, 101

Alarcon, Norma, 54–55

Alchemy of Race and Rights, The (Williams),
30, 123

Alexander, M. Jacqui, 97

Alexander-Floyd, Nikol, 38, 43, 70, 82

Allen, Jafari, 54

American Booksellers v. Hudnut, 36–37

American studies, 145n5

American Studies Association (ASA), 35–36

Anzaldúa, Gloria, 54–55, 100, 108

assemblage theory, 50–52, 54, 99–100

Association of American Colleges and Universities, 22–23

Bambara, Toni Cade, 42

Barnard College, 36, 37, 89

Beal, Frances, 6–7, 8–9, 41, 42, 72

Belkhir, Jean Ait, 40

Berlant, Lauren, 58, 116

besiegement, 56–57, 58

Bey, Marquis, 78–79

Bilge, Sirma, 6, 38, 39–40, 44–45, 64, 65, 113

black feminism: affective work of, 30, 32;
agency in, 62; aspects of, 5; besiegement and,
56–57, 58; care in, 61, 76–80, 113; critique
of intersectionality and, 46–58; death of,
112–13, 137; defensiveness in, 3, 26–28, 32,
42, 56, 73, 130–31, 136–38; as disciplinarian,
34–35; as discipline, 13–16; as felt experience, 3, 28–32; fetishization of, 19–20; on
inclusion, 15; intersectionality in, 2–3, 6–11,
13, 35–36, 40–41, 43–45, 84, 110, 112–13,
128–29; juridical tradition of, 108, 115; on
multiple jeopardy, 8–9, 72; practice of love
in, 113–21, 126, 129–30; on protection of
intersectionality, 38–39; queer theory and,
55; state violence and, 51; surrender of intersectionality by, 83–84, 104, 109–10, 114; university violence toward, 3–5, 19, 27, 63–64,
138; vulnerability in, 114, 116; witnessing in,
114, 116; women of color feminism and, 84;
women's studies and, 13–16, 28, 34, 88

Black Feminist Thought (Collins), 11

Black Lives Matter movement, 78, 79–80, 111
blackness: death and, 129; as parochial, 95–96; queerness and, 21
black queer studies, 22
black studies: on death, 20–21, 22, 130; intersectionality in, 18–22
black women: academic interest in, 29, 31; corporeal presences of, 1–2; discrimination of, 8–9, 72–73, 102; hairstyles of, 31; invisible intellectual labor of, 3, 5, 19; political consciousness of, 133–34, 135; scholarly work of, 105; self-love of, 79; as synonymous with intersectionality, 53, 71, 92, 98, 104, 138; violence against, 8–9, 10, 19, 73, 102, 111, 127, 138. *See also* women of color
Brandzel, Amy L., 51
Brawley, Tawana, 123
Brown, Simone, 111
Brown, Wendy, 12, 14–15
Brown v. Board of Education, 122
Butler, Johnnella, 92
Butler, Judith, 117

Caldwell, Paulette, 31
Camp, Stephanie, 19
Cancer Journals (Lorde), 30
Carastathis, Anna, 6, 10, 40, 44, 60, 97–98, 106
Carbado, Devon, 40, 41, 49, 65, 67, 71–73, 75
Carbin, Maria, 46
care: in black feminist practice, 61, 76–80, 113; death and, 79; ethic of, 69, 76–77, 79–80; in intersectionality, 80; in intersectionality wars, 59; politics of, 76–80; stewardship and, 77–78
Castile, Philando, 111
Chang, Robert, 99–100
Cho, Sumi, 63, 66, 67, 74
Christian, Barbara, 19, 20, 27
Chrystos, 54–55
Chun, Jennifer Jihye, 74
civil rights, expansion of, 124–26
Clinton, Hillary Rodham, 133, 134
coalition, framework of, 105–6
Cohen, Cathy, 106
Collins, Patricia Hill, 6–7, 10–11, 41–42, 112, 113
color blindness, 75, 123
Combahee River Collective, 6–8, 41, 42, 77, 108, 115

common language, use of term, 81–82
Cooper, Anna Julia, 7, 41, 42
Cooper, Brittney, 6, 7, 9, 16, 28–29, 38, 53, 112, 133–34, 147n34
corporate university, use of term, 141n36
correct citationality, 63–64
Crenshaw, Kimberlé, 6–7, 9–11, 37, 41, 55, 60, 63, 67, 69, 73, 74, 102, 108, 127–28
critical race theory, 121–23, 129
Crunk Feminist Collective, 38
Culp, Jerome, 99–100
Curb, Rosemary, 89
Cvetkovich, Ann, 30–31, 129

Davis, Angela, 93
Davis, Jordan, 111
Davis, Kathy, 11, 66–67
death: black, 111–12; of black feminism, 112–13, 137; black studies on, 20–21, 22, 130; care and, 79
decolonial scholarship, 100
defensiveness: as agency, 26–28; in black feminism, 3, 26–28, 32, 42, 56, 73, 130–31, 136–38; intersectionality wars and, 26–27, 32, 137; in women's studies, 3–4, 28
Denison University, Women's and Gender Studies Program, 17
Desai, Jigna, 103
discrimination: antidiscrimination law as, 9–10, 123, 126; multiple jeopardy, of black women, 8–9, 72, 73
diversity/inclusion complex, 22–26, 94; black feminism and, 15; vs. intersectionality, 24–25; language of, 26
domination: hegemony of, 102; matrix of (concept), 10–11; social relations in, 8; violence of, 11, 119
double jeopardy theory, 8–9, 72, 73
Douglass, Patrice D., 21–22
Du Bois, W. E. B., 31
Du Bois Review (journal), 61
duCille, Ann, 19–20, 27, 29
Dworking, Andrea, 36, 37

Edenheim, Sara, 46
Ehrenreich, Nancy, 70–71

Ellison, Julie, 101
Evans, Sara, 89–90

Falcón, Sylvanna, 107
fatigue, 101–3, 138
feminism. *See* academic feminism; black feminism
Feminist Anti-Censorship Taskforce, 36
Ferguson, Roderick, 23, 24, 55, 82–83
Fernandes, Leela, 97
fetishization, 6, 19–20, 120
fetishized marginality, use of term, 29, 44
For Colored Girls Who Have Considered Suicide / When the Rainbow Is Enuf (Shange), 26, 30
forgetting, 66–69

Garcia-Pinto, Magdalena, 82
gender: racialized aspects of, 22; ungendering concept, 20–21; violence based on, 8–10, 21–22, 79–80, 91, 102, 111–12, 120, 123–26
global South, 68, 96–99
Gonzalez, Maria C., 90
Green, Kai, 78–79
Grewal, Inderpal, 102
Grutter v. Bollinger, 23
Gulati, Mitu, 73

Halley, Janet, 38
Hancock, Ange-Marie, 6, 59, 71, 77, 80
Hartman, Saidiya, 20, 111
Heller, Nathan, 1
Hemmings, Claire, 13–14, 15, 34, 97, 104
Hesford, Victoria, 13
Higgenbotham, Evelyn Brooks, 8, 112
Hillsburg, Heather, 102
Hine, Darlene Clark, 112
holding on, use of term, 3
Holland, Sharon, 95–96, 145n6
Holloway, Karla, 95
Hong, Grace, 19, 27, 55
Huffer, Lynne, 54

identity politics, 75–76, 106
inclusion: as based on exclusion, 128–29; black feminist demand for, 15; diversity/

inclusion complex, 22–26, 94; ethic of, 70–73, 122–23
intersectionality: in academic feminism, 2, 12, 16, 82–85, 103, 133, 135–36, 138, 139n7; accident metaphor of, 9–10, 67, 126; antisubordination of, 48; appropriation of, 40, 43–45, 60; in black feminism, 2–3, 6–11, 13, 26, 35–36, 40–41, 43–45, 84, 110, 112–13; in black studies, 18–22; black women as synonymous with, 53, 71, 92, 98, 104, 138; care in, 80; colorblind, 75; as corrective to white feminism, 13, 15, 37, 46, 136; critical race theory and, 121–22; critique of, 1, 33–34, 38, 45, 46–58, 64, 66, 76, 101; deep engagement and, 60–61; defensiveness and, 26–27, 32; vs. diversity, 24–25; diversity/inclusion and, 22–26; domestic, 68; ethics of, 15; forgetting and, 66–69, 109; genealogies of, 6, 9, 39, 41–42, 71–73, 108, 136; in hiring practices, 17–18; hybrid, 70–71; identity categories and, 97–98, 107–8; institutional life of, 11–22, 94–95; intellectual history of, 6–11; intimacies in, 104–10; juridical tradition and, 9, 108, 114, 121–22, 126–27, 128–29, 130, 131; language of, 22–23, 26; metaphors of, 9–10; neoliberal regimes and, 38; originalism in, 60, 61–76; origin of term, 1–2, 6, 13, 40, 82; ornamental, 64; Other in, 52; as passé, 103; post-intersectionality, 66, 99–100; practice of love in, 114; privilege in, 70–71, 73; as program-building in women's studies, 16–18; as property, 131, 137; rescue of, 65–66; resistance and, 135; stewardship in, 77–78, 80; as stolen object, 26, 32, 43; student activism and, 1; subjectivity and structure in, 74–76; surrender of, 83–84, 104, 109–10, 114; transnationalism and, 83–84, 91–104; use of term, 35–36; vagueness of, 67; violence inflicted on, 27, 37–39; as vulnerable object, 60–61; white heterosexual male, 75–76; whitening of, 39–40, 43, 70, 75; women of color in, 38, 44, 47, 48–49, 52, 71, 84, 95–96, 101–2, 104, 107–8; in women's studies, 2, 11–12, 16–18, 40–41, 43–45

intersectionality wars, 35–45; appropriation in, 43–45; care in, 59; critic as villain in, 45, 56–58; defensiveness and, 26–27, 32, 137; identity in, 106–7; origin stories in, 39–43; use of term, 8, 27, 34, 36–37, 136

intimacies: in intersectionality/transnationalism, 104–10; women of color and, 84, 96, 106, 108–9, 131

invisibility: of black women's intellectual labor, 3, 5, 19; doctrinal, 9–10; of gender, 21–22; of raced/gendered violence, 102, 111, 120; in transnationalism, 98; witnessing and, 119

Jordan, June, 19, 107–8, 118–19
judicial activism, 62
juridical tradition: of black feminism, 108, 115; intersectionality and, 9, 108, 114, 121–22, 126–27, 128–29, 130, 131; violence of, 11, 121–22

Kaplan, Caren, 102
King, Deborah, 6–7, 8–9, 41, 72
King, Tiffany Lethabo, 28–29, 51, 103, 114–15, 147n36
Kochiyama, Yuri, 108
Kwan, Peter, 99–100

Lee, Rachel, 4, 14, 15, 28–29, 44
Leidner, Robin, 90
letting go, ethic of, 3, 35, 73, 84, 110, 114, 129–31, 137, 138
Lipsitz, George, 74
Lorde, Audre, 19, 30, 55, 78, 108, 112
Love, Heather, 129
love, practice of, 113–15; in black feminism, 113–21, 126, 129–30; vulnerability in, 116–19, 121
Luft, Rachel E., 44
Lugones, Maria, 95, 100

MacKinnon, Catherine, 36, 37
Maria, Bethania, 81
Martin, Trayvon, 111
Martina, Egbert Alejandro, 54
Matsuda, Mari, 108

May, Vivian, 6, 7, 25, 46–49, 63, 80, 149n9
McBride, Renisha, 111
McCall, Leslie, 38, 63, 67, 74, 83
McRuer, Robert, 141n36
Mendoza, Breny, 99, 100, 105
Menon, Nivedita, 68
Mills, Linda, 127
Mitchell, Nick, 66–67
Mohanty, Chandra Talpade, 24, 54–55, 97
Moore, Roy, 134
Moraga, Cherríe, 54–55, 108
Morgan, Joan, 112–13
Morrow, Colette, 82
Musil, Caryn McTighe, 88–90
Musser, Amber Jamilla, 28–29, 101

National Women's Studies Association (NWSA), 81–84; Akron conference, 88–90; archiving, 84–94; "Difficult Dialogues" conferences, 92–93; on global context, 81–83, 90–91; on intersectionality and transnationalism, 91–104; on racism in women's studies, 85–90; self-destruction of, 89–90; Women of Color Caucus, 81, 86, 89
New York Magazine, 1
Ngai, Sianne, 27, 129
Nkadi, Ashley, 134
NWSA. See National Women's Studies Association

Ohio State University, Women's, Gender, and Sexuality Department, 17
origin stories, 39–43

Parmar, Pratibha, 91
Patil, Vrushali, 41, 68
Pedwell, Carolyn, 82
Peoples, Angela, 134, 135
Pipmeier, Alison, 56–57
plurilogue, critical methodology of, 109
"Poem about My Rights" (Jordan), 118–19
politics of reading, use of term, 59–60
pornography, 36–38
post-intersectionality, 66, 99–100
Puar, Jasbir, 33, 38, 50–54, 56, 82

Quashie, Kevin, 83–84
queerness: blackness and, 21; queer of color critique, 55; theory, 30, 55

race/racism: critical race theory, 121–22; in critiques of intersectionality, 49; meta-language of, 8; violence based on, 8–10, 21–22, 79–80, 91, 102, 111–12, 120, 123–26; in women's studies, 85–90
reading practices, 59–61, 62, 63, 69; intersectionality originalism as rereading, 69–76; politics of reading, use of term, 59–60; reading sideways, use of term, 55–56
rescue work, 65–66
resistance, 18, 44, 60, 119, 135
Rice, Tamir, 111
Rich, Adrienne, 81–82, 87
Rogers v. American Airlines, 31
Roshanravan, Shireen, 95, 109
Russo, Ann, 87–88

Sales, Ruby, 88–89
Sandoval, Chela, 54–55
Santa Cruz Feminist of Color Collective, 105
Say Her Name movement, 111
Schneider, Elizabeth, 127
Scott, Barbara, 90
Scott, Joan Wallach, 12
sexuality: public life and, 30; as raced category, 8
sex wars, 36–38
Shange, Ntozake, 26, 30
Sharpe, Christina, 20, 61, 79, 111, 121
Shin, Young, 74
Signs (journal), 61
Silko, Leslie Marmon, 108
slavery, afterlives of, 79–80
Smith, Barbara, 86, 87–88
Soto, Sandra, 95
Spillers, Hortense, 20
spirit murder, use of term, 123–25
stewardship, 77–78, 80
Stewart, Kathleen, 30
storytelling, 13–14, 34. *See also* origin stories
Straehle, Christine, 116–17
Subramaniam, Banu, 24

Suchland, Jennifer, 91, 98–99
Sullivan, Andrew, 1, 16
surrender of intersectionality, 83–84, 104, 109–10, 114
Syracuse University, Women's and Gender Studies Department, 17

Tallen, Bette S., 89
Tate, Claudia, 19
Terrorist Assemblages (Puar), 52, 53, 54
This Bridge Called My Back (Moraga/Anzaldúa, eds.), 108–9
Thompson, Becky, 87
Tomlinson, Barbara, 41, 47–48, 63, 64, 67, 73–74
transnationalism: critique of, 101; forgetting, 109; genealogies of, 107; identity categories and, 97–99, 107–8; intersectionality and, 83–84, 91–104; intimacies in, 104–10; scattered hegemonies and, 102; women of color in, 95–96, 98–99, 101–2, 107–8
travel (concept), 67–68
Trump, Donald, 133–35
Truth, Sojourner, 42
truth-telling, 63, 72

ugly feelings (concept), 27
un-forgetting, 109
ungendering (concept), 20–21
University of Akron, 88–90
University of California, Berkeley, Department of Gender and Women's Studies, 17
University of Michigan Law School, 23–24

violence: of academy toward black feminism, 3–5, 19, 27, 63–64, 138; against black women, 8–9, 10, 19, 73, 102, 111, 120, 127, 138; inflicted on intersectionality, 27, 37–39; juridical, 11, 121–22; political, 106; raced/gendered, 8–10, 21–22, 79–80, 91, 102, 111–12, 120, 123–25; spirit murder as form of, 123–25; state, and black feminism, 51, 124; of structures of domination, 11, 119; systemic, 19; witnessing, 119–21, 127
Voice from the South, A (Cooper), 7
vulnerability, 114, 116–19, 121, 123

wake work, 79, 121

Wald, Gayle, 109

Walker, Alice, 91

Ward, Jane, 44

Warren, Calvin, 21

Warren, Earl, 122

Waters, Maxine, 60

white supremacy, 79–80, 89

Wiegman, Robyn, 12, 13, 42, 66–67, 113, 114

Williams, Patricia J., 28–29, 30, 120, 123–26

witnessing, 114, 116, 119–21, 127

women of color: as disciplinarians, 104; feminist traditions of, 6, 31, 33, 54–55, 77, 84, 102, 109; in intersectionality, 38, 44, 47, 48–49, 52, 71, 84, 95–96, 101–2, 104, 107–8; intimacies and, 84, 96, 106, 108–9, 131; as killjoy figure, 101; political consciousness of, 133–34; scholarly work of, 94, 97–98, 105, 109–10; sexism/racism against, 66, 70, 72, 127; in transnationalism, 95–96, 98–99, 101–2, 107–8; in women's studies, 4, 14–15, 20, 83, 92, 97. *See also* black women

women's studies: American studies and, 145n5; black feminism and, 13–16, 28, 34; black studies and, 18–22; defensiveness in, 3–4; global context of, 81–83; hiring practices, 17–18; institutional history of, 11–16; intersectionality and, 2, 11–12, 16–18, 40–41, 43–45; on intersectionality/transnationalism, 96–97; racism in, 85–90; violence of, 138; women of color in, 4, 14–15, 20, 83, 92, 97

Wynter, Sylvia, 20